Beat the Craps
Out of the Casinos

Beat the Craps Out of the Casinos

How to Play Craps and Win

Frank Scoblete

Bonus Books, Inc., Chicago

95 94 93 92 91   5 4 3 2 1

Library of Congress Catalog Card Number: 91-75650

International Standard Book Number: 0-929387-34-1

Bonus Books, Inc.
160 East Illinois Street
Chicago, Illinois 60611

Composition by Point West Inc., Carol Stream, IL

Printed in the United States of America

To The Captain and his Mate

To my sons:
Greg and Mike

And to Alene Paone,
the best partner a man could ever have.

Contents

Author's Note

The diagrams used in this book were graciously supplied by *Win Magazine*. They depict the typical Las Vegas craps table. For the purposes of playing the methods discussed in this book, the differences between the Atlantic City and Las Vegas layouts are irrelevant.

Acknowledgments

I'd like to thank, first and foremost, the Captain himself for allowing me to write about his remarkable methods, even at the risk of exposing him somewhat to casino heat. Thank you, Captain.

I'd like to thank the following members of the Crew for allowing me to quote them and/or to use them as examples in the book: Ceel, Jimmy P., Frank T., Connie, Rose, John A., Russ B., Jo, Sal, Vic, the Doctor, Joe, Helen, Phil, and Mary. I'd also like to thank two of my favorite Barnacles, Annette and Dave, for allowing me to use them as examples.

I'd also like to thank the various casino hosts and pit bosses I talked to concerning the Captain and his Crew. You gave me invaluable insights into this remarkable man and his remarkable friends. Although you wish to remain anonymous, you know who you are, so thanks.

Another thank you to A.P., my partner in blackjack and in adventure, who invariably gives me valuable editorial help, and whose beauty is only surpassed by her intelligence, loyalty, and sense of daring.

And thanks to David Greenberg, Don Paone, Lisa Vetere, David Paone, Rebecca Forman, Ernest Wendt, and Peg Paone.

Last but certainly not least, a very special thanks to Mr. Cecil Suzuki, Senior Editor at *WIN Magazine*, for supplying me with the illustrations for the book, for giving me good tips on writing and gambling, and for taking time out from his wild and busy life to give me a hand.

ONE

The Captain of Craps

He's known as the Captain and he's the leader of the Crew, a group of twenty-two high-rolling craps players. He plays an average of three times a week. In the past ten years he has been a winner at a game in which the casinos clearly have the mathematical edge. What's more, he's fully comped at the best hotel-casinos in both Atlantic City and Las Vegas. Indeed, the casinos vie with one another to gain his patronage, knowing that his Crew will follow. The casinos figure, correctly, that the Crew will dump tens of thousands of dollars monthly into their coffers so the Crew is afforded the royal treatment. The casinos think the same about the Captain. In this they are mistaken.

This book offers, I believe, the only

way to beat the game of casino craps in the long run. As you will discover in chapter two, every bet in craps has a negative expectancy for the player. This negative expectancy is called the House Edge or simply the Edge. The Edge assures the casino long-term profits from the game of craps. For years gamblers have attempted to come up with systems to beat the game of craps. All have failed. No professional gamblers make their living solely at craps because no system has ever been devised to overcome the casino Edge. Until now.

All past systems of craps have fallen into three major categories: 1) positive or negative betting progressions, 2) Best Bet strategies, or 3) a combination of these two. The Captain's methods utilize some of these systems with one crucial difference: until his "5-Count" strategy, there has never been a method by which a craps player could know in advance that he or she would be protected from truly horrendous rolls of the dice, rolls that can wipe out a gambler's bankroll with a flick of the wrist. Mathematicians call those horrendous rolls fluctuations in probability. Craps players call them cold dice.

Now, before you panic, let me tell you quite clearly that this book is not some mysterious and arcane exercise in higher mathematics. On the contrary, it is a simple guide to beating the craps out of the casinos. Although there will be charts and some discussion of math, you can skip those if you like. All you really need to do is memorize the Captain's "5-Count," pick one of the methods that best suits your personality and bankroll, and head for the casino of your choice, happy in the knowledge that you have a terrific shot at coming home a winner.

At this moment you're probably asking yourself: "If the Captain's methods are so terrific, why is he wasting his time with this book? Why isn't he applying his great strategies and making a living at craps?" I've asked the very same questions myself of other systems sellers and gambling "authorities." If their systems were any good, wouldn't they be using them? Of course they would! Would they be selling them to the general public? Of course, they wouldn't!

So what makes the Captain an exception? First, he *is* currently making his primary living playing craps in Atlantic City. As I stated previously, he has been a winning player for ten years, ever since he developed his method. Second, the impetus for writing this book was not the Captain's but mine. Indeed, the Captain balked when I first suggested the idea in November 1989 because he didn't want to alert the casinos to what he was doing. The Captain has made friends with many casino hosts and top executives who are obviously unaware of his consistent wins. For a year I have hounded him to let me write about his methods. On October 8, 1990, he relented and gave me permission to write this book.

I think he finally gave in for several reasons. The first is that he really didn't think a publisher would be interested in a book on craps because previous ones, although solid sellers, were poorly written and somewhat embarrassing exercises in feigned eccentricity and phoney philosophy. Along these lines, most knowledgeable gambling authorities have dismissed any notion that craps is in fact a beatable game. Why bother publishing another book by another eccentric? The Captain also realizes that most veteran craps players, particularly the high rollers, are a stubborn lot and would rather continue losing truckloads of money than play another way. So, while traditional craps players may read this book, odds are they won't change, and the casinos will continue to blithely think the Captain is just another high-rolling loser.

Another reason why the Captain relented concerns the nature of his method of play—particularly his revolutionary "5-Count." As you will learn, the Captain's methods do not require a great intellect. But, they do require tremendous discipline. The Captain figures, rightly I believe, that most of you reading this book, especially novices, will succumb to the glamour of the casinos and impatiently start playing hunches and betting wildly. Therefore, the Captain (and a select few of his readers) will still be able to play his methods without undue casino heat. (Heat means pressure from casino personnel.)

I also think the Captain gave in because I'm pretty persuasive when it comes to getting people to go along with my writing projects. So why aren't I simply using the Captain's methods and making my living playing craps? Why do I want to write about it instead? Because I'm a writer, and a writer is compelled to write about what he knows and what he's experienced. I've been with the Captain for over a year now. I have watched him win, week after week, month after month. I have talked to other members of the Crew, even those who do not use his methods, who have assured me that what I've witnessed is no fluke. They have watched him do this for ten years! Oh, yes, I'm a gambler as well as a writer. I love to gamble as much as I love to write. But I'm not a compulsive gambler—I want to win. Before I played craps with the Captain, the only gambling I had done was blackjack. I'm an expert card counter. I've even been banned from several Vegas casinos. (Being banned is not something to be proud of because it means you weren't smart enough to cover up the fact that you were counting!) Now I play craps, too. After using the Captain's methods for a little over a year, I'm now ahead in craps. I won't lie to you and tell you I've made a fortune. To make a fortune, you have to bet a fortune. To bet a fortune, you have to be economically and emotionally capable of losing a fortune without literally losing your shirt. I'm neither.

Finally, I think the Captain, like all of us, has a certain amount of pride, and he'll take pleasure in seeing his methods and himself extolled in print. As a writer, I get a kick (and a paycheck) when I see my efforts in print. So this book will serve us both. If it helps others beat the craps out of the casinos, so much the better. I have a suspicion that for those of you who become experts in the Captain's methods, this book could very well become your craps bible.

Who is this Captain? For obvious reasons, I'm not going to reveal his real name, but suffice it to say that he was born in December 1923 and was a gambler from the get go.

"I come from a family of gamblers, bad ones at that. Until she died at the age of eighty-seven, my mother was an inveterate horseplayer. In fact, she died at the track. So did the horse she was betting on. My earliest memories concerned my brother, myself, and several of our friends playing dice in the alleys of Bay Ridge, Brooklyn. I was a pretty good pool player and when the money was on the line, I was tough to beat. In the army during World War II, I ran craps games with my friend, Jimmy. That was quite a different type of game from the ones they now have in casinos.

"I was always astute mathematically and I was always able to exploit the ignorance of other players. I never cheated, mind you, but I always knew the odds. At craps I was a winner because I ran the games. However, I was a loser at other forms of gambling. I played the ponies, and, although I was good, in the long run I realized that the horses were too tough to beat. So now I bet games and races, but recreationally and not for serious money. Craps I play seriously. It's the only serious gambling I do today. If it wasn't for craps, right now I'd be in difficult financial circumstances. I'm heavily invested in real estate and you know what's happened in the East in that market. The bottom's fallen out. So for two years now I am literally making my living playing a game that many gambling authorities swear can't be beaten.

"The funny thing about my method is that I didn't invent it after long hours of study and calculation. It was more of a coincidence. In science that's called serendipity—you're looking for one thing, and you stumble on something else that's even better.

"I literally stumbled on my '5-Count' because I was looking for a way to be considered a high roller in Atlantic City without actually spending the time or money to do so. I had no idea when I first started using it that in reality I had stumbled on a winning key. However, I realized what I had after the first two years of playing. I was a winner. Not only was I being comped but I was taking home money too. Not a lot, mind you, but steadily.

"Realizing I had found a possible winning method, I started to experiment with different types of betting strategies. I made every stupid bet imaginable, I'll tell you. But gradually I narrowed down my betting strategies to the ones in this book. My Supersystem, as Frank, the author, likes to call it, is truly the only system I think can wipe out the House

Edge in craps when used in conjunction with the '5-Count.' It's the system I recommend most highly. However, when you use it don't expect the casinos to lavish you with anything other than scorn and hostility. You'll consider yourself lucky if they just treat you cordially because, as you'll see, the Supersystem upsets many casino personnel. I'm actually hoping that anyone reading this book opts for the other two systems because they won't bring down the casinos' ire as will the Supersystem. I'm also somewhat concerned that if enough people start employing the '5-Count,' casinos will change the rules of craps the way they did in blackjack when card counters showed they could beat the house.

"As you read this book, I want you to keep in mind that although the '5-Count' and my betting strategies are rooted in sound logic and mathematics, some of my advice is rooted in my own personal superstitions. These superstitions are not those commonly held by other craps players (like, if the dice hit someone's hand, a seven will appear, etc.) but are rather conditioned responses, you might say, to a lifetime of playing the game and over ten years of playing it steadily in casinos. So, wherever possible, Frank knows to distinguish my advice that is based on rational principles from my advice based on my own intuitive response to a lifetime of gambling occurences."

Will you definitely win if you use the Captain's techniques? Definitely not. Anything can happen in gambling just as anything can happen in life. However, if the Captain's ten years are any bellweather, you'll have a hell of a run at the casino bankroll with his methods. If you have the least bit of sporting blood in you, this book will give you the best weapon to take your best shot at casino craps. Read it carefully and you too may be able to say ten years from now: "I beat the craps out of the casinos!"

TWO

The Game of Craps

This chapter is for those who have never played the game of craps but who are curious about the rules. Some of you may have been to the casinos and seen the people cheering (or moaning) loudly at the craps tables, but when you looked at the layout you felt intimidated by its seeming complexity. Don't be intimidated.

"Craps is not a difficult game to comprehend. It can't be, otherwise all the suckers who play it wouldn't be able to. Actually no casino game is all that complicated, except possibly counting cards at blackjack, because casinos must cater to the lowest common denominator: a thrill that doesn't require much cerebral output. The casinos would go broke if they only offered games that catered to physicists who specialized in quantum mechanics. So don't be intimidated by the appearance of the craps layout. The game isn't all that hard to understand."

This chapter is also for those whom the Captain considers Crazy Crappers: craps players who make crazy bets. The material is organized from the simplest information (how the game is peopled, the basic layout, etc.) to the more serious (the odds of the various bets). If you already understand, for example, who mans the table and what their jobs are, don't bother reading that section. We don't want to waste your time if you already comprehend some aspect of the game. However, even if you've played the game before, it might serve you well to review the material on the odds and why some bets are considered sane and some crazy.

Now, if none of the information in this chapter is new to you, and you already fully understand the odds and are a conservative bettor, move on to chapter three and discover the "5-Count"—the only method that gives you a chance to beat the casinos in the long run.

The Table and the Personnel

If you take a look at figure 1, you'll see the following personnel listed: the boxman, the dealers (2), and the stickman. The boxman is the boss. He runs the table and oversees the payouts. He also serves as a referee in case there are any disputes between the dealers and the players over some point of order or payout.

"Just because the boxman works for the casino doesn't mean he's biased. My experience has been that most times the boxmen will render a fair verdict and many will bend over backwards to see the player's point of view. It's not in the interests of a casino for its staff to alienate players, so more often than not in close calls the boxman will tend to side with the players."

The boxman will always be seated. However, in very crowded games a second boxman might be called in or a pit

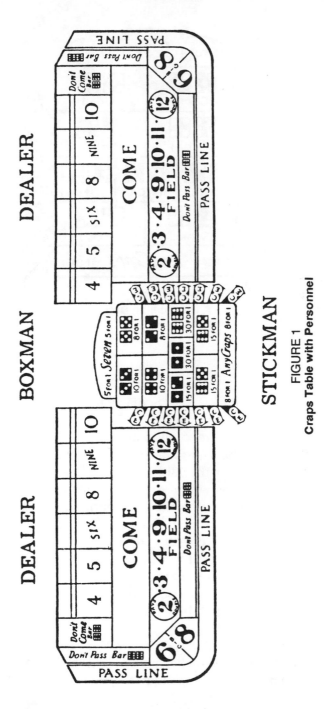

FIGURE 1
Craps Table with Personnel

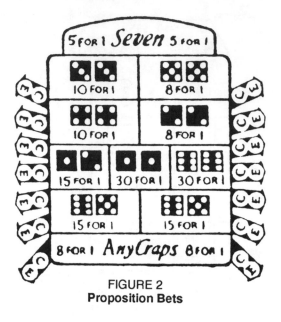

FIGURE 2
Proposition Bets

boss might oversee payoffs, particularly if some of the players are getting garrulous or upset.

There are two dealers, one on either side of the boxman. Their job is to place bets and handle collection and payoffs on their particular side of the table. The dealers will also cash your money into chips when you first enter the game.

Opposite the boxman is the stickman, so called because he has a long stick with a curved end that he uses to move the dice around the table. After the player rolls the dice the stickman will usually be the one to call out what number came up. Then he'll gather up the dice and send them back to the shooter. The stickman also handles those bets that you see in the middle of the table. These bets are called **Proposition Bets**.

"They should be called *bad* proposition bets because they are some of the biggest sucker bets found in the casino. You have more of a chance surviving a fall from a five story build-

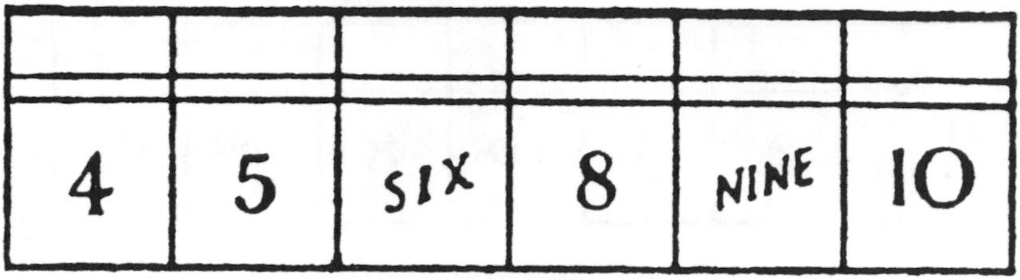

4	5	SIX	8	NINE	10

FIGURE 3
Point Numbers

ing than you do of winning those middle bets in the long run."

Craps tables come in many sizes. Some are incredibly long, and it's an effort to hit the opposite end when rolling the dice. By the way, when you roll the dice you must attempt to hit the back wall because that assures the casino of a random roll. The back wall of the table is made of rubber and you'll notice that it is lumpy with pyramid shapes. Again, this is to assure a random roll of the dice.

At the top of the craps table are grooves where the players can store their chips. Running around the outside center of the table is a shelf where players can put their ashtrays and drinks.

Now, take a look at the craps layout and you'll notice that both sides of the board are the same. In the middle, as stated, are the "bad" Proposition Bets. Later on we'll discuss why these bets should never be made. Look at the top of the layout to either side of the middle. You'll see boxes with the numbers 4, 5, 6, 8, 9, and 10. These are the **Point Numbers**. These are the only numbers we'll be truly concerned with on the board.

Right under the Point Numbers you'll notice a large area that has the word **Come** and a smaller boxed area to the upper right or left, depending on which side of the board you're looking at, that says **Don't Come**. These are types of bets that

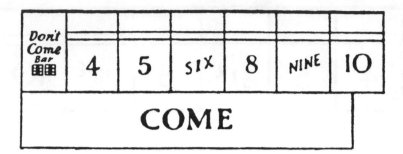

FIGURE 4
Come and Don't Come

we'll discuss shortly. They are very important for one of the systems in this book.

Under the Come section of the layout is the **Field**, another sucker area that we'll ignore. "The Field is where the casinos take the lambs to the slaughter." To the left or right of the Field, on Vegas layouts only, there will be something called the **Big 6** and the **Big 8**. "And, you have to be a Big Dope to bet them."

Finally, there are two bands that go around the entire board. One is called the **Don't Pass Line**, and the other is called the **Pass Line**.

FIGURE 5
Field and Big 6 and 8

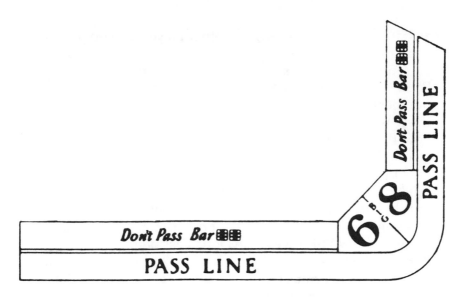

FIGURE 6
Pass Line and Don't Pass

How the Game Is Played

The stickman empties a tray containing five dice and pushes all five over to the shooter. The shooter selects two dice and the stickman takes back the remaining three. The shooter places a bet either on the Pass Line or the Don't Pass Line, and the game begins. Since the overwhelming majority of players are Right Bettors (i.e., players who bet the Pass Line and with the numbers) as opposed to Wrong Bettors (i.e., players who bet the Don't Pass Line and against the numbers) we'll limit our discussion of the game right now to Right Bettors.

Therefore, the shooter places his bet on the Pass Line, picks up the dice and shoots. That first roll is called the **come out** roll. If 7 or 11 appears, the bet is immediately paid off at even money. If a 12, 3, or 2 is rolled, the bet is lost. The shooter must have a Pass Line bet up in order to shoot. (Or, as stated, a Don't Pass bet.) The other players can opt to make a Pass Line bet or not.

The shooter will keep rolling until he makes one of the Point Numbers: 4, 5, 6, 8, 9, or 10. When he hits one of those numbers a large two-sided black/white disk is placed with the white side up in the box with that number. The number is now the shooter's point. He must make that number again before the 7 comes up in order to win his Pass Line bet. The Pass Line is always paid off at even money.

Now, let's take a look at the Don't Pass bet. With a Don't Pass bet, the shooter is betting that a 7 will appear before he makes his point. On the come out roll, things are the exact reverse. If a 7 or 11 is rolled, the Don't Pass bettor loses his bet. But, if a 3 or 2 appears, he wins. If a 12 appears he pushes (ties). (On many craps layouts, you'll notice the words **Bar 12**, or, sometimes, **Bar 2** by the Don't Pass and Don't Come. This means that when you are betting the don't wagers the 12 or the 2 will not win for the wrong bettor. The reason for this will be explained shortly.)

Those are the parameters of the game. Now, let's examine the Pass Line and Don't Pass Line bets more closely.

To do so, however, it is important to understand what the odds are of making a given number. "Craps is essentially a game of understanding the odds. So, it behooves anyone wanting to play the game to spend a little time familiarizing himself with the numbers."

Keep in mind that you're playing with two dice and that each die has six numbers on it: 1, 2, 3, 4, 5, 6. Thus, there are 36 different combinations of the dice: six sides times six sides equals thirty-six possible combinations. When you look at the following chart, you'll notice that certain combinations are repeated but in reverse order. For example, the number 3 can be made two ways, 2:1 and 1:2. Wait a minute, isn't that the same?

"Pick up two dice, one in your left hand and one in your right hand. Now, turn the one in your left hand to the number 2 and the one in your right hand to the number 1. That's 2:1. Now, turn the one in your left hand to 1 and the one in your right hand to 2. That's 1:2. Thus, there are two ways to make a 3."

Number	Ways to Make	Combinations
2	one	1:1
3	two	2:1, 1:2
4	three	3:1, 1:3, 2:2
5	four	4:1, 1:4, 3:2, 2:3
6	five	5:1, 1:5, 4:2, 2:4, 3:3
7	six	6:1, 1:6, 5:2, 2:5, 4:3, 3:4
8	five	6:2, 2:6, 5:3, 3:5, 4:4
9	four	6:3, 3:6, 5:4, 4:5
10	three	6:4, 4:6, 5:5
11	two	6:5, 5:6
12	one	6:6

Most craps books will tell you that the Pass Line bet is one of the best bets in the casinos, and they are not wrong. When the shooter is coming out, the Pass Line bet wins automatically if the shooter rolls a 7 or an 11. If you look at the chart above, you'll notice that the 7 comes up an average of six times and the 11 comes up an average of two times for every thirty-six rolls. Thus, on average, the Pass Line bet will win eight times for every thirty-six come out rolls. However, the Pass Line bet will lose four of every thirty-six come out rolls because a 12, 3, or 2 will appear. (Check the chart to see how many times each number is made.) Thus, the Pass Line will win on the come out at a rate of two to one. It will win twice for every one it loses.

"If the game of craps were only a Pass Line game and no points had to be made, the Right bettor could mortgage his house, sell the family jewels, borrow every penny he could and be confident of making a fortune. Since the odds of winning on the Pass Line favor the Right bettor by two to one, and he only has to bet even money, quite quickly every casino would go out of business and every Right bettor would be a billionaire. Unfortunately, the casinos aren't stupid, and once a point is established, the odds swing wildly in their favor. And, here's the rub: once you have a Pass Line bet down and a point is established, you can't call it off. You're stuck with it." And, because of this, the entire game favors the casino.

Again, check the chart, and you'll see that for every point number, the 7 has a probability of coming up more. Without going into complicated math, the bottom line is that the Pass Line favors the house in the long run by 1.414 percent.

So, the Don't Pass bet would appear to be a shoe-in, right? After all, if the Pass bet favors the house by 1.414 percent, wouldn't it favor the Don't Pass bettor, too?

It would, if the house didn't bar the 12 from winning on the Don't Pass line. The House wins on the 12 when the Pass Line bettor loses, but, unfortunately, the Don't bettor is not allowed to win. (In Northern Nevada, the 2 is barred.) The house has a 1.403 percent edge on the Don't bettor.

Just what does this all mean? For every $1,000.00 you bet on the Pass Line, you will lose an average of $14.14. For every $1,000.00 you bet on the Don't Pass you'll lose an average of $14.03. So, while obviously there is a difference between the two bets, that difference is inconsequential.

"But, remember this, although a thousand dollars seems like a lot of money, in reality during the course of a game you'll probably bet much more than that, even those of you who bet just $5.00. That's because as you play, you will win some rolls and play with that money also. Money is constantly going back and forth between you and the casino. So, by the end of many sessions, that tiny little percentage the casino holds over you will take its toll. My crew members will literally bet millions of dollars during a stay in Vegas or Atlantic City."

Placing or Laying Odds

Once a shooter has established his point on the Pass Line, all Right bettors can place *free odds* behind the line. That is, they can place an amount either equal to, double, or sometimes triple or higher, depending on the policy of the individual casino, behind their Pass Line wagers. These bets are called *odds* bets because the house pays them off at the true odds. Thus, if the point is 10 and the shooter makes it, the pass line bet is paid off at even money but the odds bet is paid off at two to one. So, a $5.00 Pass Line bet with double odds ($10.00) behind it will return $25.00.

"The odds bets in craps are the only *fair* bets in the casino because they pay off properly. If the entire game of craps were handled fairly, the game would result in a long-term draw with neither the house nor the player winning."

Why is that true? Just take the case of our point number 10 above. Say the Pass Line actually paid off at true odds all the time. You would lose two $5.00 Pass Line wagers ($10.00) for every one you won, *but* the one you won would pay two to one—$10.00! A draw.

When you put the odds behind the Pass Line you are *taking* the odds. However, when you're putting the odds behind the Don't Pass, you are *laying* the odds. Thus, if the point is ten and the casino allows double odds, you must lay $20.00 to win $10.00 on a $5.00 Don't Pass bet.

So which is the better bet? Should you bet with or against the dice?

"Technically the Don't Pass is the better bet but I prefer betting with the dice. First, you have to put up quite a bit more money in order to lay odds rather than take odds. You hit a bad streak where that 7 doesn't show and the shooter will wipe you out quickly. As you will learn from the next chapters, in craps *time is money*. You have to be able to last in order to take advantage of good situations. When you're laying odds, you can lose just too much too quickly.

"The second reason I prefer to bet with the dice as opposed to against them is because of the camaraderie that develops with the other players. Ninety percent or more of the craps players in Vegas and Atlantic City are Right bettors. It's an awkward situation for the Wrong Bettor because everyone's misfortune, that 7, is his fortune. That's why you'll rarely hear a Wrong bettor cheering as he wins and everyone else loses at his table. He doesn't dare. The other players might kill him.

"Next time you're in a casino [or on a riverboat], check out the attitudes of the various Right bettors when a Wrong bettor appears at their table. The baleful stares, the loathing, the hatred directed at the Wrong bettor is a powerful inducement to bet Right. Some bettors, particularly emotional ones and old timers, hate Wrong bettors with a passion. The Wrong bettor is the gambling equivalent of a plague carrier. One of my crew members facetiously believes that all Wrong bettors should be made to wear a bell around their necks as the ancient lepers did. Whenever a Wrong bettor appears at the table, he'll say: 'Captain, another bell-ringer has arrived!'

"Personally, I don't hate Wrong bettors. However, in the past, when I experimented with Wrong betting, I never got that thrill that comes with a good roll. The Wrong bettor just doesn't get that rush of adrenaline when number after number comes up. For emotional reasons, then, Right betting is the right way to go. So when that ultimate thrill, the hot roll, comes you'll be on the side of those cheering, instead of those looking furtively about hoping for an end to their torment.

"The strangest thing I ever saw at a craps table was a Wrong bettor who had a twenty-minute roll and literally wiped himself out. He was rolling number after number, point after point. Everyone at the table was cheering, yet few of us realized he was betting the Don't bets. Suddenly, he slammed his hands down on the rail and before anyone could comprehend what was happening, he walked away in a fury. He had lost every penny he had. Finally, the stickman explained the situation to the rest of us at the table. One old woman then shouted: 'God punished the bastard for betting Wrong!' and we all laughed and counted our profits."

I agree with the Captain, bet Right.

Come and Don't Come Bets

Although it is the biggest section, the Come section is often the least understood. Many authors will tell you that it

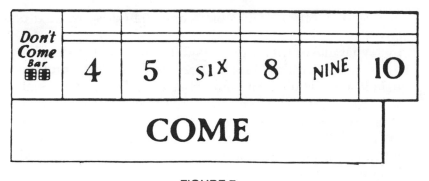

FIGURE 7
Come and Don't Come Bets

acts just like a Pass Line wager. Technically they are correct. However, the Come bets have a subtle difference that we'll mention shortly. But first, what are Come bets and how are they made?

Once the shooter establishes the point, you can then place a Come bet in the Come area. Now, the shooter rolls again. If the shooter rolls a 7 or 11, the Come bet wins. If the shooter rolls a 12, 3, or 2, the Come bet loses. Just like the Pass Line.

The Don't Come is also similar to the Don't Pass because if the shooter rolls a 7 or 11, the bet loses; but if the shooter rolls a 3 or 2, the bet wins. Again, a 12 is a push.

If the shooter rolls a number, then your bet is placed by the dealer on that number. If the shooter should hit that number again before rolling a 7, you win. If the shooter rolls a 7 before rolling that number again, you lose. Like the Pass Line, you can also place odds behind your Come bets by placing the money on the layout and saying: "Odds." The dealer will then take your odds bet and place it askew on your Come bet. Again, you can do the same with the Don't Come bets by informing the dealer that you wish to lay odds. Like the Pass Line or Don't Pass bets, the Come and Don't Come bets are paid off at even money and the odds are paid off correctly.

"What makes the Come bets different from the Pass Line bets is this: a 7 will win for you on the Come but simultaneously lose for you on all your other bets. Thus, emotionally the Come is not a satisfying bet. The same is true of the Don't Come. Emotionally, you're in the same position as the Don't Pass bettor. And again you're putting up quite a bit of money and can be wiped out that much sooner. So, although traditional experts recommend these bets, except for how I use them in the Supersystem, I would avoid them."

The Come bets also function as a game within a game. If the shooter should make his point while you have your Come bets up, the Come bets will still be working during the come out roll. That means that if a shooter rolls a 7 you would lose all your Come bets. However, during a come out roll, the odds on your Come bets are not working unless you specifically request it. In that case you would simply tell the dealer to keep your odds working.

Place Bets

The only other bets you have to understand in order to follow the Captain's methods of play are the **Place Bets**. Like the name says, this is a bet in which you place the numbers. Generally, the shooter will establish his point and after that you place the number(s) of your choice. And just because that big, white disk inhabits the point box doesn't mean you can't place a bet there. You just throw your wage onto the layout and say: "Place $5.00 on the nine" (Or on the ten, or four or five). However, you must always bet the six or eight in multiples of $6.00 because they are always paid off at $7.00 for $6.00.

If after you've placed your numbers the dice make them, you win. If the ubiquitous 7 appears, you lose.

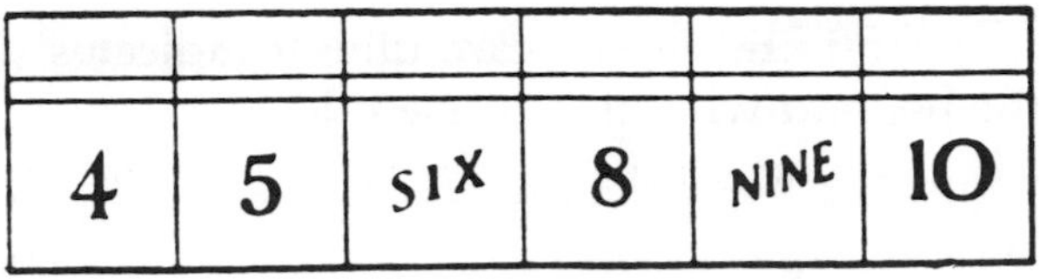

FIGURE 8
Place Bets

So how do Place bets differ from Pass and Come bets? First, Place bets can be removed at any time. Unlike the other bets mentioned, you don't have to sit on that number until a final judgment is rendered. (However, you may remove the odds portions of Pass and Come bets at any time.) Second, to pay for the privilege of discretionary removal, the Place bets are not paid off at true odds but at "house odds."

In This Place the Odds Are What They Ain't

Place bets are not paid off at true odds because the casino or riverboat must make money in order to survive. Thus, in all wagers the casino or riverboat will attempt to give itself a clear mathematical edge. You saw that with the Pass, Don't Pass, Come, and Don't Come bets, the fact that the casino paid these bets off at even money or removed the 12 from winning on the Don't bets, clearly made these negative expectation bets for the players. Simply, in the long run, the player is destined to lose.

We also explained how the odds are computed vis-à-vis the 7. Just to refresh you memory, remember that 7 can be made six ways while the 4 can be made three ways. Thus, the odds in thirty-six rolls are six to three, or two to one. To have a fair game (the definition of a fair game is one that in the long run has an equal expectation for player and house), every time you win on the number 4 you should be paid off at

2 to 1. Now, study this chart carefully. It indicates the true odds of the bet and what the house odds are.

Place Number	True Odds	House Odds
4	2 to 1	9 to 5
5	3 to 2	7 to 5
6	6 to 5	7 to 6
8	6 to 5	7 to 6
9	3 to 2	7 to 5
10	2 to 1	9 to 5

"I'll always maintain that craps is an easy game. However, the only mental ability a player needs is the ability to memorize the payoffs on his standard bets. If you're a $5.00 place bettor, you should know that if you place $5.00 on the 9 you'll get back $7.00 if you win. However, you must bet $6.00 on the 6 and 8 to get the correct house payoff of $7.00. The same holds true for the Pass, Don't Pass, Come, and Don't Come. If you put a $5.00 Pass Line bet and back it with $10.00 in odds and your number is 9, your payoff will be $20.00. That's $5.00 for the Pass Line bet per se and $15.00 for your $10.00 odds bet behind, because the 9 pays off at 3 to 2.

"In another chapter I'll explain how you can Push the Casino for even better payoffs by manipulating their own rules. That section might require you to use a little more brainpower but you've bought this book to become a winner and to beat the craps out of the casinos you have to exploit every ethical edge the casino gives you. So memorize the payoffs."

Buy Bets

One last thing should be mentioned. Casinos will allow you to *buy* the 4 or 10, when you place them in multiples of $20.00. Buying simply means that you pay a 5 percent commission to the casino or riverboat and then they give you the correct odds. So, for a $20.00 bet, you give the casino a dollar and say: "Buy the 4 for twenty or buy the 10 for twenty." This

is a definite bargain. Had you merely placed the 4 or 10 for
$20.00, your return on a win would have been $36.00. Buying
the number brings you an extra $3.00 payoff. In addition,
most casinos and riverboats will allow you to buy these numbers for $25.00 and still only pay $1.00. The Captain will have
some interesting things to say about buying the numbers in
chapter seven.

Should You Roll the Dice?

You should now know what you need to know to benefit
from the Captain's methods. However, two issues remain to
be settled before we move on to the devastating "5-Count."
The first is the question of whether to roll the dice when it's
your turn, and the second is an understanding of why all
other bets on the craps layout are for those poor souls who
want to be economically laid out by craps.

"If you're a new player and when it's your turn to shoot
you wish to pass the dice on, then do so. Quite often, if I'm
not feeling particularly hot or my previous rolls were awful,
I'll pass up my turn to roll. I realize that it's merely superstition what I've just said about passing up rolls because I
haven't been hot but man's a superstitious creature, and I'm
comfortable with my own idiosyncratic superstitions. So
pass up the dice if you wish.

"However, it is fun to roll those little cubes. I've found
that the best shooters treat the dice gently like a lady. Will
treating the dice gently assure good rolls? No. But so much of
gambling is style, actually so much of life is style. Pick up the
dice gently and let them roll a little in your hand gently and
then as gently as possible roll them down the middle of the
layout so they bounce once and hit the back wall.

"I find one of the most enjoyable aspects of craps, aside
from making money, is watching a truly skillful and stylish
shooter roll the dice. In casino craps today there is probably
no way to consciously manipulate the dice in order to guarantee certain numbers coming up. The design of the table,
the sponge rubber walls, and the fact that you must hit the

back wall, all combine to make craps shooting a strictly random activity. But so what? Life might be the strictly random activity of elementary subatomic particles, but we still prize finesse and class. So I recommend a gentle, classy approach to throwing the dice."

Having played the Captain's methods in both Las Vegas and Atlantic City, I can tell you that you'll find rough shooters predominating in Vegas. It seems that many Vegas shooters just love to whiz those dice down the tables. In fact, some Vegas shooters are so wild that if you're on the opposite end of the table and those dice go flying off, you could be in danger of being wounded. In Atlantic City, on the other hand, you'll tend to see shooters who shoot as the Captain recommends. Interestingly enough, in Vegas some shooters believe that gentle throws automatically bring out the seven. On several occasions, I had men comment unfavorably on my masculinity because my rolls are so gentle. If the commentator was an elderly or sickly and weak-looking individual, I'd tell him to mind his own business. If he was one of those large, muscular types in cowboy boots, I'd smile wanly, tell him I'd broken both my wrists in a horrible fall from a horse and continue to roll gently.

But like everything in a casino, there are rules for throwing the dice. As mentioned, you must hit the back wall. You can only use one hand to roll the dice and you can not switch them from hand to hand. You also must keep the hand holding the dice over the table at all times. This is so the casino knows you're not attempting to switch or alter the dice in any way.

Some people like to "fix" the dice; that is, set them so certain numbers are showing in certain arrangements before they shoot. I fix my dice so that the threes are in a "V" position. Thus, no matter how many sides you look at, the dice are not showing a seven. In Atlantic City, the fixing of the dice is tolerated and you'll enjoy watching the various rituals certain shooters perform before shooting. However, my experience has been that most Vegas casinos, in their attempts to keep the game moving, have very little patience for people fixing the dice. A few casino personnel can even become quite abusive when you attempt to fix your numbers. You'll have to feel your way.

"I'm never abusive when casino people are abusive to me. My attitude is to just leave the table and walk out the door. I'll admit that I have the edge here because when I walk out the door, twenty-two high rollers walk out with me. It also just doesn't pay to react nastily to someone who is being surly. You can't make someone's mood sunshine bright by barking at him. As for fixing the dice, I do it. It's a little ritual. I also fix the dice so that no seven is showing. Again, it's merely a superstition, but it makes me feel good. And if it makes you feel good, what's the harm? If the casino personnel feel I shouldn't do this, I may just pass the dice on if I've been winning but I'll stay at the table. However, if I'm losing or merely breaking even, I'll leave the table. If the casino personnel are rude, however, I'll signal my Crew and we walk out the front door and go to the next casino.

"Even if you're a low roller in the casino's eyes, your bets mean the same to you as a millionaire's do to him. Walk out."

When you're rolling and for some reason the dice leave the table or land on the top rail, the stickman will call "No roll," and you'll have to try again. If you wish, you can ask for the same dice.

"One of the two most common superstitions among inveterate craps players is that if the dice go off the table, a seven is about to be rolled. Just watch how many of them call off their odds and their place bets when this happens. The second most common superstition is that a seven invariably shows up if the dice hit someone's hand. That's why you'll hear players and personnel alike shouting 'Watch your hands!' as a shooter is about to shoot and someone is leaning over with a late bet or a late payoff. Personally, I don't subscribe to these superstitions, I prefer my own. But I'll shout 'Watch your hands!' too, because it unites the table like common prayer. (See chapter ten for a fuller discussion of craps superstitions.)

"Usually the dice will hop off the table if you're throwing

them too hard. One of the female members of the Crew, a gifted, high-stakes, winning card counter at blackjack, is so petrified of rolling the dice for fear other players will yell at her that she's bathed in sweat whenever she works up the courage to shoot. Now, this is a lady who has been banned from several Vegas casinos for card counting and has iron will when playing blackjack. But she wilts when she has to roll two little dice.

"Several weeks ago, we were at Trump Castle in Atlantic City and the table was quite cold. I was at the table, and Frank, the author, was, too. We called over A.P., our card counting lady, who was counting down blackjack games from behind the players. We figured we could use someone new to roll. She came over and right away I could see that she was sweating. We told her to roll the dice. At first she didn't want to, but we begged her. Finally, she picked up the dice in her sweaty hand and threw them. They must have stuck to her palms because the dice flew up and hit the stickman—actually, stickwoman—smack in the face. Both of them! And they fell to the table. A four! Frank and I both laughed, not at the discomfort of the stickwoman but at the absurdity of the throw. However, the stickwoman was quite upset and asked us if we thought it was funny that she had been hit with the dice. We both apologized and Frank immediately threw a $5.00 chip onto the layout and said: 'Hard four for the dealers!' That meant that if A.P. could make the four by throwing it 2:2 (the hard way), the dealers would be paid seven to one. Thus, they'd make $40.00, since they'd get to keep the original five dollar bet. The very next throw, A.P. made the hard four! Justice was served. The dealer was mollified.

"By the way, the hard-way bets are some of the stupidest bets on the craps table but as a method of tipping, they'll suffice. You'd be surprised at how many dealers are not aware of the actual odds on the various bets in craps. So a hard way bet sounds great to them."

Which brings us to the final topic of this chapter: the Crazy Crapper bets.

Crazy Crapper Bets

The following list will show you all the bets you should avoid in the game of craps. Unless you're insane and enjoy throwing away money, these bets offer nothing but the prospect of *substantial* losses in the long run. Strangely, there are some craps writers (I hesitate to label them "authorities") who insist that since most players are only occasional craps shooters, they don't have to adhere to sound betting strategies because anything can happen in the short run.

"True, anything can and does happen in the short run but, more often than not, the short run tends to reflect, over a short period of time, the long run. Yes, for a given roll of the dice, you can have wild swings in probability. I once witnessed the 12 come up four straight times. However, I would be willing to bet that even on that particular day on that particular table if you had been betting the 12 on every roll, you still would have come out a substantial loser. If you spend ten hours on a given weekend at the craps tables and you make the bets on this list, I'd be willing to put down a wager that you'll come out a loser. True, it's possible that you could win, but it's more likely you'll lose. Now, let me bet on ten players on ten weekends making the following bets and my wager would get substantially higher. These bets take such a tax out of your winnings that they're only for self-destructive individuals and compulsive losers. If you're taking the time to read this book, there's a good chance you don't want to be a loser."

We're going to take a look at these Crazy Crapper bets in a unique way. Most books tell you what the percentages are against you when betting these bets. But we're going to show you what happens when you win one of these bets! You see, the casinos and riverboats actually make their money from you when you win because by giving themselves the edge, they literally *take a tax out of your winnings*.

Let me explain how that works. If you place the number 4 and win, instead of giving you a $10.00 payoff for a $5.00 bet, the casino gives you $9.00. In reality, they handed you ten singles but at the last second they took away one and kept it. When you lose, you can't reach out and remove a chip or two, yet when you win, this is exactly (albeit symbolically) what the casino or riverboat does to you. So, still using our theoretical example of the 4, since for every one time a 4 shows, the 7 will show two times, watch what happens. If the casino gave you true odds, the two 7's would lose you $10.00 but the one 4 would win you $10.00. We did this example earlier. That's a fair game. You break even. But this is what happens when you place the 4. You still lose $10.00 when the 7's appear but instead of winning $10.00 when the 4 appears you only win $9.00. Instead of breaking even, you're a loser. Now, look at a few of these Crazy Crapper bets and don't be fooled when the Las Vegas layouts say ten *for* one and the Atlantic City layouts are saying nine *to* one because they mean the same thing. Thus, in a ten *for* one bet, the casino or riverboat returns $10.00 for a $1.00 bet, nine of its own money and one of yours. In a nine to one bet the casino or riverboat gives you $9.00 of its money and your original one dollar bet back to you. That's right you get ten back altogether. It's just another method the casinos and riverboats use to confuse those confused enough to bet the Crazy Crapper bets.

Bet	True Odds	House Odds	What You Should Win On $5 Bet	What You Do Win	Tax Casino Takes On Your Win
Any 7	5 to 1	4 to 1	$ 25	$ 20	$ 5
Any craps (2, 3, 12)	8 to 1	7 to 1	$ 40	$ 35	$ 5
2	35 to 1	30 to 1	$175	$150	$25
12	35 to 1	30 to 1	$175	$150	$25
3	17 to 1	15 to 1	$ 85	$ 75	$10
11	17 to 1	15 to 1	$ 85	$ 75	$10

The FIELD is paid off at even money even though the bet favors the house ten to nine. Although, the 2 and 12 will pay two to one if hit, this merely reduces what would have been a five to four wager down to a ten to nine wager.

These are just some of the crazy bets you can make in craps. The hard ways are no better than these, so avoid them too. Also, when in Vegas, avoid the Big 6 and the Big 8 because only people who have had their brains dehydrated by the desert make that bet. There's also a one-roll bet called a "Hop Bet" in which you call out what number combination that you want and if it hits, the house pays you twenty-nine to one on thirty-five to one bets and fifteen to one on seventeen to one bets. So hop away from these sucker bets.

If you still don't realize why these bets are crazy, just imagine a world where everything was fair and on thirty-six rolls of the dice the numbers came up exactly in proportion to their probability. Now, picture a millionaire, yourself, betting the above bets for a million shooters. In a fair world, the man would start with a million dollars and end with a million dollars. But if the casino were able to operate in this fair world as it operates in our imperfect one, then even though all the numbers appear as they should, our millionaire would go broke.

THREE

The "5-Count"

The key concept to every system in this book is the Captain's "5-Count," a deceptively simple yet revolutionary method of craps playing.

"Without the '5-Count,' all my other methods of play would just be intelligent betting strategies. I doubt if I would have been capable of a ten-year winning streak or of making my living at the craps table."

In this chapter we'll lay out the "5-Count" exactly as the Captain plays it today. Memorize it. Then we will give explanations as to what it accomplishes and why it works.

A shooter has just been passed the dice, and he is on his first come out roll. You do not place any bets. The shooter must make five successful rolls of the dice before you risk your first bet. That's the "5-Count."

What is considered a successful roll? On the first roll, the come out, the shooter must hit a point number for the "5-Count" to begin. Thus, if the shooter rolls a 4, 5, 6, 8, 9, or 10 on the come out, the count is at one (or 1-count). If the shooter rolls a 2, 3, 7, 11, or 12 on the come out, the count has not begun.

On the second, third, and fourth counts, any number rolled will be included. Thus, if the shooter rolls as his come out a 6 and then rolls an 11, the count is at two (or 2-count). Then he rolls a 12, and the count is at three (or 3-count). Then, he rolls a 2, and the count is at four (or 4-count).

On the fifth roll, which from now on we'll call the "5-Count," the shooter must again roll a point number 4, 5, 6, 8, 9, or 10 for the count to be completed. Thus, the "5-Count" starts with a point number and ends with a point number.

With the successful completion of the "5-Count," your betting will begin.

Whether the shooter makes his point or not is irrelevant to the "5-Count." For example, say on the come out the shooter rolls a 9. The count is one and his point is 9. On the second roll, he rolls an 11. The count is two. Next, he rolls a 9. The count is three. His next come out roll, **regardless of what it is**, will be the 4-count. If, for example, he rolls a 6 and then rolls another 6. The first 6 was the 4-count, and the second 6 was the 5-count. Your betting would begin.

Of course, if the shooter sevens out, the count is terminated. Also, the count does not have to begin on the first come out roll. If you arrive at a table and the shooter is in the process of rolling, the very first roll you witness will be the 1-count—if that roll is a point number. Then, you would continue from there. One important thing to note is that you do not have your bets working during a come out roll. Most casinos and riverboats do this automatically, but if you should be placing a bet after the 5-count and it happens to coincide with the come out roll, the dealers might ask you if these bets are working. Tell them no.

If a shooter sevens out within the first five counts, you begin the process over with the next shooter.

Why the "5-Count" Works

The "5-Count" is devastatingly simple yet it accomplishes what no method or system in craps has ever accomplished. It automatically eliminates in advance all the horrendous rolls; those rolls that seven out immediately after the shooters have established their points, or within several rolls. Thus, you are only risking your money on shooters who have a chance for a good roll.

"Instead of looking at craps as individual rolls of the dice, I look at the game as a series of fluctuations in probability. The laws of probability are inviolable and the odds on any given number showing up are always the same from roll to roll. However, no extended series of rolls will ever conform perfectly to probability. You will notice wild fluctuations as some numbers come up out of all proportion to their expected frequency. If a fluctuation occurs in which the 7 is not thrown but most of the other numbers repeat again and again, we call that a *hot roll*.

"However, the reverse is also true. You can have a series of fluctuations where the 7 is thrown with such frequency that many players are convinced the dice are loaded. These fluctuations would make a table *cold*. Obviously, in craps you make money at hot tables and you lose money at cold ones. The '5-Count' eliminates those fluctuations in probability in which the 7 is coming up with alarming regularity just after the come out roll."

Not only does the Captain's "5-Count" put you in a position to be at a table when a hot roll occurs, but it positions you to fully take advantage of it.

"Too many times I'll see craps players so devastated by a series of cold shooters, that when a warm or hot one comes along, they are unable to recoup their money. Remember this, a hot roll of twenty or more numbers without a seven appearing is much rarer than cold ones of five or less. When that hot one does come along, you have to be able to take full advantage of it. The way to do that is simply not to have lost too much money during the cold shooters.

"I also realize that it is possible to experience a mediocre fluctuation of the dice, in which shooter after shooter sevens out after six to nine rolls. This will occur. However, in no way does this change the impact of the '5-Count' because in the long run the craps player makes his money from the few hot rolls he encounters. The rest of the time spent at the tables is essentially an effort in reducing losses and positioning oneself to take advantage of the hot rolls. And the '5-Count' does this perfectly."

An interesting experiment for you to do right now would be to get a pair of dice (preferably casino type with the square edges and painted spots) and roll them several hundred or a thousand times. Pretend you just walked to a table and the shooter is coming out. Roll and practice the "5-Count" as it has been explained. See for yourself how many horrendous rolls of the dice you will avoid. And keep in mind, that in the real world of casino craps every horrendous role you avoid is money saved, money which is waiting to work for you on better roles.

I would also recommend this imaginary craps game as a way of testing all the systems in this book. Pretend you're at a casino and actually put in some time with the Captain's methods. See how much you would have won or lost at the betting level and system you chose. Do this so that when you go to the casino you're confident in your method of play and fully understand and appreciate the fluctuations in the game.

How the Captain Discovered the "5-Count"

"As I said before, I literally stumbled on the '5-Count' because I was looking for a way to extend my time at the tables without extending my risk. To understand why this was important to me you must first be aware of how casinos rate players and why players want to be rated.

"A casino will judge your gambling in order to determine what comps, or freebees, they'll give you. At certain betting levels for a certain period of time, usually four hours (see chapter seven), you'll get what's called RFB—room, food, and beverage—courtesy of the house. Of course, by betting so much for so long, the house edge will grind you down. At high betting levels, you're doomed to be a loser in the long run—a big loser. So the casinos aren't really giving anything away for free—you pay for it dearly.

"Now, I was looking for some method to reduce my losses to a level below what it would cost me if I paid for my room, meals, drinks, shows, etc. Say it would cost me $800.00 to $1,000.00 for a weekend in Atlantic City. Now, if I was able to put in four hours at the tables, have the casino pick up the tab, but only lose, say, $500.00, I felt I would be ahead of the game. I'd be getting a substantial discount.

"It's no secret that strong blackjack players who know the Basic Strategy can play even with the house in the long run without even counting cards. Now, if a blackjack player has a big enough bankroll and can bet substantial amounts, in the long run he'll actually be getting everything for free.

"How to do this in craps? That's what I wanted to know. Having read chapter two, you can see quite clearly how much of an advantage the house has over the craps player even when that player isn't a Crazy Crapper. I wanted to reduce my risk of going broke without reducing my chances for RFB.

"If I could reduce my time at the table but still make it *appear* as if I were putting in four hours, I would obviously be reducing my long-term risk. I had no illusions that I would actually be able to win in the long run, I just wanted to reduce my losses so my comps would be meaningful.

"So I analyzed how players were being rated. I quickly realized that in craps you don't have to bet on every roll of the dice to get a good rating. In fact, many craps players will wait until a player makes a point before placing any bets. This is a strategy called finding the Qualified Shooter. The definition for Qualified is simply that a shooter has made a point. It is a very old system of play and players who use it have no trouble being rated.

"Unfortunately, waiting for someone to make his first point has built-in dangers if you want to win some money. A shooter could roll number after number and not make his point and an otherwise good roll would be worthless for you. So through trial and error, I came upon the '5-Count.' What I wanted to be, really, was what baseball analysts call a 'tough out.'

"In baseball a hitter who rarely strikes out, who rarely defeats himself, is called a tough out. A pitcher has to use all his wiles, all his guile and ability to handle such a hitter. The '5-Count' was originally designed to make me a tough out in craps. With it I am able to stay at the tables for four hours of physical time but much less in **betting** time. Betting time is, of course, the amount of time your money is actually at risk. With the '5-Count' the casino will give you credit for your physical time at the table even though your betting time is substantially less. That alone will save you money."

While the "5-Count" is a necessary condition for winning at craps in the long run, it alone is not sufficient to do so. Your betting strategies must also work to cut down the house edge.

"If you're a Crazy Crapper, you'll lose less money utilizing the '5-Count,' but you'll still be a big long-term loser. You cannot give the casino too much of a mathematical edge, period. In craps, you tend to lose on most shooters, even when employing the '5-Count,' so you must work to reduce your losses. How is this done? Strangely enough, by maximizing what you win when you win. By using the '5-Count,' you haven't fallen victim to every cold shooter and you have been able to *stretch* your money over a longer period of time. Now, by making the best possible bets you will reduce what the casino takes from your wins in the form of taxes. Remember that the casino makes its true killing when you win because it doesn't pay you at the true odds. Thus, winning more when you do win is the other condition necessary for the '5-Count' to work sufficiently for you to have a shot at the casinos' bankrolls.

"I think of the '5-Count' and my betting strategies as long-term strategies. When I'm being comped at an Atlantic City or Vegas casino, I play my High Roller System, but I only play it for the minimum time necessary to get RFB. I never give a casino more time than agreed upon because then they will expect that in the future. When I have put in my hours, I'll leave and go to another casino and there I'll use my Supersystem. It is not unusual for me to play eight to ten hours on a given day. That's why my strategies are designed to give you the best possible long-run chances."

Considering the Captain plays three to four days a week, and sometimes more, it is quite obvious that his strategies have stood the test of time. Naturally, one could challenge his "5-Count" in several ways. Why, for example, does the count begin on a point number and end on a point number? Why five counts? Why not six? Seven? A hundred?

"I realize that some of my assumptions are based strictly on my experience. For example, I believe that numbers tend to repeat (see chapter seven), and thus I prefer a fluctuation that might be repeating numbers I'm betting on. So I don't bet until the point number's showing. As to why it's five rather than six or a hundred counts, that's quite simple: you've come to play the game. It can get pretty boring standing around the tables waiting for five successful rolls. Many of my Crew, who have watched me win year after year, still don't have the patience to do this. So five seems to be just right for my temperament. I don't think I'd have the patience to wait for a hundred rolls. So, while I think the logic behind the '5-Count' is unassailable in the long-run fluctuations of the game, I can see many quibbles with individual components in the short run."

My attitude towards the Captain's "5-Count" and his other strategies is quite simple. I've been playing craps with the Captain for a little over a year now, and I have personally witnessed his wins. I have utilized both his Limited Bankroll and his Supersystem for that time and in a year of playing craps, I'm ahead too. I play the Captain's way to the letter. I suggest you do too.

One final word and then I'll take you into the world of the Supersystem. I was once playing blackjack at a table and another player was constantly second guessing my playing strategy. Now, I'm a successful card counter and I know how to play every hand according to the particular count of the deck. But this guy was constantly riding me. I ignored him. Finally, he left the table in disgust at my "amateur play" and also because he had lost several thousand dollars. A little old lady next to me said: "Every gambler thinks he's an expert and every one of them is a loser. Why listen to him?"

Why, indeed! That little old lady was right. The Captain, however, is the exception that proves her rule. Why listen to him? Because he's a winner!

FOUR

The Supersystem or the "5-Count" Doey-Don't

A lthough not overly complicated to play, the Captain's Supersystem requires study and practice in order to execute it properly under casino or riverboat conditions. Not only do you have to understand when and how to bet, when to call bets off and put them back on, but you must be thoroughly familiar with all the possible payoffs to your bets and simultaneously ever watchful for dealers' mistakes. It's doubtful that dealers would try to cheat you, but so few of them have ever experienced a method of play like this (as far as I know only the Captain, myself, and several members of the Crew have actually played this way) that they will make mistakes and these mistakes will invariably cost you money. So, in addition to understanding what you must do, you must understand the dealer's job as well.

"I'll tell you right now that the Supersystem is not effortless to play. You cannot come to the table like a happy idiot, throw bets down, relax, yuck it up with the pit crew and cocktail waitresses, and leave it up to the dealers to figure out the monetary end of the game. You must be prepared to concentrate every moment you're at the table.

"You have to size your bets correctly, take advantage of every casino loophole (see chapter five), be aware of the fluctuations in your bankroll, stay on top of your '5-Count' and, perhaps, tolerate some antagonistic behavior on the part of pit personnel.

"In the Supersystem you'll be playing both sides of the board, the Do and the Don't—that's why I call it the Doey-Don't System—so you'll be winning and losing bets simultaneously. That's why you have to concentrate and be aware of your money and the dealers' actions at all times. You can't afford to make mistakes."

The benefits for your efforts are simple: you'll be playing the strongest game of craps possible.

The Supersystem can be played aggressively or conservatively, depending upon your temperament and bankroll. The Captain plays a moderately aggressive way. We'll use his approach as the model for our initial discussion.

Positioning

The Supersystem strategy begins the moment you walk up to the table. You must position yourself at the upper corners of the table, either to the left or right of the respective dealers. This gives you the ability to place Come and Don't Come bets without the assistance of the dealers themselves. By positioning yourself correctly, you will hopefully eliminate certain dealer errors that would be otherwise made had you been calling out your bets.

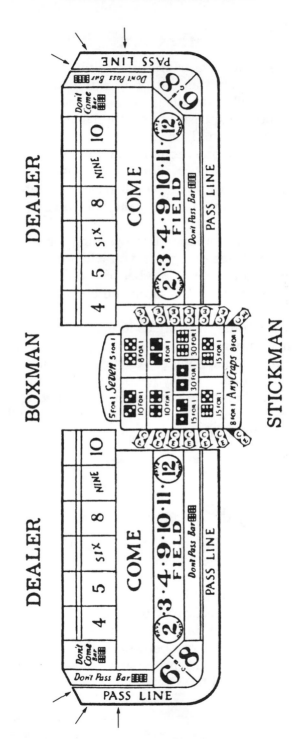

FIGURE 9
Where to stand for SUPERSYSTEM

The Count

The Supersystem starts on the 2-count. That means that the shooter has established his point and made one successful (non-seven) roll of the dice. You now place a Come and a Don't Come bet of equal value on the layout. You will continue to place Come and Don't Come bets until you have four numbers working. However, you don't put any odds behind your bets until the 5-count. Thus, regardless of how many numbers you have working (you'll have between one and three), on the 5-count you will take *full* odds behind your *Come* bets.

When you have four numbers working for you and one hits (leaving you three numbers), you will immediately place another Come and Don't Come bet of equal value until you once again have four numbers on the board with full odds behind the Come.

You will continue this way as long as the shooter makes one of your numbers *at least* once every three rolls. Should the shooter fail to make one of your numbers on three rolls, you will tell the dealer that your odds are off until you say differently. You then keep your odds off for two rolls. If the shooter doesn't seven out in these two rolls, you tell the dealers to make your odds work again. You then repeat the process.

Why the Supersystem Is Super

What makes the Supersystem so elegant and so devastating is the fact that you have almost eliminated the house edge by betting the Come/Don't Come simultaneously.

Let's examine this more closely. The shooter is on the 2-count. You place Come/Don't Come bets of equal value. The shooter rolls a 7. What happens? You lose your Don't Come bet but you win your Come bet. Standoff.

Next, the shooter rolls an 11. Same thing. You win on the Come but you lose on the Don't Come. Standoff.

However, if a shooter rolls a 2 or 3, the reverse holds true. You'll win your Don't Come bet but lose your Come bet. Unfortunately, if the shooter rolls a 12 you will lose your Come bet but only push (tie) on your Don't Come bet. The house wins this bet. That's its only edge.

How many times can you expect a losing bet as you place a Doey-Don't bet? Once every thirty-six rolls of the dice! Of course, if all you did was bet Come/Don't Come and never placed odds and never followed the "5-Count," the casinos would grind you down rather quickly. Since all your bets but one would be standoffs, that one bet would dictate the flow of your game—unerringly downstream.

However, by utilizing the "5-Count" and placing full odds behind your Come bets, you have placed yourself in a position to beat the craps out of the casinos.

"The Supersystem gives you an opportunity to play an almost even game mathematically with the casino by whittling down the house edge to a one in thirty-six probability. The '5-Count' reduces losses due to early sevening out, and keeping bets on for three rolls only, unless one of your numbers hits, helps to protect you against repetitions of numbers that you don't have."

Diligence is required at all times because when your numbers are hitting, the dealer must 1) pay off your odds bet correctly, 2) pay off your Come bet at even money, 3) remove your Don't Come bet, and 4) if you have placed a Come/Don't Come wager, replace both Come and Don't Come numbers. That's quite a bit of work for a dealer to do for one player and the tendency will be for the dealer to make mistakes. And remember, if a 12 is rolled, you will automatically have to replace your own Come bet if you had a wager down.

"I've played this system for a long time, and it's rare that a dealer handles my bets flawlessly—particularly if I'm *pushing the house* (see chapter five) with multiple chip bets. So before you place any real money at risk, I suggest you sit down with a pen and paper, analyze how much you can afford and want to bet and then work out all the possible permutations in your betting strategy."

Step by Step

In order to help you maneuver your way through the Supersystem, we'll do a step-by-step theoretical game. Let's assume that the table minimum is $5.00 and that you are on a moderate bankroll. Since $5.00 is generally the lowest table in Atlantic City casinos and a common one in Las Vegas casinos, this theoretical game will be very easy to find in practice. The casino we'll be playing in will be offering us double odds, again the norm for both Atlantic City and Las Vegas.

The shooter gets the dice and on his come out roll he rolls a 7. There is no count.

The shooter rolls a six. The 1-count. The six is now his point number.

The shooter rolls an 8. The 2-count. You now place Come and Don't Come bets of $5.00 each.

The shooter rolls an 11. The 3-count. You win on the Come bet but you lose on the Don't Come bet.

"There are several ways that a dealer can handle your winning and losing bets. Generally, the procedure differs from casino to casino. If the dealer collects your Don't Come and then places a chip next to your Come, you must immediately take that winning bet and place it on the Don't Come line. In Atlantic City, more often than not, the dealers will follow this procedure. However, some dealers will simply push your losing Don't Come bet over into the Come area. Again, it will be up to you to push it back. Still others, particularly in Las Vegas, will merely tap your chips with their finger to indicate a push. Whatever method is being used it's up to you to make sure that you have both sides of the board covered."

The shooter rolls a 9. The 4-count. The dealer now takes your $5.00 Come and Don't Come bets and places them in the appropriate boxes for the 9. You now place a Come and Don't Come bet again.

The shooter rolls a 4. The 5-count. Once again the dealer moves your Come and Don't Come bets to the appropriate boxes. Again you immediately put down another Come and

Don't Come bet. However, this time you also place $20.00 on the table and tell the dealer to give you full odds behind your Come bets.

"Once your odds are on, you have money at risk. Except for the odd 12 now and then, quite a bit of your betting in the Supersystem is money not-at-risk. With two numbers working and full double odds on a $5.00 Doey-Don't bet, you have $20.00 at risk and $20.00 not-at-risk. Obviously, the only money you need be concerned about is the money at risk since the other money will be returned to you. You also might find that because the '5-Count' is eliminating shooter after shooter, you are playing for quite awhile with not-at-risk money. However, don't become bored or lose your concentration because dealers can get sloppy and if you're not paying attention you might forget, for example, to replace a Come or Don't Come bet."

Now you have two numbers, the 4 and the 9, with $10.00 behind each. You also have put down another Come/Don't Come bet.

The shooter rolls an 8. The dealer places your Come and Don't Come bets on the 8, and you put $10.00 on the table and ask for the odds on the Come bet. You now have three numbers working for you: the 4, the 8, and the 9. Once again you place $5.00 Come and Don't Come bets.

The shooter rolls an 8. The dealer now takes your Don't Come off the board because that bet lost. However, he now pays you $12.00 for your odds bet of $10.00 (remember that 6 and 8 are paid off at true odds of six to five) and $5.00 for your Come bet of $5.00 because this bet is paid off at even money. Since your Don't Come bet lost, the dealer now takes your Don't Come bet off the layout and puts it in the appropriate box for the 8. You now put another Don't Come bet down to cover the one taken away. (Remember, you still only have three numbers working: 4, 8, and 9.) But instead of having to place another Come bet down, the dealer will have left your previous one in place because your number hit and one Come replaced the other.

The shooter rolls a 10. You place a $10.00 odds bet behind

the Come. You now have four numbers working—4, 8, 9, and 10—so you do not place another Come and Don't Come bet.

The shooter rolls another 10. The dealer removes your Don't Come losing bet. He then pays you $20.00 for your odds bet and $5.00 for your Come bet. Since you are now reduced to three numbers you place Come/Don't Come bets on the board.

The shooter rolls a 6. He has made his point number. However, this does not affect the placement of your bets. Your $5.00 Come and Don't Come bets will each be placed in the appropriate boxes of the 6 after the dealer pays off all the Pass Line bets.

Once again you have four numbers on the board—4, 6, 8, and 9. The shooter is now coming out again. On come out rolls the odds on all Come bets are automatically off, but your Come and Don't Come bets are still working. That means that if the shooter rolls a 7 on his come out you will lose your Come bets, win your Don't Come bets, and have all your odds returned to you. In short, a standoff.

"If the shooter's come out roll wipes you off the board, you just have to start over again. However, you start by placing a Pass and Don't Pass bet and when the shooter establishes his number, you immediately place your odds bet behind the Pass Line. You do not have to wait to do another '5-Count' because this is the same shooter. Then you continue to place Come/Don't Come bets until you have four numbers working for you again."

But for the sake of our theoretical game, let's assume that the shooter does not roll a 7 but, instead, rolls an 8. Since you have the 8 as one of your numbers here's what happens: (You probably guessed it!) You win on the Come, lose on the Don't Come, and have your odds returned. However, now you have a Pass and Don't Pass bet of $5.00 each on the 8. You place $10.00 odds behind the Pass Line bet.

Because you still only have three numbers, you place Come and Don't Come bets.

The shooter now rolls the 12. You lose your Come bet,

but your Don't Come bet is a push. You put another $5.00 chip in the Come area.

The shooter now rolls a 5. You have four numbers working—4, 5, 8, and 9. The shooter rolls several more times and makes your numbers. Every time you have three numbers working, you have placed Come/Don't Come bets up. However, he now rolls three rolls without once making one of your numbers. You tell the dealer: "My odds are off the Come until I tell you." You keep the odds off for two rolls.

If your odds are off when the 7 is thrown, you will get the odds back and once again you're in a standoff. However, if your odds are working when the 7 makes its appearance, then obviously you lose all your bets on the Come and are only returned your $5.00 Don't Come and your even money win of $5.00 on it. The next shooter then takes his shot.

"In the Supersystem, you have some real choices to make. You can do as I do and work with four numbers. At a $5.00 table, by placing the minimum bet, you'll be risking $40.00 on any given roll after the '5-Count.' However, some gamblers like to cover the board. If such a betting strategy appeals to you then you would start placing your Doey-Don't bets on the Pass/Don't Pass on the very first come out roll, as opposed to on the 2-count. Thus, when the 5-count comes you'll have between two and five numbers working for you when you place your odds. Keep in mind that the '5-Count' begins with a point number and ends with a point number so you will have a minimum of two numbers made when you place odds behind your bets. Obviously, covering the board is an extremely aggressive system. With greater aggression comes a greater chance for big wins and big losses.

"Of course, if you want you can play a more conservative system than the one I play. You can play three numbers or two or one. The only difference in strategy between an aggressive system of from four to six numbers and a conservative system of from one to three numbers will be when you call your odds off. On the aggressive side, you call off your odds after three unsuccessful rolls of the dice. On the con-

servative side, you'll call off your rolls in the following manner: three numbers are called off after four unsuccessful rolls,
two numbers are also called off after four rolls if the two
numbers are 6 and 8 and after five rolls if they are any other
combination. For one number, you just leave it and hope.

"I can't stress enough that it's important that you be the
judge of your own temperament and bankroll. You must set
clear and reasonable betting parameters for yourself. (See
chapter nine for money management advice.) You've bought
this book to learn how to be a winner, and you can't be a winner if you are unrealistic and overbet your bankroll. If you
can only afford to risk $10.00 on a roll, then only play one
number. However, if you can only bet $10.00 and you're in
Las Vegas or Laughlin or Reno or Lake Tahoe, that $10.00
could be enough for two or three numbers. The bottom line is
that you must be comfortable with the level of betting that
you choose, otherwise a losing session, and they'll be many
of them, will be emotionally crippling.

"All craps players experience wild swings in fortune.
Some nights it seems that shooter after shooter is sevening
out early. Other nights they'll be four or five good rolls in
succession and the money will come pouring in. Be prepared
to win some and lose some. Never lose more than you can
emotionally bear so that when you win the happiness more
than drowns out the past pain."

The Out and Up Progression

Regardless of your level of betting, however, you'll want
to get more money on the table during a hot roll. The Captain
has clear guidelines for when to increase your bets (if you
want to).

No matter how many numbers you have working for you
the formula is the same. Once you have won triple your
money at risk, you spread *out* on the board. Thus, if you're
keeping one number working for you and you win three
times, you spread out to two numbers, if you triple this
money then move out to four numbers, then six. But you

must always be winning triple the total amount at risk before you increase your outward spread.

Once you have all the numbers covered and have once again won triple the amount of money you have at risk, then you start the process of moving *up* your bet size. Instead of placing a $5.00 Come and a $5.00 Don't Come bet, you place $10.00 and $10.00. As these bets replace the lower ones, you place full odds of $20.00 behind them.

When you start betting multiple chips, your betting strategy will be altered depending on the rules of the casino or riverboat. These alterations will be covered in chapter five.

It's Simply S • U • P • E • R

Is the Captain's Supersystem—sometimes referred to as the "5-Count" Doey-Don't System—the best strategy ever devised for beating the game of craps? Without question it is. If we continue to use our $5.00 bet with double odds as a standard, you'll be able to clearly see that the Supersystem outperforms the only other viable betting strategies at craps: Pass Line bets with full odds and Place bets. Since Come bets function in the same manner as Pass Line bets, our analysis will ignore them. We will not consider any other betting strategies, including the Wrong bettors because in the long run the expectation is about the same for Right and Wrong bettors. As for the various Crazy Crapper bets, chapter two adequately covers what you can expect from them: economic suicide.

For the purposes of the following discussion, we are going to assume that the 7 never comes up in a negative way. That is, except for its winning potential on the Pass Line bet, the 7, for all intents and purposes, doesn't exist for this comparison. Why are we assuming this? Remember that the casinos and riverboats make their money by "taking" part of your winnings—that's their edge. They don't give you a fair return on your money at risk. Also, we are only interested in the money at risk in this demonstration. Thus, when you have a $5.00 Come bet and a $5.00 Don't Come bet with full odds behind the Come, you're actually only risking $10.00 as opposed to $20.00 because the Come and Don't Come bets cancel each other out. This has already been adequately covered.

Assuming thirty-six perfect rolls of the dice where every number comes up exactly as probability theory would suggest, you find that of every thirty-six rolls the point numbers come up twenty-four times. (6 and 8 come up ten times, 5 and 9 come up eight times, and 4 and 10 come up six times.)

The first chart shows how much of a tax the casino takes out of your wins when you place bets. Since the 7 never helps place bets, no explanation is necessary for this chart. Assuming once again that we are placing $10.00 at risk, except for the 6 and the 8, which as you recall must be bet in degrees of $6.00. Thus, we will be placing $12.00 behind the 6 and the 8.

Place Bets

#	Ways to Make	Money at Risk	True Odds	House Odds	Expected Win	Actual Win	Tax
4	3	$ 30	2/1	9/5	$ 60	$ 54	$ 6
5	4	$ 40	3/2	7/5	$ 60	$ 56	$ 4
6	5	$ 60	6/5	7/6	$ 72	$ 70	$ 2
8	5	$ 60	6/5	7/6	$ 72	$ 70	$ 2
9	4	$ 40	3/2	7/5	$ 60	$ 56	$ 4
10	3	$ 30	2/1	9/5	$ 60	$ 54	$ 6
	24	$260			$384	$360	$24

In Place betting, therefore, the casino will theoretically take out $24.00 in "taxes" for every $384.00 you win—leaving you with a net return of $360.

The next chart shows how much of a tax the casinos and riverboats take from you when you use what has traditionally been considered the best betting strategy in craps—the Pass Line wager. A short explanation is necessary for this chart.

You will notice that although I originally said that these charts would be based on $10.00 per number at risk, the following chart is more. Most astute Pass Line bettors will put $5.00 on the Pass Line and then place full odds—in this case $10.00—behind it. It would be unfair to analyze the Pass Line wager at $10.00—$5.00 on the Pass Line and $5.00 in odds behind—because that would give the wrong impression of the worth of this particular betting practice. Keep in mind that the Pass Line wager is paid off at even money. It would be a rare individual who would not place the full odds behind the Pass line. Thus, for this chart the total money at risk will be $5.00 on the Pass Line with $10.00 behind it. So for the number 4, the total risk is $45.00 since 4 can be made three ways and there's $15.00 at risk each time.

The second point of explanation concerns the positive expectation on the come out roll for Pass Line bettors. You will recall that the Pass Line wins immediately if a 7 or 11 is thrown and loses if a 2, 3, or 12 is thrown on the come out roll. Thus, on a $5.00 Pass Line wager a bettor would win $40.00 on the come out (eight ways of making 7 and $11 \times 5.00) but would lose $20.00 (four ways of making 2, 3, or $12 \times 5.00).

Thus, on the Pass Line wager the initial expectation is a net win of $20.00. This win will be factored in at the end of the chart to give an accurate assessment of the Pass Line bet.

Pass Line Bets

#	Ways to Make	Money at Risk	True Odds	Expected Win	Actual Win	Tax
4	3	$ 45	2/1	$ 90	$ 75	$15
5	4	$ 60	3/2	$ 90	$ 80	$10
6	5	$ 75	6/5	$ 90	$ 85	$5
8	5	$ 75	6/5	$ 90	$ 85	$5
9	4	$ 60	3/2	$ 90	$ 80	$10
10	3	$ 45	2/1	$ 90	$ 75	$15
	24	$360		$540	$480	$60

The Pass Line win of $20.00 must now be added to actual win. Thus, the actual win is $500.00. The total tax on the Pass Line wager is reduced to $40.00.

Now we come to the Captain's Doey-Don't. You will note that here we are able to place $10.00 at risk for each number. Since the Come/Don't Come wagers cancel each other out, this money is not at risk and will be ignored. We need only concern ourselves with the odds portion of this wager. However, as stated previously, the house does win $5.00 on the Come/Don't Come wager when a 12 is thrown, and, thus, we must factor in the loss of $5.00 for every thirty-six rolls of the dice. As we did with the Pass Line chart, this money will be factored in at the end.

The Captain's Doey-Don't Bet

#	Ways to Make	Money at Risk	True Odds	Expected Win	Actual Win	Tax
4	3	$ 30	2/1	$ 60	$ 60	0
5	4	$ 40	3/2	$ 60	$ 60	0
6	5	$ 50	6/5	$ 60	$ 60	0
8	5	$ 50	6/5	$ 60	$ 60	0
9	4	$ 40	3/2	$ 60	$ 60	0
10	3	$ 30	2/1	$ 60	$ 60	0
	24	$240		$360	$360	0

Since the casino won on the 12 once on the Come/Don't Come, we must now subtract our loss of $5.00 from our actual win. Thus, instead of winning $360.00, we won $355.00. The house took out a tax of $5.00.

In the interests of clarity, let me make the bottom line of each chart comparable. The following will show what the actual tax is for every $100.00 you would have won had the game been fair.

Betting System	Expected Win	Actual Win	Tax
Place Bets	$100	$93.75	$6.25
Pass Line/Odds	$100	$92.59	$7.41
Doey-Don't	$100	$98.61	$1.39

While none of the above systems will give you a fair game, that is a game in which the long-term potential is a standoff, the Captain's Doey-Don't comes the closest. What makes his Supersystem so compelling is the coupling of the Doey-Don't with the "5-Count." By doing this, you have reduced the casino's tax to its absolute minimum, and you have a workable method for avoiding horrendous rolls. In short, the Captain has done what every craps player wishes and dreams of—he's found the only practical and workable way to reduce losses and maximize wins!

Slow Is Safest

"As you can see the Supersystem's components—the '5-Count' and the Doey-Don't—require a thorough knowledge of the payoffs and a watchful eye in playing. I would not recommend going to four numbers the very first time you play the system in a casino. At a crowded table, with chips flying, you might find it hard to keep track of what numbers you have, much less whether the payoffs are correct.

"I would start with just two numbers for my first session and make sure I was completely comfortable in tracking my bets before I start going to three, four, or more numbers. When you're playing an aggressive Supersystem and a shooter gets hot, you'll find that the dealers tend to get a little harried, and the players will become annoyed because the game is slowing down which they associate with the casino trying to 'cool off' a hot shooter. If you're frimping and fumbling and asking the dealers which bets are yours, you might find some of the players becoming irritated with you. Craps players are a superstitious lot, and some believe that too much time passing between rolls will bring out the seven.

"Now, while I don't care what other players think about my methods of play or me, there's something to be said for a table of happy, friendly players. After all, gambling should be fun and certainly craps is one of the most exciting and fun ways to wager money. So if ill-feelings can be avoided, then they should be. So play two numbers your first time out until you are truly comfortable. If there's one thing I've learned from a lifetime of gambling experience, it's that you should never be in a rush to put up your money. Take your time, go slowly, there will always be a craps game tomorrow."

FIVE

Pushing the House

The last chapter showed you the most powerful system ever devised for beating the craps out of the casinos. Yet, if you want to approach the Captain's level of play, there's still more to learn.

"In reality, the Doey-Don't is at its worst in a $5.00, double-odds game. That's correct. As good as it seems compared to the other intelligent systems of play—and it is without a doubt the best— there are still even more advantageous ways of playing it. These will all depend upon the casino and its rules. There are ways of reducing the casino tax even more! And again, to do so requires that you understand certain casino practices thoroughly and have a firm grasp of your betting strategies and their payoffs."

Casinos with $5.00 minimum bets and double odds are the norm and, in most cases, the minimum in Atlantic City. Five dollar, double-odds games can be found in most Nevada casinos, too. However, there are much better games available, if you look around. For example, in Las Vegas you can find casinos that offer upwards of ten times odds! During a recent visit to Vegas, I noticed that The Frontier, Vegas World, The Union Plaza, and Binion's Horseshoe were all offering games with ten times odds. (In fact, Binions Horseshoe offers twenty times odds in June!) There were also a few casinos offering three and five times odds.

The best casino, from the point of view of the player with a small bankroll, is The Union Plaza in downtown Las Vegas. Here you can get a game with a 25¢ minimum and ten times odds. On the Come/Don't Come the minimum is 50¢. That means, you can have four numbers working for $20.00 at risk. Your tax is a mere 50¢ for thirty-six rolls. You'll be hard pressed to find a better game than this.

The other casinos offering ten times odds in Vegas had $1.00 minimum bets. Thus, you can have $40.00 working on four numbers but pay only a $1.00 tax for thirty-six rolls. Let me translate this as I did in the previous chapter. If your expected win in a fair game is $100.00, how much of a tax will be extracted in a $1.00 game with ten times odds? 28¢! If you were expected to win $100.00, your actual win would be $99.72. This is as close to a fair game as you'll ever get in a casino short of card counting in blackjack.

"Obviously, when given a choice between double odds or ten times odds you would be silly to choose the former. In Las Vegas you have a tremendous advantage because you can play for low stakes and high odds. However, casinos that offer double, triple, and five times odds, quite often in higher unit betting, Atlantic City will offer a better game. Of course, nothing can beat ten times odds and when given the opportunity to play in a casino that offers this don't pass it up. Even if you're staying at another hotel, you would be foolish to pass up an opportunity to play the Supersystem at ten times odds."

But not every craps player can play in casinos with ten times odds, and at this writing, no Atlantic City casino offers more than five times odds. For these players to gain an extra advantage, the Captain suggests a technique he calls Pushing the House.

"Pushing the House is very simple, really. What you want to find out is how much betting leeway a casino will offer you within the context of its particular game. For example, in Atlantic City's double odds games, if you are betting Come/Don't Come for $10.00, you would normally put $20.00 in odds behind the Come. However, all Atlantic City casinos will allow you to put $25.00 behind the 6 and 8. That's Pushing the Casino. The extra $5.00 the casino allows you is a fair bet."

The Captain has uncovered quite a few casino perks when it comes to multiple chip bettors.

"In games with triple odds, on a $5.00 Come bet, you can place odds of $16.00 or $18.00 behind the 5 or the 9 at the Claridge in Atlantic City. I suggest you take the $18.00. The reason this is allowed is that the 5 and the 9 are paid off at three to two and you must have an even number for a correct payoff. Since strict adherence to the triple odds format would result in a payout that has change involved, the casino allows you to go up a notch in order to make the payoff correctly."

Some other Atlantic City casinos will allow you to place $12.00 as your odds bet behind the 5 or the 9 when you have a Come bet of $5.00, even though a correct payoff can be made on $10.00 odds bets.

"The key to Pushing the House is to simply try it. If you're at a casino and you have a $5.00 Come bet on the 5 or the 9, and the casino is offering double odds, simply drop $12.00 down and say: 'Odds.' If the dealer returns the extra $2.00, so what? Quite often, you'll discover that the casino will accept the bet. In addition, different pit bosses will sometimes give you different games, so just because one shift rejects a bet doesn't mean the shift after it will reject it too. Always push them. It's in your interests."

There are a number of examples where the Captain pushes the casinos.

"In double odds games, when I'm betting $15.00 on the Come/Don't Come I've found that most Atlantic City casinos will accept a $50.00 odds bet behind the 6 or the 8, and a $40.00 odds bet behind the 5 or the 9. The 4 or the 10 is still $30.00.

"The strangest and most beneficial pushing of a casino occurs when I'm betting $15.00 at the Claridge in Atlantic City which offers triple odds. The Claridge will allow you to put $75.00 behind the 6 or the 8 and $60.00 behind the 5 or the 9. These bets are the equivalent of five times odds and four times odds respectively. Once again, the casino doesn't allow itself to be pushed on the 4 or the 10.

"At Resorts International in Atlantic City, there are some tables that offer five times odds. When I bet $15.00 on the Come/Don't Come, Resorts will allow me to place $125.00 behind the 6 or the 8 and $100.00 behind the 5 or the 9. Again, no pushing on the 4 and the 10.

"As you can see, in reality these casinos are offering you a better game than advertised, yet most craps players are oblivious to the idea of Pushing the Casino. But pushing a casino is an important part of being a winning craps player. It allows you to get more money on the table that is not taxed by the casino should you win.

"Every advantage you can get over a casino you should take. And don't be embarrassed to pluck down a $75.00 odds bet behind the 6 or the 8 on a $15.00 Come/Don't Come at a triple odds table and have the dealer look at you as if you're crazy. What do you care? In fact, if the dealer should return the bet and tell you it's too much, ask to speak to the pit boss. Inform the pit boss that this bet is acceptable in other casinos, so why not here? If you're polite, the worst that can happen is you'll have to reduce your odds bet to $45.00. But there's a good chance the pit boss will let you push the casino, if not for $75.00, then for $50.00 on this bet.

"I'm always looking for ways to push the house, not only

in my Supersystem but in my High Roller system (see chapter seven)."

The Pushing of Atlantic City

As far as I've been able to ascertain, the Captain is the originator of the concept of Pushing the House. It was through him that Atlantic City casinos started to offer flexible odds bets. Members of the Crew who have been with the Captain since the beginning have given me an insight as to how the Captain accomplished the Pushing of Atlantic City.

According to Jimmy P. of Bay Ridge, Brooklyn, a member of the Captain's crew and a high roller of the first magnitude, "The Captain opened up the game of craps in Atlantic City. No one ever placed the kind of odds money behind Come and Pass Line bets that the Captain did. He's responsible for it. He was the first to do it. You should have seen the looks on the pit bosses' faces in those early days of Atlantic City when the Captain started pushing them."

John A., another high rolling member of the Captain's crew, echoed Jimmy P.'s assessment: "The Captain literally pushed the Atlantic City casinos into offering those odds bets because he kept dropping them on the table. At first, the pit personnel would push the bets back at him. But the Captain was persistent. Finally, the casinos were pushed."

But according to another high-rolling member of the Crew, Russ B. of Staten Island, it wasn't just the Captain's persistence at the tables that pushed Atlantic City casinos into offering such wide swings in their odds formulations. It was also the Captain's personality and power.

"You have to understand," said Russ, "that the Captain is a man of enormous personal charm and charisma. He was and is on very friendly terms with many of the casino bosses and pit personnel. In fact, it is not unusual for casinos to ask his advice in the handling of their craps games, or for casino hosts and executives to ask for personal advice concerning their career moves. Add to this the fact that as the leader of

the Crew he wields a tremendous economic power. No casino wants to lose the play of twenty-two high rollers. So
they are more than willing to give his ideas a hearing."

"Of course, none of the casinos are aware of the fact that
the Captain is a winner," said Jimmy P. "Although perhaps
some suspect it. I mean you can't play as much as he does,
for the amounts he does and not have someone wonder."

"Thank God," laughed John A., "that most of the Crew
loses or the Captain would probably be banned."

Whether the Captain was actually the originator of Pushing the House or not, the fact remains that he's a major prac-
titioner of the idea. In fact, a review of all the literature
concerning craps only vaguely suggests that it's possible to
get slightly better odds on some propositions than stated by
the casinos. No book or article ever published, as far as I
know, has ever detailed just what type of pushing a casino
will tolerate and to what degree. Indeed, because of the Captain and his Crew, you will now see many veteran Atlantic
City craps players pushing the casinos for odds that are actually much greater than publicized.

As Russ B. states: "The Captain is the greatest craps
player of this generation. I know that many people like to ro-
manticize Nick the Greek, probably because he won millions
and lost even more millions, and that many craps writers pretend to be great craps players. But no one, *no one*, has ever
done what the Captain has done for the period of time he's
done it. The fact that only a select group of people have
known about his exploits and that the casinos are totally unaware, or just barely aware, of his success is just another indication of his greatness."

Of course, Pushing the House has some disadvantages.
You are gambling more money, for example. "You must keep
in mind that when I recommend playing a certain way, I'm
recommending it *if you can afford it*. You would be an absolute
fool to go to a casino and play the Supersystem for $15 on the
Doey-Don't in order to take advantage of five times odds if
your bankroll was limited. One bad day and you could lose it
all."

There's a psychological factor at work here, also. When you are in a casino that allows five times odds, there's a tendency to feel that you're missing out on something if you don't take full advantage of the situation. In reality, the situation is taking advantage of you.

"When you play over your head, the casino has a tremendous advantage because it can break you quickly. A casino isn't interested in how long you play as much as how much you lose. If you have $500.00, the casino is happier taking that money in one minute than in one hour, because then you leave and a spot is open for another sucker to take your place. The casino's primary reason for being is to take your money. All other considerations are secondary. Naturally, they want to make taking your money as painless as possible so they offer fine accommodations, a pleasing gambling environment, good food, and all the liquor you can handle while you're playing. This is to distract you from the main purpose—the separating of you from your bankroll.

"There's a running joke among the Crew concerning the various casino hosts we deal with. A host's job is just what it sounds like. He or she is there to see that your stay is pleasant and to offer you the services your gambling level warrants. When the Crew and I arrive at a casino for a stay, the host on duty greets us and tells us what dinner and show arrangements have been made and so forth. But in reality, to the Crew the only job of the casino host is to see that your wallet is safely escorted to your room and then the casino."

In fact, one evening over drinks, several Crew members and I engaged in a little game called *What They Say/What They Really Mean/What the Host Really Hears*. Despite its sophomoric humor, there is a great truth here and a lesson worth learning if you desire to gamble in casinos.

Host: (to High Roller) "Good to see you again, sir." (What he really means: "Good to see your wallet again, sucker.")

High Roller: "Thanks, it's good to be back." (What the Host hears: "Thanks, I'm here to make a donation.")

Host: "I hope everything has been fine." (What he means: "You haven't had any financial setbacks, have you? You brought enough to lose at your regular levels?")

High Roller: "Everything is great." (What host hears: "My wallet's bulging. Business couldn't be better.")

Host: "Good. Everything is taken care of. Your dinner reservations are made. If you need anything let me know. We value your patronage." (What he means: "Good. After we fatten your stomach, we're going to trim your wallet. It's good that you're a loser, and I'll commiserate with you whenever you want. Just keep coming to us instead of our competitors.")

High Roller: "Great! Great! I can't wait to get back into the action." (What Host hears: "I'm really anxious to lose again this time and maybe if I'm really unlucky I can lose even more than I did last time.")

Host: "Ha! Ha! Welcome back." (What he means: "Hee! Hee! What a jerk!")

Keep in mind that you must play within your bankroll at all times, even if it means passing up the opportunity to push the house. If you can't afford to push the house and you do anyway, there's a good chance the house will push you— right out the door.

SIX

Casino Heat and Other Discomforts

You now know everything you need to know about the Supersystem in order to play a technically proficient game. You understand the "5-Count" and how it reduces losses due to horrendous rolls. You understand where to position yourself at the table. You understand how the Doey-Don't reduces the casino tax. And, you know about Pushing the House. You have also started to assess what type of betting level to maintain so as to avoid emotional and economic strain (see chapter nine). The last things to cover before you make your first assault on the casino or the riverboat (or your first assault with the Supersystem), are the various types of reactions you'll get from the pit personnel, the dealers, and the other players when they witness you playing this unique way.

"If you've never played craps before, I don't recommend running to a casino, pushing your way into the proper position at the table, and starting your '5-Count.' Instead, watch for at least an hour and get a feel for the game and the people who run it. You'll notice that some dealers are personable and friendly, and some are grumps. Some are lightening quick in their payoffs and calculations; some are slow and methodical. Some are rarely challenged for mistakes, while others rarely have a roll go by where someone is not grousing about an incorrect payoff. After you've watched the games, pick the table that is running smoothly for your first try with the Supersystem.

"In the next chapter, I'll explain how to look for a *good* as opposed to a *bad*, table. But for now I'm only interested in seeing that you get to play correctly without too much concern over dealer errors. You may run into enough petty annoyances playing the Supersystem without having to worry about dealers who can't figure out your payoffs."

This advice is really for first-time craps players, but even veterans would do well to listen. The first time I played the Supersystem in Atlantic City was at Trump Plaza. I had a gracious and competent dealer. Even though the table was crowded, he was able to handle my bets flawlessly. I was playing the exact way mentioned in chapter four—$5.00 Come/Don't Come bets with $10.00 odds behind my numbers (except when I had a 5 or a 9, then I had $12.00 odds). I kept four numbers working when I had money at risk. There were no really hot shooters, and I was basically even for two hours of play. (Most of the others at my table were down.)

Since I was intent on the game and making sure I had the right bets up, etc., I wasn't aware of the fact that a small crowd had gathered behind me. Most of them were senior citizens, who probably had taken the bus down for the day. They were intensely debating me, or, rather, my "bizarre" way of playing! One of them tapped me on the shoulder.

"I never seen that way of playing before," he said.

"Not many people play this way," I said.

"What is it that you're doing?" another asked.

I explained the Supersystem. I told them about the "5-Count," and the Doey-Don't, and even about Pushing the House. As I was doing this, I was trying to keep track of the game and my betting. It wasn't easy. The senior citizens were discussing my system among themselves whenever I turned to make a bet or collect a payoff.

"You ever seen a system like that before?" one asked the dealer.

The dealer shook his head and said: "Never."

"He winning with it?" asked my original contact.

The dealer smiled and pointed at me. "Ask him," he said.

"I'm holding my own," I said.

"That's some crazy system," one said.

They chatted a little more and then wandered away from the table. The dealer turned to me and said: "They're not the only ones interested." He gestured over his shoulder. Sure enough, there were the pit boss and two other pit personnel huddling just to my left.

"How long have they been there?" I asked.

"Oh, about a half hour," he said.

"I guess people are interested in the way I play," I shrugged.

I had a very odd feeling, call it déjà vu, that I was going to be banned. Now, intellectually I know that Atlantic City cannot ban players in blackjack and that no casino has ever banned a player at craps (except if that individual was a nuisance or a threat to the other players). But, the pit personnel were whispering and giving me furtive looks—the very same way the pit personnel talked and looked just before I was banned from playing blackjack at casinos in Las Vegas. Was it possible that I was about to get the old heave-ho at a craps table?

I turned to the pit people. "Interesting system isn't it?" I said.

One of them turned from me pretending that he hadn't been watching, a second smiled, but the pit boss walked over to me and said: "Yes, it is. I've been here quite a few years, and I never saw anyone play quite like that."

"Not many people know about it," I said.

"Where'd you learn it?"

"Oh," I said, "some old-time craps player."

"He must be pretty good," said the pit boss.

"Yeah," I nodded.

Of course, I wasn't banned. I'm sure it wasn't even in their minds. They were interested in the way I was playing, just as the senior citizens were. But the fact remains—the Supersystem will, at times, draw attention to you. More often this attention will simply be polite and inquiring, as it was in my first time out. However, on rare occasions it will be hostile and abusive.

One particularly unnerving time for me occurred just two weeks after the above incident. I was playing in another Atlantic City casino which shall remain nameless (Why tarnish a place for the actions of a few employees?). This time I was placing $10.00 Come/Don't Come bets and placing $20.00 (or $25.00 if my numbers were 6 or 8) in odds behind the Come.

I was to the left of the dealer. The player on my left made polite conversation as I started placing my Come/Don't Come bets on the first 2-count. He was interested in what I was doing so I told him in general what my system was. (I have since learned that silence is golden. Most people I've spoken to in the midst of a game are interested but not receptive to what you're doing. My standard response now is to say that it's a complicated system and takes too much time to explain, but they can watch if they like.) The player next to me laughed politely and said there's no way I could win with such a crazy betting scheme. He then threw four $25.00 chips on the table and called out: "All the hard ways!"

The dealer, a young woman with a razor thin mouth and, as I soon learned, an even sharper tongue, seeing my bet, shouted out: "We got a wackoo betting the Do and the Don't!" I laughed because at first I thought she was just fooling around. She turned to me and said: "Do you know what you're doing?"

"I think so," I said.

"How can you expect to win? The bets cancel out," said the boxman.

"I'll be taking odds at times," I replied and I began to realize that the dealer was making faces at me.

"You're the one who's odd at times," she said and laughed uproariously. I started to feel a little uncomfortable. I should have simply waited for a judgment on the bets I had up and left immediately. But sometimes even experienced players can do stupid things. I stayed.

It so happens that shooter after shooter was sevening out within the first five rolls, so for the first twenty minutes I never got to place any odds. Every time that I placed a Come/ Don't Come bet this dealer would ride me. She had nicknamed me Dr. Do and Mr. Don't. It seems the other members of the pit crew found her jokes hilarious and they were guffawing every time she poked me with her forked tongue. Foolishly, I stayed at the table.

Finally, it was my turn to roll.

The female dealer was now on stick, and she shot the dice over to me. "Pick two," she said. Then she played to the crowd: "That's one," she held up one finger, "And two," she held up a second finger. At that moment I desired to hold up a third finger but being a gentleman I merely smiled and took two dice. "Very good Dr. Do and Mr. Don't," said another dealer. Just as I was rolling, the pit boss strolled over. The female dealer announced: "That's Dr. Do and Mr. Don't rolling!" The pit boss smiled. I rolled a 7. My Pass Line bet won, and my Don't Pass bet lost.

"So sorry you lost Mr. Don't," said the male dealer to my right, as he scooped up my Don't Pass bet. "So happy you won Dr. Do," he said again as he paid off my Pass Line bet.

"You're never going to win any money that way," said the pit boss genuinely concerned. "You'll lose on the twelve."

As if to prove his prophetic powers, my next roll was a 12.

"You see?" he said and shook his head and went to the table adjacent to mine.

"Too bad, Dr. Do," said the female dealer/stickperson as she shot the dice my way again. Then she became inspired: "Dr. Do-Do on the come out!"

By now the entire table was aware of her ribbing me and, unfortunately, as these things are want to be, the other players seemed to be in her corner. Still, I stubbornly stayed at the table.

"Don't call me Dr. Do-Do," I said politely. "You're embarrassing me."

"I'm just kidding," she said offended.

I rolled. Another 7!

As the Pass Line bettors were being paid off, the boxman turned to me and said: "Dr. Do-Do, if you knew how to play the game, you would have won just now."

"Don't call him Dr. Do-Do," shouted she of the acid tongue. "He's sensitive. Aren't you Dr. Do-Do-oops!" Everybody laughed.

I wish I could tell you that I had a fabulous roll, but I didn't. I sevened out just as I placed my odds on three numbers. I stayed at the table for a few more shooters, took some more abuse from Ms. Merciless and finally, common sense prevailing at last, I left.

As I walked away from the table, I heard her say: "That guy oughtta get a book and learn how to play."

"Probably he can't read," said another dealer, and everyone laughed heartily.

Obviously there are two points to this story. The first concerns the negative attention you might get as you play the Supersystem. The second concerns my stupidity in staying at a table that was not only cold but cruel! The first situation you might not be able to avoid. Some people will think that you have no idea of how to play craps when they watch you place your bets and use the "5-Count." This will be especially true when the table is cold and shooters are sevening out early. It will appear that your system of play has no chance for winning money because you're not putting up the odds.

The other players will not be aware that you are saving money while they are losing at a cold table. In these situations, the "5-Count" can save you money. But it may not be able to save you face. If the table personnel become the least bit abusive, learn from my mistake—leave. In addition, learn from my other mistakes, and don't bother to try to explain the Supersystem while you're playing because generally people won't quite understand what you're talking about.

I don't want you to get the wrong idea and think you're putting your life or dignity to the test when you play the Supersystem in a casino. You're not. Ninety percent of the time the dealers and pit personnel will simply handle your bets as if nothing is unusual. I just want you to be prepared for the times that either players, spectators, or the pit and table personnel will be interested in what you're doing. The degree and kind of attention will be more a function of the individual's personality than anything else. However, the dragon lady who breathed her scornful fire on me was an exceptional case. The Supersystem is indeed unique and will elicit commentary. Be prepared, but not panicky.

"When you use the Supersystem, you can put all ideas of being rated for comps aside. Unless you're betting maybe $200.00 or $300.00 on the Come/Don't Come, the casinos will figure that the only potential profit they're going to make from you is piddling—a mere one winning bet for them (losing bet for you) in thirty-six rolls. They'll figure that the odds bets are break even bets in the long run for them, and, thus, you aren't worth a rating. Actually, they're correct. The purpose of the Supersystem is to win money. When you play it, you're not interested in comps for dinners, shows, rooms. The only thing you want out of the casino is its bankroll."

As one who employs the Supersystem, my only fear concerns what will happen when this book becomes widely circulated. Will the casinos and riverboats begin to change the rules of their games (as was done when card counting became general knowledge)? The Captain does not share these concerns.

"You'll recall that with the card counting explosion of the

1960s, the casinos panicked and changed the rules to such an extent that many people just quit playing. The casinos then went back to their original games with some modifications to offset the poorly prepared counters. Most people who say they can count cards can't. And most people who will attempt to play the Supersystem will probably lack the discipline to do so. Those undisciplined players will simply add to the casinos' bankrolls, as those would-be card counters do. I don't really think the casinos have much to fear. I think people have a tool in the Supersystem that can enable them to win. But they must play intelligently and not get carried away. I don't think that many craps players can do that. The reason I say this is that my own Crew, with few exceptions, continues to play their old ways."

SEVEN

So You Want to Be a High Roller?

C raps tends to attract high rollers because of its excitement and the opportunity to win (and lose) quite a bit of money quickly. Some people confuse the term high roller with the idea of an expert gambler. However, in a nutshell: a high roller is someone who bets a lot of money.

Indeed, sometimes a high roller is an expert gambler; however, more often than not, the high roller is just another sucker who happens to have more money to lose. The high roller obviously didn't get his (or her) money from gambling. He or she either earned it, inherited it, stole it, or some combination of the three.

Unfortunately, there are a significant number of people who believe that because someone is called a high roller that person must know what he's doing. You'll see this quite often at a low-limit table. A high roller will appear, cash in for several thousand dollars, proceed to bet in direct proportion to his gambling IQ (that is, make the stupidest bets imaginable) and suddenly others at the table will mimic him.

Oh yes, the high roller is wined and dined by the casino. He'll receive RFB—room, food, and beverage—compliments of the house. He'll get the best seats for all the top shows. He'll get complimentary tickets to see all the great fights and other sporting events put on by the casino. He'll even be invited to elaborate parties and get to hobnob with celebrities and other high-profile high rollers. Quite often, he'll have his airfare refunded or be picked up in a private jet and flown into town. Naturally, he'll also be driven to the casino in a limousine. Sounds great, doesn't it?

"Being a high roller makes you feel good. You're treated like a king. When you show up at a table and put down that wad of hundred dollar bills, the other players take notice. The casino personnel fawn all over you. There isn't a thing that they won't do for you. The casino and its resources are at your service.

"Of course, in reality, the casinos couldn't care less about you as an individual. They care about your money—taking it, that is. To the casinos, a high roller is what a penned hen is to a fox—their lifeblood and their prey. The 'free' room, food, and beverage probably cost the high roller twenty times what it would cost the average person paying for them. It is not unusual for a high roller to lose $10,000.00 or more in a weekend of playing. It is also not so rare for some high rollers to lose ten times that!"

So why do these high rollers bet so much? Are they compulsive? Are they candidates for Gambler Anonymous?

"I think you can eliminate compulsive gamblers from our discussion, because most compulsive gamblers sooner or later crash and can't afford to play anymore. Most of the high rollers I know are successful individuals who simply enjoy the thrill of gambling. Although you might say that they're addicted to the thrill, they are in control and are not bankrupting their lives to gamble. By the way, many high rollers, myself included, are actually involved in high-risk investments, real estate ventures, and the like.

"No, I think the key to understanding the mentality of the high roller, or any gambler actually, revolves around that word THRILL. The high roller bets at a level of risk that gives him a thrill. If you're a millionaire, a five dollar bet would be meaningless. You wouldn't feel you were risking anything. However, a hundred or a thousand dollar bet would get your blood pumping. I think you have to have an acceptable level of risk in order to make gambling a thrilling experience. If the level of risk is too high, then gambling will destroy you—emotionally as well as financially; if the level of risk is too low, gambling would be boring. By acceptable level of risk I mean a level that makes you care if you lose even though you can afford it, and makes you excited if you win even though you don't need the money. It's not a gamble if you're not risking something.

"The acceptable level of risk for a high roller is, quite simply, higher. He sets his level of excitement at a manageable thrill. What makes the high roller different from the other gamblers is that his level of thrill makes the casino take notice, and he'll receive the RFB treatment. That treatment just adds to his enjoyment."

But the Captain has words of caution for would-be high rollers.

"Never play to impress the casino. Never. With that said, I must tell you that in the beginning I was interested in the RFB and the royal treatment. I had only one problem—I didn't want to lose the money that went along with being a high roller. As I stated in chapter three, I actually developed the concept of the '5-Count' as a way of getting RFB. I had no idea when I started using it that it would be the secret not just to that but to winning. Of course, my Supersystem won't get you rated, and it might even get you an invitation to leave (particularly in Nevada where the casinos are free to ban skilled blackjack players and anyone else they wish to), but my High Roller System will. I must tell you right now, however, that unless you can afford to gamble a substantial amount of money you're better off sticking to the Supersystem. Although my High Roller System only utilizes good percentage bets, nothing cuts down the house edge the way the Supersystem does.

"In the High Roller System, you'll have to overcome a house edge of 1.5 to 3.8 percent, depending on the rules of the individual casino in which you play. However, my experience has shown that the '5-Count' is quite capable of neutralizing the house edge in the long run. By using the methods of table selection, money management, and progressive betting that I'll recommend in this and subsequent chapters, aside from getting RFB with my High Roller System, you stand a good chance of actually winning. There's no feeling like that. You get everything for free, you're treated like a king (or queen), *and* you take home the casino's money to boot!

"Even if you don't actually win the casino's bankroll on your visit, if my High Roller System keeps your losses to an acceptable level so that your RFB costs you less than it would had you actually paid up front and out of pocket, then you've actually come home a winner. If, for example, you would have paid $800.00 for a weekend for room, food, beverage, shows, what-have-you and instead you lost $500.00 at the tables and received all that gratis, why then you're $300.00 up on the deal!

"I have used my High Roller System the longest of any mentioned in this book and for ten years I'm ahead with it. How is that? I get my RFB, and I've taken small withdrawals from the casino banks as well. It's quite possible you'll do the same."

To bet at the level required for RFB, you have to know the '5-Count' perfectly, play it exactly as described in chapter three, bet exactly the numbers in exactly the proportions indicated by the Captain in this chapter and exploit every advantage the casino you're staying at gives you. While the Supersystem requires concentration every moment you're at the table, the High Roller System is going to require judgment on your part, and the ability to convince the casino that you are indeed what you appear to be—just another high rolling loser!

Just as we were able to Push the House in the Supersystem to help us exploit a casino practice, so too you must exploit other casino practices in the High Roller System—some of them are simply time-management situations. Therefore, you must be sharp in order to be a high roller, without actually taking the risks that a high roller takes.

Now, we'll go step by step through the Captain's High Roller System.

Betting Level

You need to put down a minimum bet of approximately $150.00 in Atlantic City. The same would probably hold true for the more glamorous casinos in Vegas (such as the Mirage, Caesar's Palace, The Flamingo Hilton, The Golden Nugget, etc.). However, some of the less glamorous casinos might require substantially less.

"When in doubt, just ask a casino host what betting level and for how many hours you would need to sustain it in order to qualify for RFB. Most casino hosts will be more than happy to tell you. If you run into a place that hems and haws, go to another one if you can. Remember, you may be registered at one casino in Vegas, say, for a week, but you probably don't have to stay there the entire time. What if another offers you a free room? Just cancel the remainder of your stay with the previous one, as long as you don't have to pay a fine for cancellation, and go to the one that offers you RFB."

Usually, you'll have to bet the minimum over a four hour period. So for every day that you're a guest in that casino, the casino will expect four hours worth of action from you. Some casinos will actually expect less. For example, the Riviera has offered junkets where the betting minimums are substantially lower than $150.00, and they only ask for two hours of play a day. While you're not given the full high roller treatment, the hotel will pick up plane fare, room, and non-gourmet meals. Of course, it's always best to inquire at the hotel because policies change overnight.

Bankroll

How much of a bankroll would you need for a weekend, say, in Atlantic City or Vegas when your minimum bet will be $150.00 for eight hours of play spread out over 48 hours?

"I usually bring $3,000.00 to a weekend session of play, with another $3,000.00 in reserve. I realize that many authors would say that that is far too little to sustain a betting level that is so high. However, no gambling authors know about the '5-Count,' so their advice can now be considered outdated. Unless Lady Luck has taken a strong dislike to you, $3,000.00 will be more than adequate to sustain you for a weekend." (See chapter nine for a more complete discussion of money management and betting levels.)

Betting

We will be using Place bets in this system because Place bets make the casinos smile. After all, some of the Place bets give the casinos big edges. However, high rollers are notorious Place bettors. This system mimics the high roller, with two exceptions. First, you'll only be making those Place bets that give the house the smallest edge. Second, and more importantly, you'll be utilizing the "5-Count" to limit your losses, extend your playing time, and increase your potential to be in on the better rolls.

This is the Captain's procedure:
1. Use the "5-Count" (review chapter three).
2. On the 5-count, place the 6 and the 8 for $60.00 each.
3. Buy the 4 or the 10 for $35.00.

That's correct. In Atlantic City the casinos will allow you to buy the 4 or the 10 for $35.00 and still only pay a one dollar commission! To my knowledge, no craps book has ever mentioned this fact. As far as I can ascertain, the Captain was the first Atlantic City craps player to push the casinos into allowing a one dollar buy of the 4 and the 10 for $35.00. As you are aware, it is a common practice to allow the twenty-five dollar or green chip bettors to buy these numbers and only pay the $1.00 commission. Well, now you know you can buy them for $35.00. That substantially reduces the house edge on the 4 and the 10.

Unfortunately, many Las Vegas casinos do not have this policy, so you'll have to shop around and find those that do. If you must, buy the 4 or the 10 for $25.00. But, by doing this, you give the house a rather large edge on the bet.

4 *or* 10? That Is the Question!

How do you decide which of the numbers, 4 or 10, to buy? Now we have come to what the Captain facetiously calls his Law of Repeating Numbers or the LTDD (Let The Dice Decide). These laws correspond to another of the Captain's credos: the NGSGR—the No Guess Second-Guess Rule.

"Before I tell you to commit to memory how to select the buy numbers, I must tell you that there is not a shred of mathematical evidence to support my views. I arrived at my Law of Repeating Numbers just by observing that quite often numbers come up in bunches. I arrived at my LTDD because I was tired of trying to figure out what I was going to do next. I realize that the dice have no memory and no will, so why should I try to guess which numbers might come up next? I let the dice decide my bet. That eliminated guessing. If after placing a bet, I lost, I never second guessed my no-guess system.

"So my system for selecting the 4 or the 10 is quite easy. It is based on that one assumption—numbers repeat; and two articles of faith—let the dice decide and don't second-guess yourself.

"Do numbers repeat? It seems to me they do. I can't tell

you how many times over the years I've seen a string of long odds numbers come up in a row. I once saw this sequence on a come out roll: 2, 2, 12, 2, 2, 12, 12. Countless times I've witnessed one number get 'hot.' Of course, these are nothing more than random fluctuations in probability, and there is obviously no way to predict in advance when such a repetitive cycle will develop. (The Supersystem really takes advantage of repeating numbers.)

"But let us say that we could predict that a number was about to repeat. The shooter rolled a 4, and you knew another 4 was on the way—what would you do? Naturally, you'd buy the 4. Now, let's go back to reality. You don't know what number is coming up, and the shooter rolls a 4. Why not bet on it? It has the same mathematical expectancy on the next roll as it did on the previous one. And, if I'm right and numbers repeat, you might get in on a sequence. If I'm wrong, so what? The cold probabilities didn't change because you followed my intuition.

"And, please, don't fall for the fallacy that just because a number hasn't appeared in awhile that it is due. Just because a 6 or an 8 or whatever hasn't been thrown in twenty rolls doesn't make it any more likely to appear on the next roll than on any previous roll. I realize when I'm offering my intuitive advice that it's not based on mathematical precepts. But, my advice won't do you any harm. You were going to bet anyway. But if you buy into the popular misconceptions, it can cost you dearly. If the 4 hasn't shown in a hundred rolls and you decide to bet your entire bankroll on its being due, you'll probably be out your entire bankroll."

On the 5-count, if the dice are showing a 4 or a 10, buy that particular number for $35.00. Let us pretend that on the 5-count a 4 was thrown. Now, you buy the 4 for $35.00. Your Place betting now looks like this: $60.00 on the 6 and the 8 and $35.00 on the 4. You have $156.00 at risk. (Remember, you have $155.00 on the numbers and the $1.00 commission on the 4.)

However, if on the 5-count the dice are not showing a 4 or a 10, then follow this betting list:

Number Made	How It Was Made	Buy
5	4:1	10
5	3:2	4
6	5:1	10
6	3:3	4
6	4:2	4
8	4:4	10
8	6:2	10
8	5:3	4
9	5:4	10
9	6:3	4

"The purpose of using the formula is simple. You don't have to think. The dice decide for you which number you'll buy. A 4:1 appears, you bet the 10, period. The less you have to think about what you're going to do at the craps table, the more relaxed you'll be, and the better you'll be able to make sure your payoffs are correct."

But what happens if you buy the 4 and the 10 is rolled on the very next roll?

"Bet the 10. If your bankroll permits, then just buy the 10 for $35.00. However, if you're working with $3,000.00 as your bankroll, then just tell the dealer to move your 4 to the 10."

And if the shooter should roll a 4?

"Keep your 10 and don't second-guess yourself."

Sitting Until Infinity or a Seven?

Once you're up on the initial three numbers, how long do you stay up? Do you wait until the shooter rolls a seven?

"If after three rolls of the dice one of your numbers hasn't hit, then tell the dealers to take you *off*. Don't tell them to take you *down*, because they'll return your bets. You want to sit out two rolls. If after sitting out two rolls, the shooter hasn't sevened out, tell the dealer to make your bets work again. If once again the shooter hasn't made one of your numbers within three rolls, take your bets off again. Continue this process until one of your numbers hits once. Now, once it hits, you're in the game until the end of time or the seven appears. Chances are it will be the seven."

Pilgrim's Progression

The next thing to learn is when to increase your bets. Remember: the keys to successful gambling are to limit losses and maximize wins. In order to maximize wins you have to get more money on the table in favorable situations. In craps, unlike card counting at blackjack, you can't tell in advance when a situation will be favorable. However, the Captain does have certain guidelines for getting more money into action. He also has certain cautions.

"Never, never, never increase your bets when you're losing. That's called chasing your losses. You put down your $60.00 on the 6 and the 8 and your $35.00 on the 4 or the 10 and bang! the shooter rolls a seven. It hurts and it will happen. Don't be a fool and immediately come back with a $120.00 on the 6 and the 8 and $75.00 on the 4 or the 10. No, you just play the next shooter as you did the last one. Utilize the '5-Count' and bet appropriately.

"If you're hit with a losing streak at one table or several tables, and you lose one-third to one-half of your stake, quit and go for a walk or a drink or a nap. The tables will still be there when you get back. Also, don't be afraid to leave a table after losing several bets. If the table loses for you three times in a row, or the dice have made a complete circuit of the players and your money is being whittled away, leave and go to another table.

"If a table is cold it won't necessarily stay cold, but it won't necessarily get hot either. However, leaving a losing table will make you feel better, and feeling better is important. Much of gambling is psychological, and a player who is not psychologically right will make the wrong moves. He'll throw his money away, not follow conservative betting principles; he'll pray to every god whose name he ever heard of, but all for nothing. I've seen it happen a million times. So, despite the fact that probability theory does not recognize the concept of a cold table, your emotions do. Leave if you've been losing and go to the next table."

In chapters nine and ten we'll have more to say about the psychology of gambling. But right now, you're going to learn the Captain's method for getting more money on the table.

"I call this betting method the Pilgrim's Progression because it's slow but correct. You won't chase your losses, but if you're winning, you'll begin to increase at a steady but very, very conservative pace."

On the 5-count you placed $156.00 at risk. If your numbers hit *four times*, after the fifth win increase your bets as follows: make the 6 and the 8 $90.00 each. You will have been paid $70.00 for your fifth win no matter what number hit. Thus, you're betting $60.00, but you're keeping $10.00. Remember, however, that if your buy bet wins, you have to pay another $1.00 commission to keep it working. In that case, you will keep $9.00 of your winnings.

You now have $35.00 on the 4 or the 10 and $90.00 on the 6 and the 8. If you win two more times, on the third win buy either the 4 or the 10 (whichever you don't have) for $35.00. You'll now have $35.00 on the 4 and the 10, and $90.00 on the 6 and the 8.

After two more wins, increase the 6 and the 8 to $120.00 each. You'll now have $35.00 on the 4 and the 10 and $120.00 on the 6 and the 8.

After two more wins, increase one of your buy bets to $55.00. (You'll now have to pay a $2.00 commission.) On the very next roll, as long as a seven isn't thrown, whether you won or not, increase your other buy bet to $55.00. You now have $55.00 on the 4 and the 10, and $120.00 on the 6 and the 8.

Now, should Dame Fortune really be smiling on you, and you win two more times, on the third win increase your bets as follows: buy the 4 and the 10 for $75.00 each and increase the 6 and the 8 to $150.00. And finally, after two more wins, increase your buy bets to $95.00 each.

"When I get to the point where I have $95.00 on the 4 and the 10, and, believe me, that is a rare occurrence, I stay and

just keep collecting. If you ever reach a roll that gets you to
this point, then you can continue to increase your bets intermittently. If you do this, however, remember to always increase the 6 and the 8 in units of $30.00 and the 4 and the 10
in multiples of $20.00. Personally, since the roll that's just
been outlined might occur once in a blue moon, I wouldn't
recommend constant escalation. Be happy with a big win.
Often you'll notice players pressing their bets (pressing
means doubling a bet) like crazy only to have it all swept
away when the seven comes. Easy betting increments, as outlined above, will guarantee that you get to take home some
money."

Tricks for Some Treats

"One of my Crew, I'll call him Joe, is a very big bettor. It is
not unusual for him to start placing numbers at $500.00 each
and press and press until he has thousands riding. Joe will
sometimes tell the dealers to put $3,200.00 across which
means he's covering all the numbers. Compared to him, I'm a
piker. Yet, when Joe calls the casino hosts, they cringe. You
see, Joe is a spoiled child and doesn't know how to act in
public.

"Joe's been a brat ever since he grew up and went to his
first casino. Yet, in many other ways, he's a kind and generous man. But something happens to Joe when the casinos
lavish him with the RFB treatment. He becomes an ingrate.
He becomes a bore. Now, although no casino will tell Joe to
take a hike until he takes etiquette lessons, they are not particularly happy to see him. They want his money, but they
don't necessarily want him.

"One time at The Imperial Palace in Vegas, a dealer made
a mistake in paying off one of Joe's big bets. Instead of just
politely informing the dealer of his error, Joe roared something to the effect that the dealer was an idiot and should be
sweeping garbage off the street. The dealer shot back that the
first thing his broom would sweep would be Joe. Well, that
set Joe off. He proceeded to ask for $500.00 worth of dollar

chips and he played all day on the Don't Pass line. The minimum bet was $2.00. Joe was being fully comped and had played his needed time so he was just doing this to bust chops. Finally, I got a call in my room to come down and see if I could talk Joe into some semblance of sanity. Luckily, Joe listens to me, and he finally stopped his childish behavior.

"Another time, a dealer scolded Joe for not hitting the back wall on one of his rolls. Usually a dealer will wait a few rolls before he makes this caution because on any given roll you might not hit the wall. But this dealer was a cantankerous guy and wanted to bug Joe. He obviously didn't know him. On the very next roll, Joe hit the back wall all right—but it was the back wall of the casino, fifty feet away! Trying to lighten the situation, I ran to where the dice fell and yelled out: 'He made his point!'

"What is the purpose of telling you these stories? Obviously, to show you what not to do. Joe and I go back a long way. I know him in other situations where his finer qualities come out. If I didn't, however, you wouldn't catch me dead with someone who acts as childishly as he does.

"Although the casinos are only interested in your money, many hosts and pit personnel and dealers are good people who are trying to do the best job that they can. I've always found that by being nice and respectful in return you will sometimes reap rewards. Whereas many times Joe will not be able to get the front row ticket to a big fight at the last minute, I have never found that to be the case with me. When my wife wanted to go to the Miss America Pageant several hours before it began, I called Resorts International, and she was seated in Merv Griffin's box. Joe's wife, who had called about the same time, had to settle for the back row of the orchestra.

"Now, I realize that you didn't purchase this book for a lesson in manners, but if you want to be a high roller then be a classy high roller. It's to your benefit.

"For example, in addition to the Crew, I have some sixteen other couples who like to go to Atlantic City. Most of them are five dollar bettors. However, when we descend on Atlantic City, some forty strong, the casinos will comp the whole lot. They do that because, with the exception of Joe, the Crew is composed of classy high rollers who are not truculent. They have a good time, make people around them happy. They cheer and applaud good rolls. They tip the waiters and waitresses and maids and bellhops generously. In short, between the Crew and the Barnacles (we call the little bettors Barnacles), the casino has the kind of guests it wants. If the Barnacles sometimes order a little too expensively from the menu, if they have endless bottles of champagne sent to their rooms, if they order the limousine service to go shopping, the casinos never say a word to me because they know in the long run we're worth their effort, not just in the money they think they'll win from us, but in the kind of atmosphere we help to generate in a gambling hall.

"With that said, I must confess that we're not always angels. Quite often, members of the Crew and I will use casino policies to our own benefit. For example, several Crew members might chip in to make a stake. You might have three Crew members who chip in $1,000.00 each and use it jointly. Player A will go to a table, place the $3,000.00 down and play for an hour. With the '5-Count' and my High Roller System, more than likely the player will be up a little, down a little, or even after this time. For a second hour, he now slowly removes green chips from his chip rack, until he's removed some $1,500.00. Now, he'll go to the bathroom and give the $1,500.00 worth of chips to Player B who'll cash them in. This player now heads for a table and cashes in for $1,500.00. He now does the same thing as Player A. By the time he's siphoned off $750.00, Player A is finished with his four hours of play. Now, the third player gets into the act and takes whatever Player A has left of the original stake plus the $750.00 from Player B. He now puts down his money and plays. In this way, one weekend's stake has been sufficient to get three players the RFB treatment. Of course, if one of the three players hits a cold streak and gets wiped out, this method would fail. But with sharp players who know the betting strategies and are not afraid to leave a table, a great time to pocket some chips by the way, the system works."

Okay, you now know what you need in order to become a high roller. If you've never played craps before, however, it might be better if you start your RFB career by observing the other high rollers in a casino.

Naturally, the majority of people can't be high rollers, and some of you might not want to play the Supersystem because of the requirements it places on table selection and concentration. For you, the Captain has devised the Limited Bankroll System. This system is covered in the next chapter.

EIGHT

Limited Bankroll System

N ot everyone can or wants to be a high roller. Some individuals just don't have the bankroll; others don't have the need to be treated like a high rolling big shot; and still others don't have the bankroll or the need. In addition, not everyone can play the Supersystem. If concentration is not your strong point, and you become impatient with the Doey-Don't method, or worse, if you become confused, then you'd be better off playing the Captain's Limited Bankroll System.

Now, just because we call the system a Limited Bankroll System doesn't mean it can't be used for stakes almost up to those of the High Roller System. The difference between the Captain's High

Roller System and the Limited Bankroll System is in the nature of the bets placed. In the Limited Bankroll System, except at casinos offering 25¢ and 50¢ games, you will not be placing any bets (initially) on the 4 or the 10 because of the high tax these numbers incur when you win.

"I developed the Limited Bankroll System for those players who hung around the Crew but obviously couldn't afford the big stakes (i.e., the Barnacles). Quite a few of the Barnacles didn't want to play the Supersystem because it required a set place at a table or too much effort. But, whatever their reason, and some were just plain not interested, these people still wanted the action of craps without being taken for a ride."

The Limited Bankroll System gives you an excellent shot at the casino's money because, as always, the heart of the system is the "5-Count."

For the purposes of explication in this chapter, the $5.00 minimum will again be the unit of betting. However, as we go along, we'll make conversions to take into consideration lower and higher stakes.

The Limited Bankroll System starts once again with the successful completion of the "5-Count." Once on the "5-Count," you will place $6.00 on the 6 and $6.00 on the 8. (Remember that in place betting the 6 and the 8 are paid off at $7.00 for $6.00.) You will leave the 6 and the 8 working for five rolls. If one of the numbers doesn't hit at least once in five rolls, you will tell the dealer that your bets are off. Keep the bets off for two rolls and then put them back on. This time keep them on for three rolls. Again, if one of the numbers doesn't hit within three rolls, take your numbers off for two rolls.

However, let's assume that one of the numbers hits within the first five rolls. When that number hits, give yourself another five rolls for either the 6 or the 8 to hit again. Each time the 6 or the 8 hits, you give yourself another five rolls for it to hit again.

If you're at a game that allows lower betting levels, you can place the 6 or the 8 for $1.50 each (payoff will be $1.75), for $3.00 each (payoff will be $3.50), or for $4.50 each (payoff will be $5.25).

"You will find all of the lower betting level games will be in Nevada. But, no matter what the level of betting is, first ask the dealer what the minimum bet is on the 6 and the 8 in order to get the proper odds. Some casinos will tell you you can place 50¢ on the 6 and the 8, but they won't tell you that you'll only get paid even money if you do so. It is always a good rule that when you first play in a given casino to ascertain what the house rules are before you put a given bet on the table."

If you desire higher betting levels, you can place the 6 and the 8 for $12.00, $18.00, $24.00, $30.00, etc., up to $60.00. Of course, if you can afford to place the 6 and the 8 for $60.00 each, then you should seriously consider playing the High Roller System and take advantage of the extensive comps that go with it.

"You'd be surprised at how many comps you can actually get with the Limited Bankroll System, especially in moderate-sized casinos in Nevada. In Atlantic City, betting $6.00 on the 6 and the 8 may or may not get you comped to a sandwich or an ice cream sundae, but in Nevada it could very well get you a comp to one of the fine, inexpensive buffets. Of course, don't put in time just to get comped. But, if you're playing, you have nothing to lose in asking."

Higher and Higher

As with all the Captain's previous systems, there is a method for determining when and how to increase your bets. Once again, you never increase your bets when you are losing. In the Limited Bankroll System, if your numbers hit a total of six times, on the seventh hit you will tell the dealer to press the number that just hit. Thus, if a 6 hit, the dealer would double the amount of money you had on the six and return a dollar to you. You would now have the 6 for $12.00 and the 8 for $6.00. If the next hit is an 8, then you would ask the dealer to press the 8 also. He would return a dollar to you and now you would have $12.00 on the 6 and the 8.

From this point, everytime the numbers hit a total of five times, on the sixth time you would press the number that just hit. On the seventh hit you would press its opposite. Thus, if the 6 hit, you would press the 6 up to $24.00; then, if the 6 hit again, you would press the 8 up to $24.00. If the numbers hit a total of five times again, you would continue the procedure.

However, once you get to $48.00 on the 6 and the 8, the next increase is not a press but simply an increase to $60.00 on each number. If one number hits within five rolls, you immediately go to the High Roller System and buy either the 4 or the 10 for $35.00. (See chapter seven for how to determine which number to select.) You would now play the High Roller System until the shooter sevened out. Then you would return to playing the Limited Bankroll System.

"The chances of someone going from the Limited Bankroll System to the High Roller System during one shooter's roll is highly unlikely. However, truly hot rolls tend to produce a hell of a lot of 6s and 8s because of the probability involved."

Out and Up Progression

There are two other methods the Captain "tolerates" for raising bets when you're winning with the Limited Bankroll System. I say "tolerates" because the Captain is not high on this way of betting but realizes that many limited bankroll players want more action than just the 6 and the 8. Thus, here's the first alternative to the betting progression of 6s and 8s: once you have the 6 and the 8 at $12.00 each, the next progression is outward. Thus, if 6 or 8 hits five times, the sixth time either hits, you'll place the 5 and the 9 for $5.00 each. From this point it gets a little more complicated because you have to consider total money at risk.

With $12.00 on the 6 and the 8, and $5.00 on the 5 and the 9, you have $34.00 at risk. When you have won a total of

$118.00, the next win, regardless of which number or how much, you will raise all your numbers up one unit. (A unit in betting means your minimum bet, in this case $5.00 on the 5 and the 9 and $6.00 on the 6 and the 8.) Thus, you bring the 6 and the 8 to $18.00 each and the 5 and the 9 to $10.00 each. Now, everytime you win more than $118.00 total you will continue to raise each number by one unit of betting, until you get to the point where the 6 and the 8 are at $60.00. When they've reached this level, you stop increasing the 5 and the 9 and switch to the High Roller System.

The second method for increasing bets in an outward progression will only work in casinos that have minimum bets of 50¢. Instead of spreading to the 5 and the 9 only, when the 6 and the 8 reach $18.00, the 5 and the 9 reach $10.00, buy the 4 and the 10 for $5.00 each. This will cost you a 50¢ commission. Then, with every win of $128.00, you will increase all your numbers by one unit until you get to $60.00 on the 6 and the 8.

"Personally, I don't like betting anything other than the 6 and the 8 on the Limited Bankroll System because I think you're giving the house too much of an edge on the other bets. However, you are using money that has been won and that lessens the emotional impact of these weaker bets. So if you need the feel of more action, then bet across as well as up, but do it as outlined. For those of you who stick strictly to the 6 and the 8, remember to take your bets off if five rolls go by without a hit. If the 6 or the 8 hasn't hit once in five rolls, you're probably in a fluctuation where other numbers are repeating, so take them off.

"If you do decide to move out to other numbers, take your bets off if your numbers don't hit once in three rolls. Keep in mind that if you have four numbers working you'll need a minimum of four hits to make money. So what if you have one of your numbers come up once when they're called off? I've noticed that if your numbers are going to hit, they'll start hitting and repeat quickly. So don't be afraid to call off your bets."

Although the Captain grudgingly tolerates a slight deviation from perfect play for emotional reasons, he is adamant when it comes to the purity of the "5-Count."

"Without the '5-Count,' you'll be just another intelligent craps player if you follow my High Roller or Limited Bankroll Systems. These systems minus the '5-Count' are really nothing more than intelligent betting systems. The '5-Count' is what gives you an opportunity to defeat the casino by exploiting the better rolls. The '5-Count' stretches your money over time and in that time you have a shot at a hot shooter. So although you can fiddle around a little with my Limited Bankroll System if you must in order to feel you're in the action, don't ever change the use of the '5-Count.' If you do, you might as well write a check payable to the casino of your choice and just mail it. You don't have a chance at being a winning player in the long run."

NINE

Money Management and the Mental Edge

Perhaps no subject comes in for more discussion and debate among gamblers and gambling writers than that of money management. Some writers consider money management the heart and soul of gambling, while others dismiss the notion of money management as a smokescreen that obscures the purpose of gambling—which is, to gamble! To the Captain, the matter of money management is mostly in the mind.

"You might say I'm a believer in mind over money. What I mean by this is quite simple—you have to look inside yourself and figure out what it is you hope to accomplish by gambling. Are you looking for a thrill that lasts for several seconds? If so, take all your gambling money and

place it on red or black in Roulette. In a few seconds, you'll either be ecstatic or miserable.

"Are you looking to enjoy an exciting, high-roller lifestyle
with penthouses and yachts and your own private helicopter? If so, then make sure you secure a good job or have great
business acumen, because there are only a handful of people
who can actually live that lifestyle and finance it with gambling wins. You will probably have to work at a real job to be a
high roller.

"Are you looking to get out of debt, finance your kids' ed-
ucations, buy a new home, or car? Gambling won't do it for
you. But, if you're looking to enjoy a challenge that is afforda-
ble and, perhaps, profitable, one that offers the kind of
adrenaline rush associated with athletics, and you're in control of yourself, then gambling is a suitable enterprise for
you. It's to you that I'm addressing my money management
and mental edge remarks."

The Captain's first principle of money management is
simple and self-evident. Never play with *scared money*.

"Scared money is, obviously, money you're afraid to lose.
Gambling money must be money over and above what you
need to live, educate the kids, give presents on holidays, etc.
It must be money specifically set aside for gambling and not
needed in other areas of your financial life. Its loss will hurt,
all losing hurts, but it won't devastate you. Otherwise, don't
gamble it.

"I sometimes like to compare playing craps with boxing.
Actually, you can compare it with any sport, if you like. Playing with scared money is the equivalent of a fighter being so
afraid of losing that his very fear of losing sets up the necessary condition for him to lose—he freezes and doesn't fight
his fight. The same is true of playing with scared money. If
you are afraid to lose it and you start to, you'll panic and
probably chase your money (increase bet size when losing) or
make high-odds bets in order to recoup. The high-odds bets
pay the worst because of the tremendous amount taken out
in taxes. But a scared gambler usually creates the very thing
that scares him—a major loss.

"The key to being a winning player is to be in control and absolutely steeled to the fact that you could lose every penny you're playing with. You have to be comfortable with the idea that you can lose. The greatest fighters have lost fights— Muhammed Ali, Joe Louis, Sugar Ray Robinson, Sugar Ray Leonard—and they were better fighters after they lost. Their greatest fights came after their first losses. Don't be terrified of losing, and you won't set up the psychological conditions that will result in a major loss, as opposed to a minor one. There is actually something called a smart loss as opposed to a stupid loss. A smart loss is where you realize it's not your day, and you walk away. A stupid loss is where you stay in, sweating out every roll, increasing your bets as you lose, taking out markers (markers are IOU's to the casino), and generally lose your cool and your self-control along with your money. Your mental management systems are every bit as important as your money management systems."

The Captain's second principle of money management is to decide whether you're gambling for the short or the long run.

"If you picked up this book in a Nevada or Atlantic City bookshop and this is your first and probably last trip to a gambling city, then you're a short-run player. If you go once, twice, maybe three times a year for only a day or two, then again you can consider yourself a short-run player. However, if you gamble once a month or more and consistently think in terms of gambling in casinos, then you're a long-run player."

The difference between the short-run gambler and the long-run gambler has to do with the element of ruin. That is, how much of your total gambling stake are you willing to risk losing in a day or two? Keeping in mind that this advice is for people gambling with non-scared money, the Captain suggests that the short-run player should be more willing to lose all his gambling stake on a given visit, whereas the long-run player should never go for broke. A *gambling stake* is defined as the total amount of money set aside specifically for gambling.

"If you come to Atlantic City once a year and you bring

$3,000.00 as your gambling stake, then win or lose, you're not coming back for another year. You can afford to take certain risks that a person with a $3,000.00 gambling stake and twenty visits planned cannot take. As a once-a-year player, you would probably want to play the High Roller System if you desire to be treated like a big shot. The better option is to play the Supersystem betting $10.00 or $15.00 on the Doey-Don't with double or more odds. You could also afford to play a more aggressive Supersystem, having four numbers working. You must play perfectly, however. Don't violate the '5-Count' and don't make Crazy Crapper bets. If the table is cold, walk away. However, if your visit is just two days and you want to gamble your two days away, then treat your entire bankroll as a single-session bankroll and follow the single-session guidelines found later in this chapter."

Some gambling writers would obviously disagree with the Captain's advice. Some suggest that as soon as you're up 20 percent, quit and go home.

"The problem with advice like this is that your home may be several thousand miles away, and your plane doesn't leave for two days, and you haven't even had dinner or seen your hotel room yet! What are you going to do for two more days? You've come to a gambling city on this once-a-year trip to gamble. So gamble! Gamble until you don't want to gamble anymore and then leave the tables and do something else. The worst feeling in the world is to leave a gambling city and feel that you didn't really give it a good shot, that because you won early you frightened yourself out of playing as much as you really wanted to. That's as bad as playing with scared money. Or as bad as winning and giving it all back because you got greedy. But, it's up to you to assess yourself and your finances before you ever place that first bet. And just because I'm telling you to enjoy your once-a-year excursion doesn't mean I'm suggesting that you place stupid bets or not follow the advice I gave in the other chapters concerning how to play, when to play, and when to move to another table. I'm saying simply that a short-run player should think in terms of his total stake."

The Captain has different advice for long-run players. The Captain has worked out from his own personal experience a money management system designed to help you stretch your gambling stake and weather bad times at the tables.

"When you're in the long-run game, quite often you must walk away in order to live (economically speaking) to gamble another day. Let us say, like the short-run gambler above, that your total gambling stake is $3,000.00, but you intend to go to a casino twice a month, hopefully for the rest of your (very long) life. You will not go with the attitude of risking your entire gambling stake at the tables in a few sessions. Even with perfect play of the '5-Count' and the Supersystem, or the High Roller System, or the Limited Bankroll System, there will be sessions when nothing goes right, when shooter after shooter seems to have been hired by the casino to take your money."

With a total gambling stake of $3,000.00 the Captain recommends dividing the total stake into *session stakes* with each session stake composed of 10 percent of your total stake. A session is defined as a trip to the tables. You might have two or three sessions in a day. But at every session, the most you will allow yourself to lose is $300.00 or 10 percent of your total stake. If you lose this, you quit until the next session.

"Don't play games with yourself. Plan your sessions carefully. You might want to play a session in the morning, one in the late afternoon, and one in the evening. Don't lose $300.00 and dig into your pocket and pretend that another session is taking place. Make a rule for yourself that you can't have back-to-back sessions without, say, three hours passing between them. This is very important if you don't want to get caught up in a gambling frenzy and lose your entire stake through stupidity. And never, never think of your gambling stake as chips or tokens. Always talk and think in terms of money. It's not a nickel chip—it's $5.00. It's not a quarter chip—it's $25.00. It's not a black chip—it's $100.00. You do this, and you'll never lose sight of the fact that you're playing for real stakes and not pretty colored chips."

But win or lose in that first session, your next session stake is always 10 percent of your total stake. So if you lost all $300.00 in your first session, your next session stake would be $270.00 because your total gambling stake has been reduced to $2,700.00. However, if you won $300.00 your next session stake would be $330.00 because your total stake is now $3,300.00.

"Don't wait until you lose your entire session stake to quit. If the tables are cold and you're getting clobbered early, quit and do something else until your next scheduled session. Quite a bit of gambling requires intuition and that's something I can't really teach you. You'll have to learn from your own experience. But, as a rule of thumb, quit immediately if the first three rolls on the 5-count are 7s. That means you've been wiped out three times in a row. Quit if after an hour of your money going back and forth, you're down one half of your session stake.

"Probably the hardest thing to decide is when to quit when you're ahead. Again, I can only give you rules of thumb, because you'll have to develop a feel for the game. First rule: never quit *while* you're winning. A shooter is in the midst of a torrid roll, and you've tripled your session stake. He's about to roll again. Don't call off your bets, unless the shooter's lost his rhythm (see chapter ten). Yes, he might roll the seven and you lose. But the guy's hot and you're winning. Let him roll. If he rolls the seven then you're losing and you can quit.

"Rule number two: bank your wins. Say you've won $200.00 and you've been playing a half hour. Take your original stake of $300.00 and $50.00 of your winnings and put them aside. That's your bank account and you will not use that money anymore at this particular session. Gamble with the $150.00 that remains of your winnings. When you've doubled that, put another hundred into your 'bank account.' Now, you are gambling with $200.00. Keep putting $100.00 away as you win. Just keep playing with the $200.00. As long as you win, you will stay at the table. However, as soon as you lose the $200.00, no matter how much you've won for that session, the session is over."

The simplest way to keep track of your money at a table is to divide the money among the various grooves on the rim of the table. In the top groove, you will keep your initial money. When you win, you will replenish the initial money until it matches your session stake. Anything over that session stake money will go in the groove beneath it. In this way, you can keep track of your wins and losses. After every shooter, or during prolonged payoffs, you should count your money. Always know how much money you have at the table.

"I want you to keep in mind that my money management rules are not written in stone. Quite a bit of your gambling will be based on your personality and how much you want to risk. You might decide that you'll double your session stake or go bust. If that's the kind of gambling that you want to do, and you can afford it emotionally and economically, then do it. My guess is, though, that very shortly you'll go bust all the way.

"Personally, I prefer to manage my money in a conservative way. My session stakes are obviously quite a bit higher than the average player's, but my method of money management is based on percentages and not dollar figures. So I might leave a table if I get blown away on three consecutive bets after the 5-count. But rather than quit a particular session, I'll go to another table or another casino. If you're betting conservatively, it's rare that you'll get blown away in a session."

If each session stake is 10 percent of your total bankroll, how much of your session stake should you bet on the 5-count?

"Again, as a rule of thumb, don't bet more than 10 percent of your session stake on any one roll. If you're playing the Supersystem, that means for the $300.00 a session player, the maximum he'll have on the table will be $30.00 at risk. So he'll have three numbers working with $10.00 in odds behind the Come on each one. For the Limited Bankroll player, however, don't place more than $12.00 each on the 6 and the 8 for an initial bet. Truthfully, I wouldn't even go for the 10 percent maximum. Instead, I'd let two numbers work for me on the Supersystem, and I'd have $6.00 working on the 6 and the 8 in the Limited Bankroll System if my session stake was $300.00."

Naturally, if your total stake is more, your session stake would be more. The following charts give recommended betting levels for various stakes based on aggressive, moderate, and conservative betting levels. They are only guidelines. Keep in mind that if you're an aggressive bettor, you have a better chance of going bust more quickly than a conservative bettor. But the aggressive bettor also has a better chance of making a lot of money quickly if he encounters a hot roll early in a session. The Captain believes you have to decide for yourself what type of bettor you are and that your temperament will be the determining factor.

According to the Captain, Polonius' advice to Laertes in Shakespeare's *Hamlet* is perhaps the best money management advice anyone can give a gambler:

> Neither a borrower nor a lender be,
> For loan oft loses both itself and friend,
> And borrowing dulleth the edge of husbandry.
> This above all, to thine own self be true,
> And it must follow as the night the day
> Thou canst not then be false to any man.

"Polonius' advice is doubly true for anyone who wants to gamble. Never borrow money to gamble with, and if you should lose your entire stake, be it $3,000.00 or $300,000.00, make a second total stake by working for it and saving the money. For low-limit players, that might mean getting a second job for awhile in order to build up a sufficient minimum stake to get back in the action. For big stakes players, it might mean simply taking some time off from the tables to let your outside profits build up sufficiently to put together another big stake. Whatever: be true to yourself; be honest with yourself, play within your capacity, both your economic capacity and your emotional capacity. Play my systems perfectly and you'll be the toughest out in the casino and there's a great chance you'll come out a winner."

The following charts are based on playing in casinos that offer double odds with a minimum bet of $5.00. In addition, the Supersystem indices are based on non-pushing of the casinos. Obviously, you will have to adjust your betting to reflect the different rules of the casinos you play in, particularly if you can push them in your wagering. As a handy guideline to money management, the aggressive systems bet approximately 7 percent to 10 percent of the session stake on one roll, the moderate systems somewhere around 4 percent, and the conservative systems 1 percent to 3 percent. Thus, think in terms of the total amount wagered as opposed to how many numbers must be covered when you chart the money management system that you'll use. Also, short-run players should consider their total stake to be their first session stake. Thus, if you go to a casino with $500.00 do not divide the $500.00 into session stakes of $50.00 each but rather look at the chart under session stakes of $500.00 to gauge the kind of betting suitable for you.

SUPERSYSTEM
$5.00 Doey-Don't with $10.00 Odds on Come

Total Stake	Session Stake	Aggressive Betting	Moderate Betting	Conservative Betting
$1,000	$100	$10 (one number)		
$2,000	$200	$20 (two numbers)	$10 (one number)	
$3,000	$300	$30 (three numbers)	$20 (two numbers)	$10 (one number)
$4,000	$400	$40 (four numbers)	$30 (three numbers)	$20 (two numbers)
$5,000	$500	$50 (five numbers)	$40 (four numbers)	$20 (two numbers)
$6,000 to $8,000	$600	$60 (six numbers)	$40 (four numbers)	$20 (two numbers)

SUPERSYSTEM
$10.00 Doey-Don't with $20.00 in Odds on Come

Total Stake	Session Stake	Aggressive Betting	Moderate Betting	Conservative Betting
$ 9,000	$ 900	$80 (four numbers)	$60 (three numbers)	$40 (two numbers)
$10,000	$1,000	$100 (five numbers)	$60 (three numbers)	$40 (two numbers)
$12,000	$1,200	$120 (six numbers)	$80 (four numbers)	$40 (two numbers)
$15,000	$1,500	$120 (six numbers)	$100 (five numbers)	$60 (three numbers)
$20,000	$2,000		$120 (six numbers)	$80 (four numbers)
$25,000	$2,500			$120 (six numbers)

SUPERSYSTEM
$15.00 Doey-Don't with $30.00 in Odds on Come

Total Stake	Session Stake	Aggressive Betting	Moderate Betting	Conservative Betting
$15,000	$1,500	$150 (five numbers)	$90 (three numbers)	$60 (two numbers)
$18,000	$1,800	$180 (six numbers)	$90 (three numbers)	$60 (two numbers)
$21,000	$2,100	$180 (six numbers)	$120 (four numbers)	$90 (three numbers)
$25,000	$2,500		$180 (six numbers)	$120 (four numbers)
$30,000	$3,000			$180 (six numbers)

LIMITED BANKROLL SYSTEM
$5.00 Minimum Bet: Total is split between the numbers 6 and 8

Total Stake	Session Stake	Aggressive Betting	Moderate Betting	Conservative Betting
$ 1,000	$ 100	$ 12		
$ 1,500	$ 150	$ 12		
$ 2,000	$ 200		$ 12	
$ 2,500	$ 250	$ 24	$ 12	
$ 3,000	$ 300	$ 24	$ 12	
$ 3,500	$ 350	$ 36	$ 24	$ 12
$ 4,000	$ 400	$ 36	$ 24	$ 12
$ 4,500	$ 450	$ 48	$ 36	$ 12
$ 5,000	$ 500	$ 48	$ 36	$ 24
$ 6,000	$ 600	$ 60	$ 36	$ 24
$ 7,000	$ 700	$ 72	$ 48	$ 24
$ 8,000	$ 800	$ 84	$ 48	$ 36
$ 9,000	$ 900	$ 84	$ 60	$ 36

Total Stake	Session Stake	Aggressive Betting	Moderate Betting	Conservative Betting
$10,000	$1,000	$ 96	$ 60	$ 36
$12,000	$1,200	$120	$ 72	$ 48
$15,000	$1,500		$120	$ 60
$20,000	$2,000		$120	$ 90
$25,000	$2,500			$120
$30,000	$3,000	HIGH ROLLER	SYSTEM	$120
$35,000	$3,500	HIGH	ROLLER	SYSTEM

TEN

The World of Craps: Stories, Insights, and Superstitions

Without question, craps is the most exciting casino game. Even generally laid-back or staid people can suddenly be overcome by the thrilling rush of adrenaline that courses through their bodies as a hot shooter makes point after point, number after number. You'll hear them cheering, see them throwing their fists in the air, enjoy their antic dispositions as they collect bet after bet. God-fearing Aunt Millie is suddenly doing a rain dance. Laconic Uncle Laurence is bumping and grinding as the dice make their way down the table to another favorable decision. Even doddering, traditional, bun-topped grandma suddenly yells: "Come on you little monsters—give us a ten!" Indeed, newcomers to craps are sometimes embarrassed as they realize that they've been carried away by the flow of the game. Occasionally you'll see them looking around to make sure no one realized they were the ones who had let out those loud war-whoops.

"You cannot believe the level of excitement that a craps game can generate. I've heard people make all kinds of involuntary sounds as a hot shooter rolls. One guy, a well-dressed, balding businessman, very dignified and well-mannered, suddenly started crowing like a rooster as a shooter caught fire. This guy's face became beet-red as he crowed with delight. Another man howled like a wolf one night as he won his bets. One older woman would do a little pirouette everytime her numbers hit. She was quite a sight, spinning and bleating with joyous abandon."

Of course, in such an exciting environment, there can be twists and turns of fate that are not necessarily desired. Aspects of human nature and the nature of the gambling drive can be revealed that we might be better off not knowing.

"Several members of the Crew and I were at the Claridge in Atlantic City. This was sometime in 1986, I think. This monstrously large, ham-handed man was having the roll of a lifetime. In fact, that's what it turned out to be. Everytime he rolled the dice, which looked like grains of sand in his gigantic hands, he'd scream out at the top of his lungs: 'Ye-oheleven!!!' Those dice would go ripping out of his hand as if shot from a cannon. He was at the forty-five minute mark of his roll. There were people ten deep at the table. Not only were they onlookers but many were attempting to squeeze in, hoping to get in on a hot roll. There were many high rollers betting thousands on every roll. With each number, a roar would go up at the table. The level of excitement was fantastic, made even more so by the deep roar of the shooter everytime he rolled.

"The shooter was a high roller, too, betting the table maximum on every number. He was also throwing Crazy Crapper bets down and, as fate would have it, winning an incredible percentage of them. He had the grooves in front of him filled with purple ($500.00) and black ($100.00) chips.

The casino personnel were streaming to the table with new deliveries of chips to replace the ones won by the players. As I watched him roll next to me, I could see that the veins on his forehead were getting more and more pronounced. He had just established another point number and had covered just about all the Crazy Crapper bets. He picked up the dice. The table was silent, awaiting another roll, another number, more winnings. He shook the dice violently and screamed his war cry: 'Ye-oheleven!!!!' A roar went up as the dice rocketed to the opposite wall. Then a hush, then the stickman calling out into the hush: 'Seven! Seven out!' There was a moment of suspended time, and in slow motion almost I turned to the shooter. I saw his eyes bug out crazily as he reached up for his neck. And like a huge tree falling majestically in the forest, smashing the trees surrounding it, the shooter plowed through the people near him on his way to the floor. He was dead.

"I bent over him and tried to feel for a pulse. None. But as I was doing this, the following happened almost simultaneously: the stickman passed the dice to me and looked down and asked me if I wanted to roll, a man practically leaped over the body of the fallen shooter to take his spot at the supposedly hot table, and a rat-faced spectator made a lunge for the fortune in chips that the man had left as his legacy at the table. I jumped up and stopped both the new player and the would-be inheritor by thrusting my body between the table and them. I then shouted to the boxman that the man had fallen (he already knew, obviously), and then one of the Crew, who is a doctor, pushed his way through the crowd from the opposite side of the table and began artificial respiration on the fallen shooter. And you know what I did next? I counted the man's chips and informed the boxman of how much money was to be given the man's wife or estate! Why did I do this? Because the pit boss was insisting that the chips be handed to him and I felt that in all the excitement, a miscount of his funds was quite possible with the resulting error perhaps winding up in the pockets of someone other than a close relative. But here's the true crux of the story:

while all this was going on—*the game continued!* While the doctor worked to save the man's life (he couldn't), while I counted the chips, while friends of the stricken man gaped in horror, the game went on. Even as the ambulance arrived and the stretcher bearers came into the casino and lifted the huge hulk off the floor and onto a stretcher, attaching him to whatever you attach a man to as you deliver him to the hospital, the game continued! It was almost as if death was a secondary consideration to the pursuit of Lady Luck."

Perhaps craps brings out some primal sensibility in us as we challenge the gods of chance. And the strange noises and movements, the indifference to what otherwise would be tragedy, the rising levels of expectation and dread, combine to put us into an altered state of consciousness where it's just us, the dice and fate. Craps can be viewed as a metaphor for primeval man and woman straining to force their will on the blind and uncaring forces of the universe, in this case the roll of the dice. Perhaps this explains why veteran craps players are such a superstitious and idiosyncratic lot.

"I think one of the reasons I can't get most of my Crew to play my methods is that probably once in the past they won big one night, however they were playing, and have somehow or other conditioned themselves to that style of play in the unconscious hope that it will win for them big again and again. Of course, every so often on a hot roll they'll win, regardless of what Crazy Crapper bets they'll make. In the long run they lose, but they have a good time and I don't correct them or lecture. I never push any Crew member to play my way because they are my friends and they enjoy the game the way they play it. You can push a casino but you can't push a friend."

In no other casino game are there so many superstitions and non-casino protocols (protocols fashioned over time by the players and not a matter of casino practice). And in no other game will you find the player so willing to make it known, sometimes quite forcefully, that these protocols and superstitions are being violated or are about to be violated.

The Ten Superstitions of Craps

1. *When the dice or a die leaves the table, the next roll will be a seven.* This might be avoided by making sure that the dealers give you the same dice for your next roll. This is why you'll hear the shooter yell out: "Same dice!"

2. *When the dice hit someone's hand, that roll will be a seven.* This is why you'll hear so many people shouting: "Watch your hands!" as the shooter starts to roll. Even the casino crew will shout this out and be careful of where they place their hands. Many a craps player has accused the casino of jinxing the roll by letting the dice hit a dealer's hand.

3. *When a good roll is in progress never throw money on the table to cash in while the shooter is shooting.* If the dice hit the new money, the next roll will be a seven.

4. *Never speak to or touch a person who is having a good roll.* And be especially careful about barging into a space between the shooter and someone else while he's in the midst of a hot roll. That will definitely result in a seven and many angry glares on the part of the other players.

5. *Never mention the number seven when someone is rolling.* If you mention it, the next roll will be it. Generally, craps players will refer to the seven as *It*, as in: "As long as *It* doesn't show, everything will be alright!" Still other craps players refer to the seven as the *devil*. "If that devil jumps up, we're in trouble."

6. *A woman who has never rolled the dice will have a hot roll the first time out.* This is the *Virgin Principle*. Female dice virgins are a much sought after breed. When one appears, the veteran players will sometimes place bets for her to win her and her gods' favors.

7. *Men who have never rolled the dice before will have bad rolls.* Who said sexism doesn't exist in craps? We prize virginity in our female rollers and despise it in our males. The males must have experience to know how to give a good roll!

8. *Never open a table or be the first or only player at a table.* Dice are cold at a new table and have to be handled before they can warm up.

9. *A wrong bettor at the table will increase the likelihood of the seven coming up.* And the more wrong bettors at a table, the more the seven will come up.

10. *No one can beat craps in the long run because of its inherent negative expectancy.*

As silly as some of these superstitions seem, the Captain sees a thread of truth in some of them.

"There is no way to show a mathematical proof of what I'm about to say, but my experience has shown me that some of these superstitions actually have some logical foundations. For example, the ones that revolve around the disruption of a shooter have a limited merit (numbers one through four). I call this my *Rhythmic Roller Principle*.

"A shooter who has been rhythmically grinding out a good roll, who picks up the dice a certain way, shakes them just so, hits the back wall in the same spot time and again, rolls one roll almost exactly like every other roll and has been rolling number after number suddenly becomes distracted, or he loses his rhythm because someone jostled him or talked to him or whatever, that shooter will more than likely roll a seven, if not on the very next roll then shortly thereafter. I know this sounds silly but here is why I think the superstition developed and has some merit.

"The shooter who is rolling rhythmically, will be in a *non-seven mode*. That is, whatever he is doing, however he is doing it, when those dice leave his hand they are rolling in a way that the seven is not coming up. This non-seven mode will continue until his roll is altered in some way. Maybe he arcs his dice a little higher than usual, or the dealers tell him to hit the back wall because his dice are lagging, or someone talks to him and he throws the dice a little harder. He has broken his non-seven mode, the roll has become random again, and the seven is back to its normal one in six probability.

"In street and carpet craps (craps played on a carpet or blanket with a smooth wall to hit), there were individuals who could consistently control which numbers came up. These numbers would come up out of all proportion to their probabilities. In the good old days of the thirties, forties, and early fifties, I knew several people who made their livings playing craps. They would travel the country and beat game after game. You don't see that any more, but every once in a while a shooter, without realizing it, will get into a non-seven mode. Rhythmic Rollers have the best chance to have hot rolls."

The Captain believes that you can actually capitalize on such a shooter if you know what to look for and what to do when you see it.

"Here is how to take advantage of a rhythmic rolling, non-seven mode shooter. Although this is exactly what I do, it will take quite a bit of experience to gain the insight necessary to use this technique effectively.

"Play your normal game but watch the shooter closely. If he is a rhythmic roller, see what his rhythm is and the second you notice a disruption in his rhythm, take your bets off. Did he just change how he picks up the dice? Did he fix his numbers faster or slower than before? Was he just told to hit the back wall? Was he told to speed up his rolling? Did someone jostle him and make him move to the left or the right? When the dice left the table did he get flustered? Did he just turn to the player next to him or his companion and exult in his good roll? If the answer to any one of these questions is yes— immediately shout to the dealers that your bets are off.

"When you learn how to read a non-seven mode shooter, you will save quite a bit of money. I believe this technique has allowed me to fully capitalize on hot rolls by rhythmic rollers.

In fact, when I'm truly comfortable with a rhythmic roller, I tend to put up more money than I normally would because I'm confident I can call my bets off at the least change in the shooter's flow. I don't recommend you attempt increasing your bets with a rhythmic roller unless you've been playing for quite awhile and have been successful when calling off your bets. Don't be in a rush to become an expert in recognizing the rhythmic roller because you might find yourself deluding yourself. But with more table time and an astute and intuitive mind, you'll be able to do it."

But is every hot shooter a non-seven mode shooter?

"No. Most shooters have no rhythm and have no predictable patterns to their throws. Sometimes the dice fly down the table and at other times they hobble limply. These shooters are just having a lucky roll. There's no way to judge them, so just have fun while the hot roll lasts. That's why I prefer soft shooters to shooters who throw the dice furiously. Remember that the craps table has pyramid-shaped foam rubber walls so as to insure random rolls. I believe the harder you hit these walls the harder it is to have a sustained non-seven mode roll.

"Of course, any shooter can get hot, but the non-seven mode shooter is in a different category. There's a consistency of execution that is almost mechanical in its components, and these shooters can be read, so to speak. I believe my rhythmic roller concept explains the phenomenal success of one of my Crew members at rolling. (See chapter eleven.) Personally, I attempt to be a rhythmic roller, but I'm not consistent. On rare occasions I can feel myself in a non-seven mode, with number after number hitting, but I would never bet on myself in advance as I would a truly rhythmic roller.

"Once you play enough and gain that all-important experience, and if you are a deliberate and precise roller, that is, someone who rolls or attempts to roll the dice the same way time and again, then you'll find that every once in awhile you too will be in a non-seven mode. What's more, you'll be able to sense the exact moment when the rhythm has left you. Generally this will be done in retrospect until you become a truly experienced player. You'll be into a non-seven mode roll and all of a sudden you'll feel that something's different and bang! the devil will jump up! If you are aware of your own rhythm during a hot roll, you'll sense when you've changed and be able to capitalize on it, too, in time."

Are any of the other ten superstitions accurate?

"Except for the non-seven mode rolls, the dice hitting someone's hand is irrelevant. However, the non-seven mode roll is obviously changed for that one roll when it hits the hand of another player or dealer, or if it hits a chip or money or whatever. That will merely give the 7 a one in six chance of appearing. If the shooter hasn't lost his rhythm, then he'll continue in the non-seven mode for subsequent rolls.

"As for the other superstitions, I haven't found novice shooters to be any better or worse, be they male or female, than veteran shooters. I have noticed, of course, that the deportment of some of the more cantankerous male craps shooters is somewhat more gentlemanly when a pretty young novice picks up the dice, than when her macho boyfriend does."

Of course, in gambling as in all other areas of life, particularly where superstitions abound, there are charlatans who cunningly prey upon the unwary. In both Las Vegas and Atlantic City there are young women (I have facetiously dubbed them *Virgin Marys*) who go from casino craps table to casino craps table pretending to be novices in order to get superstitious craps players to place bets for them. Quite often these young (and not so young) ladies are hookers looking to score during and after the craps game. Generally, they'll work with a male accomplice.

Here's how the scam works: The man will arrive at the table several minutes before the woman, but he doesn't necessarily place any bets. Several moments later, the woman arrives and, if possible, takes a position at the table some distance from the man. She will then proceed to let everyone know in as girlish and/or innocent a manner as possible that she doesn't know what she's doing and has never played the game. Naturally, the veteran craps players (usually men) will gallantly take her under their wings and explain the rudiments of the game to her. She'll cash in for maybe four times what the table minimum is—thus, allowing her four minimum Pass Line bets when she rolls. As the game progresses the dice are making their way around the table, she just watches and absorbs the advice of the various veterans explaining the game. She lets everyone know that she doesn't have much money and really wants to save it so she can roll.

Meanwhile, her companion is placing intermittent but minimum bets. When it comes time for our Virgin Mary to roll, she places a minimum Pass Line bet and rolls. If luck has it and she hits her number, her accomplice, pretending to sense a hot roller, will call out in a loud voice as he throws a minimum bet down: "For the shooter!" The accomplice will select either a Crazy Crapper bet or a number for the shooter. The hope is, of course, that other players will also start placing bets for the shooter. Naturally, if enough players place different bets, the team has a great chance of making some decent money. Indeed, quite often it isn't even necessary for this Virgin Mary to make her first point before players will start placing bets for her.

Sometimes, however, the accomplice will wait until the Virgin Mary is down to her last bet before he pipes up: "She's gonna get hot! I sense it! Ten bucks on the hard ten for the shooter!" This will hopefully motivate others to start laying money across the board for our virgin shooter. Of course, if our lady is also hooking, she'll probably have two or three gents falling over each other to place bets for her believing that the more generous their bets, the more generous will be her favors. The Virgin Marys who work this scam, by the way, rarely look like hookers. That's the secret to their success.

Of course, you don't have to be a con artist or a novice shooter or a pretty young woman to have other craps players place bets for you. During hot rolls, it is not unheard of for other players to place bets for a shooter who has just made them some money. It doesn't happen all the time, or even much of the time, but it does happen frequently enough to be a part of craps lore. Second only to the dream of a monster roll, craps players sometimes imagine a high roller placing bets for them because they're making money for him.

In fact, one of the most disheartening and annoying things that ever happened to me at a craps game involved a high roller with a penchant for placing bets for others. I was at Trump Castle, playing with the Captain and two other members of the Crew. A man to my left in the upper left hand corner of the table had just cashed in for $6,000.00 and started making the typical high roller bets. He placed most of the numbers, without even buying the 4 or the 10 until a dealer reminded him to, and made several Crazy Crapper bets for himself and the table crew. Now, there was one man between me and this high roller, a pleasant-looking yuppie-type who was betting the Pass Line with odds and one Come with odds.

During the course of play, while the dice made the rounds of the shooters, this high roller, who reminded me superficially of W.C. Fields sans the wit, would place bets for the shooters. The table was cold and the high roller was down to his last thousand dollars. When it came my turn, I was hoping for a decent roll, figuring he might place some bets for me. I don't remember what my point was because I never made it. I had a decent roll and hit several numbers before sevening out. However, I hit quite a few Crazy Crapper numbers that this man was on. For my roll he had bet, in various ways, his entire thousand dollars. He had $100.00 on the 11, $100.00 on all the hardways. My very first roll after the come out was an 11. At fifteen to one, I had just made him $1,500.00. He placed another $100.00 on the 11. I hit a hard 6. He lost his $100.00 on the 11 but won on the hardways bet. He was paid $900.00. I hit a hard 6 again. He was paid another $900.00. Then, I threw a 12 and low and behold, he had just bet the 12! That was a $3,000.00 jackpot for him. He then took another 12 and a 2. I rolled some point number. By now I was really excited, figuring that I had won him his money back and surely he'd place a few bets for me. He again placed $100.00 on the 12 and the 2. I rolled the 2! Another $3,000.00

in his kitty. Then he upped all his hardways bets to $400.00 each. I rolled a hard 10. He was paid $2,800.00. I hit a couple of point numbers that he was on. Of course, I still hadn't made my point. But surely he'd place a bet for me? He had, after all, placed bets for the other shooters who had sevened out and lost him money. But I had made him quite a bit of money. Thinking these thoughts, I sevened out.

The next shooter was up, the yuppie. On his come out, he rolled a 5. Immediately, the high roller says: "Give me all the hardways for $500.00 each and give the shooter the hard 6 for $100.00." I don't have to tell you what happened because I wouldn't be writing this anecdote if the yuppie didn't within two rolls roll that hard 6 and make $1,000.00 on the deal (he got to keep the original bet, too). The yuppie then sevened out. To say I was annoyed is an understatement. As the yuppie jumped up and down, and unctuously and profusely thanked the high roller, I felt like taking the stickman's stick and doing something obscene to the yuppie with it. But I refrained. However, when the yuppie turned to me and the rest of the table and effusively exulted in his good luck with his hard 6, I was hard pressed to contain my rising ire. "Isn't that something!" he cried triumphantly. "He gave me a thousand dollars!"

"Yeah," I said, feigning good will.

"Did you ever see anything like it?"

"No," I said and thought: I never hope to again—unless it's me.

Sad to say that, although I've seen bets placed for others before and since that incident, so far I've never had a bet placed for me except by me or the Captain, who'll sometimes place bets for Crew members who are having a rough night.

Interestingly enough, the Captain does believe in placing bets for shooters who make you money because he feels that such a practice brings goodwill to a table.

Now, let us return to some of the other superstitions and see what the Captain has to say about them.

"The idea that the dice are cold when a table opens or that being the only player at a table is a losing proposition is nonsense. I've had some of my best rolls starting a table or being the only player at a table. I think this superstition can be observed throughout the casino gambling scene. Very few people like to be the only ones at the blackjack tables or baccarat tables, also. Take a stroll around a casino in Vegas where there are dealers waiting for a player to begin a game and notice that as soon as that first daring person picks up the dice, or tells the dealer to deal, seemingly out of nowhere, hordes of people will appear ready to play. Maybe people are embarrassed to play alone because they fear that their gambling habits will be scrutinized or mocked by the professional dealer who now has time to notice them. Whatever the reason, the overwhelming majority of gamblers have plugged into this superstition."

But can saying the word "seven" actually give it flesh? "Of course not. Saying the word 'seven' doesn't bother me, and it doesn't have any effect on the game except if it upsets a rhythmic roller. So, I don't say seven only because it will upset some of the superstitious players. At a craps table, the concept and definition of vulgarity take a peculiar turn. Otherwise racy conversationalists will find it the height of bad manners to say the word 'seven.' These fellows will be cursing and muttering under their breaths all manner of improbable obscenities but just utter 'seven' and it's as if you said something truly raunchy to a roomfull of nuns.

"As for superstition number nine, I don't think wrong bettors at a table bring out the 7, but they certainly bring out the anger of their fellow craps players. If I notice several wrong bettors at a table, I'll pass it by. The reason for this is simple. Since there are very few wrong bettors percentage-wise in the craps-playing population, the fact that several have congregated at one table probably means that they're having some success there. Why bother walking into the lion's den? Remember the advice I gave in a previous chapter? If a table is cold and that seven is coming up too frequently and you're losing despite the '5-Count'—move to another table!

"And number ten is a commonly held myth because *al-*

most all gamblers *are* losers. It certainly isn't always true, and it certainly isn't true in my case, but it's the one common misperception that is more often true than not. Except for myself and the small handful of experienced Crew members who are playing my Supersystem, I have never met anyone who has beaten the game of craps in the long run. And as far as I know, I'm the only one making a living at the craps tables playing the game honestly without scamming. I've seen people ahead for months, but eventually their betting style and poor play catches up with them and they inevitably join the ranks of losers. Craps is a game that was designed by the casinos so it could not be beaten in the long run. And please don't delude yourself into thinking that having once read this book, you can quit your job and make a fortune playing craps. That kind of thinking will be the surest way to economic ruin. So, take my Supersystem, play it perfectly and there's a good chance that you'll join the few of us who have been beating the game over the long run."

The Captain has an interesting and unique view of the craps playing public and their many superstitions.

"I like to think of the craps table as another country, with a culture all its own. I respect the culture and try not to offend its believers. Even if I think that what they believe is silly and what they do is idiotic, I gain nothing by letting them know of my feelings. All I can do is ruin a fun experience for them and me. I mean, you will see players talking to the dice, kissing the dice, fixing the dice in all sorts of ways. Some will rub their hands on the table as it to rub off some magic onto themselves. Still others will pray and make incantations. It comes with the territory of craps. It comes with the country. So when in another country I follow the customs of that country."

The Captain's advice extends to the superstitions of individual players as well as to their idiosyncratic behaviors.

"You have to be tolerant. Actually, I enjoy the idiosyncrasies of the various players. In my Crew, for example, are many craps-playing eccentrics, or should I say eccentric craps players, because in real life they are fine, upstanding members of society. But get them near a craps table, and they are right out of Damon Runyon. You have to realize that at a craps table, the inner person is sometimes revealed and for many men that inner person is an energetic little boy who wants to play, play, play and not come in for dinner when mommy calls."

ELEVEN

The Crew

You already met Joe in chapter seven, but some of the other Crew members deserve mention because in a very real way they represent types of players you're likely to encounter. Of course, they are types of players only in the positive sense, because with the exception of Joe, the Crew members tend to be aggressive only in their betting and not in their behavior. The negative types of players—the obnoxious and the disdaining, the accusatory and the complaining, the stupid and the supercilious, the know-it-alls and the naggers—won't be found gracing the Captain's Crew. The female craps shooters in the Crew are not the stereotypical female gamblers, either, but fearless, good-humored, witty, and astute individuals, successful both in their lives and careers. (There's quite a bit of sex-stereotyping in gambling, and it can be exploited profitably by expert players, but that's another book.)

"I enjoy playing with members of my Crew because there's immediately a sense of camaraderie at the table. There's a hidden danger, however, in playing with your friends, and that is that you'll change the nature of your game. In my earlier years, I would bet on every member of my Crew who was rolling right off. I wouldn't follow the '5-Count.' I'd bet more than usual feeling that I would hurt my friends' feelings if I didn't. And more often than not, I'd wind up the poorer for it. It took me awhile to realize that you have to play your game regardless of who's at the table with you. My Crew realizes now that I play my game no matter who's shooting, even myself. I don't bet on myself until a successful completion of the '5-Count.' "

As I write this, I've been with the Captain for a little more than a year. I guess I could be considered a Crew member in training. Although I have successfully applied the Captain's strategies both in Las Vegas and Atlantic City over the course of this time (I spend about a third of my life in casinos), I can't even pretend to have a feel for the game as he does. Perhaps I never will. After all, there's only one Captain. He's unique.

As for the Crew, a greater bunch of men and women you'll never find inside a casino, or outside for that matter. Forthwith and in no particular order of importance are some of the Captain's Crew. Those members of the Crew who did not wish to be profiled, for whatever personal or professional reasons, I have respected their wishes for anonymity and have not used them as examples, either directly or pseudonymously.

First, there's Jimmy P., a World War II veteran who compares playing craps with "being in the barracks!" A major player who sometimes follows the Captain's advice— "Captain, I swear I'll follow the '5-Count' into battle this time!"—but more often gets carried away and throws caution to the winds—"Bet it up—it's Anzio all over again!" ("He wasn't at Anzio but during a craps game he thinks he was."—

The Captain.) He's the rooter at the table. He cheers. He talks to the dice. "They got little ears, I swear to God, Captain, they got little ears them dice!" When Jimmy P. is at a table, win or lose, you're in for a great time. A great bear of a man, Jimmy P. is the First Mate.

"Before I met the Captain," Jimmy P. relates, "I used to come to Atlantic City with my friends, and while they gambled, I would feed the pigeons on the boardwalk. Now, when I'm in Atlantic City, the ocean could dry up and I'm not sure I'd notice. If it wasn't for the Captain, I would never have discovered craps. Now, if it wasn't because of him, I'd be losing my shirt. When I go crazy at a table I generally lose, but when I follow the Captain's Supersystem, I'm happy to find that I make a lot more withdrawals than deposits. The Captain does something else for us guys, too. We think of ourselves almost as an assault force on Fort Knox. I don't know about the rest of the gamblers, but me and the Captain, we come to beat the casinos' heads in."

Then there's Rose, a good rhythmic roller. You'll know it's Rose shooting because of her disarmingly charming good looks and her fierce concentration. She is riveted to the dice. "I always worry that if I throw that 7 people will be upset. I want to see everyone make money."("Rose is a banker so she likes to see people in the green."—The Captain.) Rose tends to play craps very conservatively, making Pass Line with odds bets. "I go to Atlantic City to unwind from stress, so although I gamble and enjoy it, winning or losing isn't what brings me to a casino. I enjoy the shows and dinners as much as the action. That's what's so good about the Captain and his Crew, we all get to do what we like. We enjoy all aspects of what a casino-resort has to offer."

There's John the Analyzer, who finds a logical reason for anything that happens at a craps table. If the dice go flying off the table—"Captain, the guy's having trouble with his wife, his palms were sweating, and the dice stuck and off they went."—or if a 7 appears three times on a come out roll—"She's slanting the dice, Captain, and they're skidding."—or if anything bad happens—"If the dice didn't hit that chip,

Captain, the 6 would have been hard instead of easy." But mostly John is known as the Jekyll and Hyde of betting. A normally calm and even-tempered gambler, quite conservative in his betting approach, John will order his friend Jack (Daniels, that is) and after a couple of drinks—WHAM! He manages to make every wild bet imaginable. "I'll bet that in the next five rolls the dice will leave the table!" "We don't take bets like that, sir." "Well, you should!" ("John is a fashion designer but sometimes his explanations of why something just occurred are made from wholecloth."—The Captain.) John is the Second Mate.

According to John: "During the weekdays, when the Captain and several of the Crew take day trips to Atlantic City to play the Supersystem for the best odds, I'll go and play it just right. No place bets, no hardways, no pressing. I think to myself that this is the way to go. You never really make a killing, but you do to the casino what it usually does to the player—grind it out. But on the weekend and extended trips to Vegas, I get into the flow of the action, have a couple of drinks, and I find my mouth saying: 'Hard 4 for two hundred!' " At those times John dances with Lady Luck, but sometimes she steps on his feet, hard.

There's Connie, a warm, caring woman with sparkling eyes who doesn't want to see anyone lose, ever. "It's just no fun when luck isn't with you." Connie will slip unobtrusively into a spot at the table and inquire of each and every Crew member how he or she is doing. In many ways she's the philosopher and personal therapist of losing players. "I always give words of encouragement to everyone, and I can sympathize because I know what it feels like to lose and how good it feels to have someone care about you when you're down." ("Connie is the nurturer of the Crew and when she's around we feel more like a family."—The Captain.)

"I enjoy the action of the casinos, but I also enjoy the shows and dinners and just walking along the boardwalk in Atlantic City, or shopping. I think many of the men in the Crew are far more addicted to the thrills and action than most of the women. Of course, I say that now, but when I'm at the table and I have those dice in my hand and my heart is pounding and my blood is pumping, I only have one wish—to roll until the end of time."

There's Phil the Forgetful, who once forgot to pick up $3,000.00 in chips at a table and someone else walked off with his money. "What numbers do I have, Captain?" Phil is so busy planning his future strategy that he sometimes fails to recall what his past one was. "Place the 6 and the 8 for $90.00 each!" "You already have them, sir." "Oh, then, forget it." ("Phil's forgotten more money in one night than most people earn in a month!"—The Captain.)

There's Russ the Breather. He's called the Breather not because he makes obscene phone calls, but because he has emphysema and must bring a vanload of equipment with him to the casinos. "I will not miss a craps game as long as I am able to stagger to a table, pick up those little cubes, and throw chips on the layout." A high roller of the first order, Russ's room looks like a scene out of *2001: A Space Odyssey* when he goes to a gambling city. "I take as much oxygen in my room as I can and then me and my inhaler hit the tables. My whole muscle structure is falling in but I can still throw a hard 4!" ("Russ is an intellect and a wit, a man with a dry sense of humor and an appreciation for dry wine. When Russ is at the table, we surround him with three Crew members on either side to help keep the smokers away."—The Captain.)

Russ's interests are far-reaching, and he's a man who is quick on the uptake. One evening in Atlantic City, over a second bottle of Pouilly Fuisse, I was relating to Russ my adventures as a card counter in Las Vegas. I was explaining to him the system of card counting that A.P. and I use to beat the casinos. I explained to him the difference between a positive and negative deck, the former favors the player, while the latter favors the house. The conversation then turned to an individual we both knew. I was trying to find the right description for her and I couldn't quite put my finger on it. Russ looked at me with his half-closed eyes, took a sip of the wine, then a hit on his inhaler and said: "Frankie, she's a negative deck." Precisely!

There's Vic, an expert blackjack player and a follower of the Captain's systems in craps. Vic is often aghast at the devil-may-care attitude of other Crew members. "Captain, these guys are crazy!" To Vic the purpose of gambling is to win and then have a good time. "I follow the Captain to victory, and then we'll have dinner and a good time. But I gamble to win." ("Vic has the ability and determination to be a long-term winner in both craps and blackjack. This man is truly a tough out."—The Captain.)

Vic is an expert at figures and figuring odds and percentages. Vic learned blackjack strategy in a very unusual way. We were at Resorts International in Atlantic City one weekend in late summer. Vic had been playing blackjack for several months when he asked me for a written explanation of the basic strategy of blackjack. In one hour he was able to memorize and understand the entire sheet I gave him—all 260 variations of hands he or the dealer could be dealt. It usually takes the average person, me included, at least several days, if not weeks, of memorizing and practicing to be able to play blackjack effectively in a casino. I had given Vic the basic strategy at breakfast, by the afternoon he was playing like a well-oiled machine in a high-stakes game.

Then there is the legend—Ceel "The Arm." The Crew members all call her "The Arm" because in the past ten years she has consistently had monster rolls. (A monster roll is defined as one that lasts a minimum of a half hour.) It is rare that a week, much less a month, will go by when "The Arm" won't have a thirty-minute or longer roll. ("She is simply the best rhythmic roller I've ever seen. When she gets into a non-seven mode, forget it, we all make big money."—The Captain.) When "The Arm" walks into a casino, the members of the Crew let out a cheer, and the people part like the waters of the Red Sea to let her get to the table to roll. It seems to me that she goes into a trance at the table. She sets the dice, rolls carefully, and never seems to be paying attention to the results of her rolls. She just stares at the table. "I feel a great responsibility when I roll because I know everyone is looking for a monster from me. And sometimes I deliver it."

Her rolls are certainly the stuff of legend. She's had several hour-long rolls, one in which the players collectively wiped out a table's bank. More importantly, she can almost be counted on when a hot roll is needed. If there is such a goddess as Lady Luck or Dame Fortune, then Ceel has an inside channel to her. It is quite evident to me that Ceel is the lady with the luck who has made a damn fortune for many a craps player.

Two incidents that I personally witnessed come to mind to give you some idea of how this lady can roll those dice. Once I was playing blackjack at the Claridge, and I could see the Captain and the Crew at the craps table directly across the room. It was about three o'clock in the morning and the tables had been cold all day and night. No matter which casino the Captain went to, he just couldn't seem to get untracked. He was down. Most of the Crew were down considerably. It looked like one of those horrible weekends where bad luck followed swiftly by still worse luck was the norm. Finally, Jimmy P. shouted out: "We need to wake up 'The Arm,' Captain, or we're all gonna take a beating."

The Captain left the table and went to Ceel's room. Groggy from sleep and a persistent, nagging cold, Ceel was gently led from her room to the elevator and into the casino. ("To this day, I have no recollection of getting dressed or of going down in the elevator with the Captain," she says.) A roar went up when the Crew members saw her coming to the table. I started to get up from my blackjack game, intending to rush over to the table and get in on the action, but even before I could color in my chips or stuff them in my pocket, the craps table was overcrowded. Almost every member of the Crew was there. So I colored in my chips anyway and decided to watch from the high roller baccarat pit. This area at the Claridge is elevated and gives you a good view of the craps tables on the main floor.

Since the table was mostly Crew members, when the current shooter had sevened out, which he did rather quickly, everyone passed up his or her chance to roll so that "The Arm" could get started.

She picked out her dice and carefully set them. Then she rubbed them gently on the layout in a small circular motion and arced them slightly to the opposite side of the table. By the way, Ceel prefers to be on the left side of the stickman and, naturally, this is where the Crew positioned her. Her first roll was not memorable. She established her point, made a few numbers, then sevened out.

The players at the table passed up their rolls again and Ceel had the dice a second time. Again, she sevened out rather early. Once again, the other players gave up their turns to roll and Ceel had the dice. ("By my third roll, I had fully awakened, and I concentrated on setting my dice just so and smoothly rolling them down the center of the layout. I like one slight bounce before they hit the back wall. If I'm rolling right they'll just die when the hit the back wall and plop down still on the table—hopefully without the seven showing.")

On her third roll, she started to click. She made two points and a dozen numbers before sevening out. By this time, the stickman realized that no one else was interested in shooting, so he immediately gave the dice back. For the next fifty straight minutes she rolled. She made dozens of points and hit dozens of numbers. The Crew and the ubiquitous crowd that always gathers during a hot shoot were cheering wildly. Trays of black and purple chips were brought to the table to replenish what the Crew was winning. Above the din and cheering I could hear Jimmy P.'s voice saying: "Let's break the bank again, Ceel!"

Ceel seemed mesmerized. She ignored the personnel at the table, even when they told her to throw the dice harder. (Sometimes casino personnel and pit bosses like to disrupt hot shooters by getting them to change their deliveries. But as long as the shooter is hitting the back wall, however lightly, he is fulfilling his obligation to the casino.) She would do her setting of the dice, stare at the table, rub the dice lightly against the felt in a circular fashion and roll. The dice seemed to float on the air, bounce once, hit the wall and lie still. In that fifty-minute roll, the greatest roll I ever personally witnessed (and, unfortunately, could not take part in), Ceel threw sevens only on come out rolls. Her last sequence of numbers was 6-6-6, the number of the Beast in the *Book of Revelation*. But unlike that mythical monster, Ceel's monster roll had been for the good of her fellow Crew members, most of whom had walked away from that table with a small fortune in chips weighing down their pockets.

When she finally sevened out, she turned to the Captain and said: "Now, can I go to bed and get some sleep?"

In the elevator on the way up to her room, surrounded by the grateful Crew members, Ceel counted her own winnings. She had only placed a twenty-five dollar bet on the Pass Line ("I wasn't interested in playing, just rolling.") but with her wins and the money the Crew had bet for her, she was up almost $3,000!

The second roll had more significance for me, personally, because on a Sunday afternoon, ten minutes before I was scheduled to leave Atlantic City and return home a loser one weekend, Ceel came to my rescue. I was saying my goodbyes to the Crew, when I noticed that it was her turn to roll. I was down to my last fifty dollars, so I placed a $5.00 Pass and a $5.00 Don't Pass bet. Ceel rolled a 4. Since I was playing at Resorts International, I was able to place $25.00 in odds behind the 4, since the Resorts Casino allows five-times odds. (You'll notice that I was also violating the "5-Count" when she was rolling.)

She immediately came back with another 4. She had made her point and I had made $50.00. She rolled again. Another 4! I placed $25.00 behind it in odds and placed a $5.00 Come/Don't Come on the layout. She rolled a 10. I put $25.00 in odds behind the 10. She rolled another 10. I had just made another $50.00. I placed another $5.00 Come/Don't Come and she rolled a 4, the point number. I had made another $50.00. I placed odds behind my Come bet and waited for her come out roll on the Pass Line. She rolled a 6. I placed the odds behind the 6. She rolled a 4. I had won $50.00 on my Come odds. I placed another $5.00 Come/Don't Come. She rolled another 4! I took the odds again. This time I placed an-

other $5.00 Come/Don't Come, figuring to go to three num-
bers on the next roll. She rolled another 4!!! Then she rolled,
you guessed it, another 4. I was still up on the 4, since my
Come/Don't Come bet had been up. She then rolled a 3, followed by an 11. Finally, for good measure, she rolled another
4! She then sevened out. She had made nine fours in fifteen
rolls. And I went home slightly ahead for the weekend.

How does "The Arm" or, as she is also known, "The
Queen of the Monsters," explain her phenomenal rolls over
the past ten years?

"I can't explain them," she says. "I have a little ritual I follow when I set my dice up, and I try to throw them the same
way each and every time. Also, I focus my mind just on the
mechanical things that I'm doing. Truthfully, I can't explain
it, and I just feel that I'm lucky."

The irony with Ceel is that she spends very little time at
the tables. She prefers walking or reading, going to shows or
having a conversation to gambling. "I don't like to gamble all
that much. I know that the Crew would like me to roll two or
three straight days when I'm with them, but I would find
that too much. Maybe I'll play craps for two or three hours on
a weekend. I'll also play a little baccarat but I'm not really
much of a gambler. I like casinos for the excitement and the
electricity in the air."

According to the Captain: " 'The Arm' is the ultimate
rhythmic roller. It was probably because of her that I formu-
lated my idea that numbers repeat." Who knows? Maybe
someday Ceel will challenge the fabled "Golden Arm" of Ha-
waii for the Guinness rolling record.

Of course, to be in on a truly scorching roll is the ultimate
experience for a craps player. In my year or so with the Crew,
I've seen only three Big Monsters (let's define a Big Monster
as a roll lasting forty-five minutes or more), the one I just related by Ceel, one by a drunken young man at Bally's Grand
in Atlantic City and one by an old-timer at the Union Plaza in
Las Vegas (which my partner, A.P., and I fictionalized and
used as the basis of a short story for *Win Magazine* titled
"Steak and Eggs"). Luckily, the latter two rolls I was in on.

The feeling as you collect bet after bet and see your bankroll skyrocketing is nothing short of exhilarating. Naturally, during a scorching roll the Big Monster will make all players money, regardless of how stupid their individual betting patterns. In fact, during a scorcher, the idiot bettors will make more money than an individual who is playing the Supersystem. On the other hand, the amount these poor souls have lost in the past due to their poor betting habits probably will never be recouped in a month of Big Monsters. When you play the Captain's way, however, the monster rolls will propel you into the black, if you were in the red, or give you a hefty profit if you were already in the black.

Unfortunately, I've never known the feeling of actually being the monster roller. I've had some mediocre rolls that have made me some money but I've never known the thrill of having a whole table clapping and cheering for me. Well, maybe someday, right?

But let me get back to the Crew.

There's Frank T., who worries that he has no luck. He does. It's just mostly bad. Frank has the uncanny ability to place all the numbers that won't hit. At least that's what he claims. "You want to make money at craps? Just check out the numbers I'm on and bet the other ones and you'll make a fortune. I have the gift of not doing anything right."

(Dear Readers: You realize that in the writing of a book some not inconsiderable time passes between first draft and second draft of a manuscript and still further time passes between a completed manuscript and its actual publication. Between the first draft and the completed draft of this book, Frank T. passed away. He was one of the Captain's oldest friends. They met at P.S. 102 in Brooklyn in 1933 and went to high school together.)

Frank's passing is truly something of a story in and of itself. If I didn't know it to be true, I'd say that it was made up. But let the Captain tell you himself: "We were in Atlantic City the previous weekend and he had an unusual streak of good luck. You know, of course, that any good luck with him was unusual. He was the only craps shooter I know who would call off his own bets in mid-roll. Even as the dice were leaving his hand he'd scream 'bets off!' He had absolutely no confidence in himself as a gambler. He never wanted any of the Crew to bet on him when he rolled. His wife, Helen, on the other hand, is the complete opposite. We've labeled her a crapaholic because she loves the game and rarely leaves the tables. You can see her tall, stately figure at the tables and you sometimes wonder how any game that such a classy woman could play would be called craps.

"Helen is the picture of confidence and grace under pressure. She is as cool and calm a craps player as you'll ever see. But Frank? He's all jangling nerves and noticeable worry. Before a trip to Atlantic City or Vegas, Frank would roll the dice in his basement for hours trying to decide what 'hot' numbers would come up. He would practice his rolling technique. But in a casino, he just...well, he just wasn't too lucky. He never played any of my systems because he'd let the game carry him away.

"Now, although he was a big player, he'd never leave a casino with an outstanding marker. He'd write a check at the end of a weekend when he lost, which he usually did, and settle his accounts. Me and the other Crew, whether we win or lose, pay off markers when they come due, in forty-five days. That's an interest-free loan for us. It's a perfectly ethical thing. But Frank couldn't stand the thought of leaving a casino with a marker, so he'd pay up promptly.

"But last weekend all the years of bad luck and skittish play must have had the Lord thinking, 'Let Me give him one good one before he goes,' because for a whole weekend Frank was hot. He made his point numbers and he had many good rolls. In the midst of one of his final rolls of the weekend, as the dice left his hands, instead of calling off his bets, he twirled his hand and made a fist and looked over at me and said: 'How's that, Captain!' as the dice made another number. He was truly in his glory.

"Some days later he died of a heart attack. At the wake for Frank, Helen, who is a great, great lady, placed two dice in his coffin as the Crew members paid their respects. Jimmy

P. summed it up best at Frank's funeral: 'The son of a bitch didn't even leave 'em with a marker!' True. Take care, Frank, my friend, and smile on our games."

There's Sal the Staller, who's always slowing down the game and the meals because he has so many questions. He once asked a waiter to explain every item on the menu because he was genuinely interested!

There's Jo the Wanderer, who can't make up her mind whether to stay at the craps table or go to her first passion, the slots. Of the women, Jo is the most avid player; she is a pure gambler. "I love to gamble. I once spent twenty-three straight hours at a slot machine. I've won huge jackpots and lost small fortunes. Craps is so exciting that after an hour or two, I have to go to a slot machine to relax. But gambling is in my blood. I'll gamble on anything. That's why I like Vegas so much, you can gamble from the second you leave the plane to the second before you board to return home. You can gamble during your meals. If they could figure out a way for you to gamble in your sleep, I'd probably do that, too." She summed up her philosophy succinctly: "All I want out of life is a bigger bucket—to put my wins in."

There's also the Doctor. A devotee of the Captain's Super-system, the Doctor (that's what the Crew calls him) is a gifted surgeon; he is also an outstanding card counter in blackjack. Perhaps because he has to deal with life and death issues everyday, he is somewhat cavalier to the vicissitudes of fortune. Once one of the Crew had to go to him for some surgery, and as she was coming out of the anesthetic, she mumbled to the Doctor: "How did everything go?" He looked at her, smiled and said: "I'm afraid your horse lost."

When the Crew member's eyes welled up with tears, the Doctor asked her what was the matter. "How long do I have to live?" she sobbed.

"Twenty, thirty years, maybe more. Who knows?"

"I don't understand," she said.

"Understand what?" he asked.

"I thought you said I was dying."

"Whatever gave you that idea?" he asked.

"You said my horse lost," she said.

"It did. The horse you wanted me to place a bet for lost. Got killed." Then the Doctor smiled: "But mine won."

Those are just some of the Crew members. Of course, there's me and there's A.P., who could be the best female card counter in the States, certainly the best I know of, and my playing partner for two years now. A.P. says, "I hate to gamble, but I love to win!" And there are naturally the assorted Barnacles who enjoy the good company and accommodations with the Captain and the Crew. Two of my favorite Barnacles are Annette and Dave.

Annette has no interest in gambling, but since she's married to Dave, she finds herself in Atlantic City quite often. Dave, on the other hand, is a study in expertise, concentration, and discipline. At first Dave's interest in gambling was related strictly to roulette, an unbeatable game. Then he moved to baccarat, another unbeatable game. These he played for small stakes. Before he played these two games, however, he read everything he could get his hands on about them. Now, he's starting to move into blackjack and craps, my games. But Dave does not just jump in the pool and start swimming. He has bought hundreds of dollars worth of programs and software, systems and analyses for blackjack and is reading most of the good books on the topic. He has watched the Captain's craps systems in action. He has spent endless hours rolling the dice in his home and playing casino games on his home computer. "So far, I'm ahead in these games," he says.

Now, what makes Dave truly unique to me is the fact that he can spend quite a bit of time in Atlantic City, he goes almost weekly, *and not gamble much!* He'll watch and analyze, discuss and debate. He is slowly becoming a scholar on gambling. Yet, with all his knowledge, he's a cautious swimmer, always testing the waters before taking a plunge. So when Dave turned to me the other day as he placed $200.00 on the craps table at Bally's Grand in Atlantic City and said: "No doubt about it, Frank, in craps it's the Captain's system to win," I knew the time had come to tell the world.

If you love to win, then follow the Captain's advice to the letter and go on and beat the craps out of those casinos. And may the goddess of fortune favor you in your pursuit!

TWELVE

The Captain's Ten Commandments of Gambling

1. Never gamble with *scared* money.

2. Never gamble when you are *unhappy* or *depressed*. Negative emotions result in negative cash flow.

3. Never gamble when you are *tired*.

4. Never *chase* your money when you're losing. It is better to decrease your bets than increase them when you're on a losing streak.

5. Never let other players annoy you. You can only control your own actions and not the actions of others.

6. Never be *impatient* to place bets.

7. Never play to impress casino personnel. A free meal has ruined many a gambler.

8. Never play to impress friends. If they're not impressed by your personality, they're not going to be impressed by your gambling.

9. Never ask the casino for credit when you're high or drunk. Drinking and gambling work well for the casinos, but not for the players.

10. Always keep in mind that the real struggle is not between you and the casino. *The real struggle is between you and yourself.*

THIRTEEN
Terms, Jargon, Concepts, and Constructs

Action: The amount and type of betting a player does in the casino. The longer a player plays, the bigger the bettor bets, the more *action* he gives the casino. All ratings of players are based on the total action they give the casino.

Any Craps: A one roll bet. The next roll of the dice will be 2, 3, or 12. A Crazy Crapper bet and not recommended.

Any Seven: A one roll bet. The next roll of the dice will be a 7. A Crazy Crapper bet and not recommended.

Back Line: Another term for the Don't Pass Line.

Bankroll: The total stake a player has to gamble with.

Banning: The practice by Nevada casinos of barring skilled players. The Captain: "This is a despicable and un-American practice."

Barnacles: Low-limit players, usually $5.00 bettors, who hang out with the Crew.

Bar the 12: The 12 does not win for wrong bettors on the come out roll. It is a tie. This gives the casino an edge over the player. Some casinos bar the 2 rather than the 12.

Big 6 and Big 8: An even money bet that either the 6 or the 8 will come up before the 7. A Crazy Crapper bet and not recommended.

Boxman: The seated supervisor at the center of the craps table.

Buck: Another term for the black/white disk used to delineate which number is the shooter's point.

Buy the 4 or the 10: Giving a 5 percent tax to the casino in order for the 4 and the 10 to be paid off at correct odds of two to one when they are placed. A poor bet unless used exactly as the Captain outlines in the High Roller System.

Center Field: The number 9 in the Field section on the craps layout.

Chasing Your Losses: Increasing your bets when you're losing in order to make back your money. Or, placing Crazy Crapper bets to get bigger payoffs. A poor way to recoup and not recommended.

Cold Dice or Cold Table: When the dice aren't passing and shooters are sevening out early in their rolls. A losing table.

Come Bet: Betting that the dice will repeat a number established after placing a bet in the Come Box. Similar to a Pass Line bet.

Come Out: Rolls of the dice before a point has been established. Usually referred to as the come-out roll.

Comp: Free goods and services given to players in exchange for their action.

Craps: The roll of a 2, a 3, or a 12. On the come out roll the stickman will call "Craps out!" when these numbers are rolled.

Crazy Crapper Bets: Big odds bets where the house takes a heavy tax out of the player's winnings. A Crazy Crapper is a person who makes these bets.

The Crew: The name for the group of high rollers which travels with the Captain. Also the term for the four dealers at the craps table.

Dealer: Name for any casino personnel who works a game.

Devil ("The devil jumped up!"): Another name for the 7. An expression for sevening out.

Die: Singular of dice.

Discretionary Removal: The ability in place betting to call off or remove your bets. Odds bets are also discretionary.

Disk: Two-sided black and white circular device that designates which point number is the shooter's.

Doey-Don't: Betting both the Pass Line/Don't Pass Line and the Come/Don't Come sides of the board.

Don't Come Bet: A bet made against the dice representing a number established by placing a bet in the Don't Come Box. Similar to a Don't Pass bet.

Don't Pass Bet: A bet made on the come out roll that the dice will not repeat the point number established before a seven is rolled.

Easy Way: The opposite of a hard way, where the numbers 4, 6, 8, and 10 are made with any combination but a pair. 3:1 is an easy 4.

Edge: The amount, usually expressed as a percentage, of advantage that the house has over a player.

Even Money: A bet paid off at $1.00 for $1.00.

Fair Game: A game that theoretically doesn't favor the house or the player. Given a sufficiently long playing time, the game would end up a draw. In craps a fair game would be to pay off all bets at their true odds.

Field Bet: A bet that the next roll of the dice will be any of the following numbers: 2, 3, 4, 9, 10, 11, or 12. A Crazy Crapper bet and not recommended.

"5-Count": The revolutionary system developed by the Captain to avoid horrendous rolls of the dice, stretch the amount of time your money gives you at the table, and position you to take advantage of good rolls.

Fixing the Dice: The setting of specific numbers or the arrangement of the dice a specific way by the shooter before he rolls.

Floorman: The person who supervises a portion of the pit under the direction of a pit boss.

Fluctuation in Probability: Sequences of numbers appearing out of proportion to their probability.

Free Odds: A bet made behind the Pass/Don't Pass or the Come/Don't Come wager that is paid off at true odds. Free odds are fair odds.

Front Line: Another name for the Pass Line.

Gambling Stake: The amount of money specifically set aside for gambling purposes only.

Hard Way Bets: A bet that the numbers 4, 6, 8, or 10 will be made as 2:2, 3:3, 4:4, or 5:5 respectively before a seven is rolled. Crazy Crapper bets and not recommended.

Heat: The psychological pressure that a casino can put on a player. The casino is placing heat on a player when the pit personnel take a more than casual notice of him or constantly question him about his method of play. In blackjack, casino heat has resulted in the banning of card counters and other skilled players from casinos in

Nevada. The Supersystem on occasion will draw some casino heat.

Higher and Higher: The Captain's method for increasing bets during a good roll. Used in the Limited Bankroll System.

High Roller: The term for individuals who bet large sums of money.

High Roller System: The Captain's method of play for large stakes that reduces the house edge and stretches your time at the table. Involves precise use of "5-Count" and intelligent place betting strategies.

Hop Bet: A one roll bet on any number the player wants. A Crazy Crapper bet and not recommended.

Horn Bet: A one roll bet that any one of the following numbers will appear on the next roll: 2, 3, 11, 12. A Crazy Crapper bet and not recommended.

Horrendous Rolls: Rolls where the shooter sevens out within a few rolls after establishing his point number.

Hot Dice or Hot Table: Rolls of the dice where numbers and points are being made and the 7 is nowhere to be seen. A winning table.

House Odds: Odds paid out to place bets and Crazy Crapper bets that are not true odds. House takes tax out of winnings.

Inside Numbers: The place numbers 5, 6, 8, 9.

Law of Repeating Numbers: A term for the Captain's belief that numbers tend to repeat.

Lay Bet: A place bet against the number being rolled before a 7 appears. Paid off at house odds.

Lay the Odds: An odds bet placed by the Wrong bettor that the 7 will appear before the number is rolled.

Limited Bankroll System: The name for the Captain's system for players who don't wish to play the Supersystem or find it too demanding. Also, for those players with limited funds.

Long Run: The concept that a player could play so often that probability would tend to even out. That is, you'd start to see the total appearance of numbers approximating what probability theory suggests. A long run player is one who intends to play a lot.

Money at Risk: Money that when wagered can be lost. In the Supersystem, odds bets on the Come and the initial Come roll where the 12 loses for the player.

Money Not-At-Risk: Money that is on the layout but cannot be lost. Bets that have been called off. Bets that cancel out as in Come/Don't Come.

Monster Roll: A hot roll where numbers and points are coming and the 7 is nowhere to be seen. The roll lasts a minimum of a half hour. Ceel "The Arm" is known affectionately as "The Queen of the Monsters."

Nickel Chips: Term for $5.00 chip. The Captain doesn't recommend thinking of money as chips.

Non-Seven Mode: A roll in which a rhythmic roller is positioning and rolling the dice in such a way that the 7 doesn't appear. Can be taken advantage of by an expert player.

No Second Guess No-Guess Rule: A tongue-in-cheek rule that the Captain recommends so you don't castigate yourself for making wrong guesses.

Numbers: The numbers 4, 5, 6, 8, 9, 10.

Off ("Take my bets off!"): A verbal call that some or all of a players bets will not be working on this and/or subsequent rolls. Any bet that is not working.

One-Roll Bets: Bets determined by the next roll of the dice only.

On ("My bets are on!"): A verbal call that some or all of the player's bets are working. Any bet that is working.

Out and Up Progression: The Captain's method in the Super-system and the Limited Bankroll System for having more numbers working and then more money on the table.

Outside Numbers: The numbers 4, 5, 9, 10.

Pass: The point number being made.

Pass Line: The area of the layout where a Pass Line bet is made.

Pass Line Bet: A bet that the dice will make the shooter's number before a seven appears.

Payoff, Payout: The paying of a winning bet by the casino.

Pilgrim's Progression: The Captain's method for getting more money on the table during a hot roll. To be used in the High Roller System.

Pit: The working area for casino personnel inside a group of tables of the same game.

Pit Boss: The supervisor of the entire pit.

Place Bets: A bet placed directly on any, some, or all of the numbers: 4, 5, 6, 8, 9, 10. Paid off at house odds.

Point: The number the shooter must make before a seven is rolled.

Point Numbers: The numbers 4, 5, 6, 8, 9, 10.

Pressing a Bet ("Press it!"): To increase a bet, usually by doubling it, after a win.

Proposition Bets: Bets in the middle of the layout. These are all Crazy Crapper bets and not recommended.

Push: Term for a tie in gambling.

Pushing the House or Pushing the Casino: The term coined by the Captain to describe a player placing more money in odds behind the Pass or Come bets than is indicated by the casino. Making the casino give you a better game than advertised. The Captain has been credited with the Pushing of Atlantic City. A recommended technique for getting more money on the table at correct odds.

Qualified Shooter: A shooter who has already made a point. This concept has been the basis of several systems in craps. An interesting but archaic way to play in light of the Captain's revelations.

Quarter Chips: The term for $25.00 chips. The Captain does not recommend thinking of money as chips.

Rails: Another term for the grooved area where players keep their chips.

Rating: The casino's appraisal of a player's action to determine the level of his comps.

RFB: The expression used to indicate that a player is fully comped by the casino. Literally means room, food, and beverage. The Captain and his Crew are all RFB.

Rhythmic Roller: The Captain's term for a shooter who rolls the same way over and over in a set rhythm. Such a shooter can get into a non-seven mode and be exploited by an expert player.

Right Bettor: A player betting with the dice and against the 7.

Ruin or Element of Ruin: Losing every penny of your gambling stake. The possibility of losing every penny of your gambling stake.

Scared Money: Money the player is afraid to lose because he cannot afford to. Money not set aside specifically for gambling.

Session Stake: The amount of money specifically set aside for a single session at the tables.

Seven-Out: The 7 being rolled after a point was established. All right bets lose on a seven-out.

Shoot: All the rolls of a single shooter until he sevens-out.

Shooter: The player rolling the dice.

Short Run: A limited time at the tables where numbers may fluctuate sharply from probability. A short-run player is one who plays infrequently.

Stickman: The dealer calling the game and carrying the big stick.

Supersystem: The Captain's ultimate system, the dynamic combination of the "5-Count" and the Doey-Don't.

Take the Odds: Free odds bets behind the Pass Line and Come bets that are paid off at correct odds.

Tapped Out: Losing your session stake or your entire bankroll.

Tax: The amount of money the casino takes out of winning bets.

Toke: A tip.

Tough Out: A player who doesn't beat himself. A player who through skill, insight, and intuition has the potential to hurt the casino's bankroll. Readers of this book who effectively put into play the Captain's principles.

Vigorish, Vig: A gambler's term for the house edge. Heard less and less in casino circles.

Virgin Principle: The superstition that a female who has never rolled the dice before will have a hot roll the first time out.

Wager: A bet.

Working ("My bets are working!"): A verbal call that bets are on. Bets are on and can be lost.

Wrong Bettor: A player who bets against the dice and with the 7.

Index

Outdoor
Family
Guide ™

Rocky Mountain
National Park

Third Edition

Outdoor Family Guide™

Rocky Mountain
National Park

Third Edition

LISA GOLLIN EVANS

THE MOUNTAINEERS BOOKS

The MOUNTAINEERS BOOKS
is the nonprofit publishing arm of The Mountaineers,
an organization founded in 1906 and dedicated to the exploration,
preservation, and enjoyment of outdoor and wilderness areas.

1001 SW Klickitat Way, Suite 201, Seattle, WA 98134

First edition 1991, second edition 1998, third edition 2011

Manufactured in the United States of America

Copy Editor: Joan Gregory
Cover and Book Design: The Mountaineers Books
Layout: Jennifer Shontz/Red Shoe Design
Cartographer: Benjamin Pease/Pease Press Cartography
All photographs by the author unless otherwise noted
Frontispiece: *A young hiker enjoys the view of Longs Peak at Bear Lake.*

Library of Congress Cataloging-in-Publication Data

Evans, Lisa Gollin, 1956–
An outdoor family guide to Rocky Mountain National Park / Lisa Gollin Evans.—3rd ed.
   p.   cm.
Includes bibliographical references and index.
ISBN 978-1-59485-498-9 (ppb)
1. Hiking—Colorado—Rocky Mountain National Park—Guidebooks. 2. Outdoor recreation—Colorado—Rocky Mountain National Park—Guidebooks. 3. Family recreation—Colorado—Rocky Mountain National Park—Guidebooks. 4. Trails—Colorado—Rocky Mountain National Park—Guidebooks. 5. Rocky Mountain National Park (Colo.)—Guidebooks. I. Title.
GV199.42.C62R6245 2011
917.88'69—dc22

2011011781

ISBN (paperback): 978-1-59485-498-9
ISBN (e-book): 978-1-59485-499-6

CONTENTS

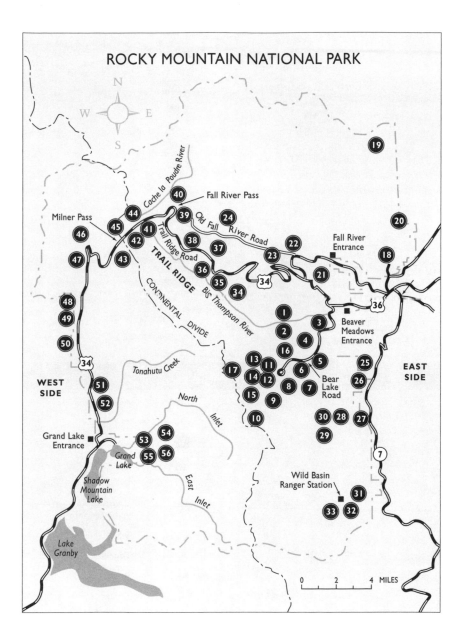

ROCKY MOUNTAIN NATIONAL PARK

N / W / E / S

Cache la Poudre River

Milner Pass

Fall River Pass

Old Fall River Road

Trail Ridge Road

TRAIL RIDGE

CONTINENTAL DIVIDE

Big Thompson River

Fall River Entrance

Beaver Meadows Entrance

Bear Lake Road

EAST SIDE

WEST SIDE

Tonahutu Creek

North Inlet

Grand Lake Entrance

Grand Lake

East Inlet

Shadow Mountain Lake

Lake Granby

Wild Basin Ranger Station

0   2   4   MILES

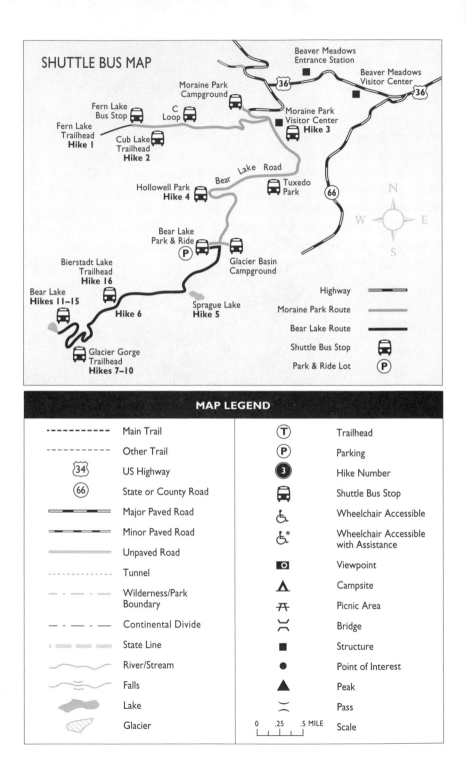

SHUTTLE BUS MAP

Beaver Meadows Entrance Station

Beaver Meadows Visitor Center

36

US 36

Moraine Park Campground

C Loop

Moraine Park Visitor Center
Hike 3

Fern Lake Bus Stop

Fern Lake Trailhead
Hike 1

Cub Lake Trailhead
Hike 2

Bear   Lake   Road

Hollowell Park
Hike 4

Tuxedo Park

66

Bear Lake Park & Ride

Glacier Basin Campground

Bierstadt Lake Trailhead
Hike 16

Bear Lake
Hikes 11–15

Hike 6

Sprague Lake
Hike 5

Glacier Gorge Trailhead
Hikes 7–10

N
W   E
S

Highway	
Moraine Park Route	
Bear Lake Route	
Shuttle Bus Stop	
Park & Ride Lot	(P)

MAP LEGEND

`- - - - - - - - - - -`	Main Trail		(T)	Trailhead
`- - - - - - - - - -`	Other Trail		(P)	Parking
{34}	US Highway		(3)	Hike Number
(66)	State or County Road		🚌	Shuttle Bus Stop
▬▬▬	Major Paved Road		♿	Wheelchair Accessible
▬▬▬	Minor Paved Road		♿*	Wheelchair Accessible with Assistance
═══	Unpaved Road		[o]	Viewpoint
`· · · · · · · · · ·`	Tunnel		△	Campsite
`— · — · — · —`	Wilderness/Park Boundary		⊼	Picnic Area
`— · — · — · —`	Continental Divide		⏝	Bridge
▬ ▬ ▬ ▬	State Line		■	Structure
∿∿∿	River/Stream		●	Point of Interest
∿∿∿	Falls		▲	Peak
	Lake		⏜	Pass
	Glacier		0 .25 .5 MILE	Scale

HIKE FINDER

KEY TO SYMBOLS:

Handicap access: (H) = Yes, according to uniform federal standards of accessibility; (H*) = Yes, with assistance

Mileage: RT = Round trip; OW = One way

Difficulty: NS = Nature stroll; E = Easy; M = Moderate; S = Strenuous; VS = Very Strenuous

Usage: L = Low; M = Moderate; H = High

Point of interest: G = Geological formation; NT = Nature trail (self-guided); P = Peak; H = Historical interest; I = Interpretive signs

		Difficulty	Mileage	Usage	Backpacking	Fishing	Scenic Views	Fall Foliage	Wildlife	Point of Interest
EAST SIDE HIKES										
1.	Arch Rocks and the Pool	E	1.5/1.7 OW	H	•	•		•	•	G
2.	Cub Lake and the Pool Loop	M	2.3/6.0 OW	H	•	•		•		
3.	Moraine Park (H*)	NS	0.25 OW	M						G
4.	Mill Creek Basin	E	1.6 OW	M	•			•		H
5.	Sprague Lake (H)	NS	0.5 OW	H	•	•			•	NT
6.	Boulder Brook/Alberta Falls Loop	S	5.6 RT	L/H	•		•	•	•	
7.	Alberta Falls	E	0.8 OW	H			•	•		
8.	Mills Lake	M	2.8 OW	H			•	•	•	
9.	The Loch	M	3.0 OW	H	•	•	•	•	•	
10.	Timberline Falls, Lake of Glass, and Sky Pond	S	4.2/4.4 4.8 OW	M	•	•	•	•	•	
11.	Bear Lake (H*)	NS	0.5 OW	H					•	NT
12.	Nymph Lake	E	0.5 OW	H			•	•		

		Difficulty	Mileage	Usage	Backpacking	Fishing	Scenic Views	Fall Foliage	Wildlife	Point of Interest
13.	Dream Lake	E	1.1 OW	H		•	•	•		
14.	Emerald Lake	M	1.8 OW	H			•	•	•	
15.	Lake Haiyaha	M	2.1 OW	H		•	•	•	•	
16.	Bierstadt Lake	E	3.0 RT	M			•	•		
17.	Flattop Mountain	S	4.4 OW	H			•	•	•	P
18.	Gem Lake	M	1.8 OW	H			•	•	•	G
19.	Deserted Village	M	3.0 OW	L				•		P
20.	Bridal Veil Falls	M	3.2 OW	L	•			•		G
21.	Deer Mountain	S	3.0 OW	H			•			P
22.	Alluvial Fan Trail (H*)	NS	0.8 OW	H						H
23.	Beaver Boardwalk (H)	NS	0.3 RT	H					•	I
24.	Mummy Range	S	1.5/2.4/3.5 OW	L			•		•	P
25.	Lily Mountain	M	1.5 OW	M			•			P
26.	Lily Lake (H)	NS	1.0 RT	M		•	•			
27.	Eugenia Mine	E	1.4 OW	M	•					H
28.	Estes Cone	S	3.3 OW	M	•		•			P
29.	Chasm Lake	S	4.2 OW	H	•	•	•		•	
30.	Longs Peak	VS	8.0 OW	H	•		•		•	P/H
31.	Copeland Falls (H*)	NS	0.3 OW	H				•		
32.	Calypso Cascades	E	1.8 OW	H	•			•		
33.	Ouzel Falls	M	2.7 OW	H	•		•	•	•	

TRAIL RIDGE HIKES

		Difficulty	Mileage	Usage	Backpacking	Fishing	Scenic Views	Fall Foliage	Wildlife	Point of Interest
34.	Indian Game Drive System Trail	E	0.75 OW	L			•		•	H
35.	Upper Old Ute Trail	M	2.0 OW	M			•	•		H
36.	Forest Canyon Overlook (H*)	NS	0.25 OW	H			•		•	I
37.	Sundance Mountain	M	0.5 OW	L			•			P
38.	Tundra Trail at Rock Cut (H*)	NS	0.5 OW	H				•	•	G/I
39.	Marmot Point	E	0.5 OW	M					•	P

		Difficulty	Mileage	Usage	Backpacking	Fishing	Scenic Views	Fall Foliage	Wildlife	Point of Interest
40.	Fall River Pass Tundra Trail	E	0.25 OW	H			•			I
41.	Fall River Pass to Forest Canyon Pass	E	1.9 OW	L			•	•		
42.	Milner Pass to Forest Canyon Pass	M	2.3 OW	L			•	•		
43.	Milner Pass along the Continental Divide	S	2.1 OW	L			•	•		
WESTSIDE HIKES										
44.	Poudre River Trail	E	1.0/2.5 OW	L				•		
45.	The Crater	M	1.0 OW	M			•	•		
46.	Lulu City	M	3.6 OW	M		•		•	•	H
47.	Grand Ditch	S	3.4 OW	L	•		•	•	•	H
48.	Holzwarth Historic Site (H*)	M	0.75 OW	M						H
49.	Kawuneeche Valley at Bowen/Baker Mountains (H*)	NS	0.5 OW	L				•	•	
50.	Coyote Valley Nature Trail (H)	NS	1.0 RT	L		•			•	I
51.	Green Mountain Loop	S	7.0 RT	L	•					H
52.	Big Meadows	E	1.8 OW	L	•				•	H
53.	North Inlet Meadows (H*)	NS	1.2 OW	M	•					
54.	Cascade Falls	S	3.5 OW	M	•					
55.	Adams Falls	E	0.3 OW	H						
56.	East Inlet Meadows Trail	E	1.7 OW	L	•			•	•	

WILDLIFE LOCATOR CHART

The following chart lists Rocky Mountain National Park's most popular birds and mammals and describes their habitats and likely locations. Be mindful that for the great majority of wildlife, dawn and dusk are the best viewing times. Another tip is to be aware of other viewers. Cars in pullouts (with people pointing) often mean a sighting of interest. Park rangers are also excellent resources for information on wildlife activity. Most of all, remember to watch wildlife ethically (from a distance) and safely.

TIME = Time of day most often seen   SEASON = Season of activity   Information supplied in part by NPS, RMNP

Animal	Time	Season	Habitat	Likely Locations and Trails
Chipmunk	Day	Sp, Su, F	Open areas from forest to tundra	Abundant parkwide
Golden-mantled ground squirrel	Day	Sp, Su, F	Mixed and coniferous forest	Abundant parkwide
Abert's squirrel	Day	Sp, Su, F	Ponderosa woodland	East side at lower elevations; hikes 18, 25
Red squirrel (chickaree)	Day	Sp, Su, F	Dense forests of spruce and fir, Douglas-fir, or lodgepole pine	Parkwide at lower elevations
Wyoming ground squirrel	Day	Sp, Su, F	Parks, open valleys, and meadows, 6,000–12,000 feet	Parkwide; hikes 3, 4
Pika	Day	Sp, Su, F	Talus slopes and rock outcrops near and above treeline	Parkwide at higher elevations; hikes 6–10, 14, 15, 17, 24, 29, 30, 34–43, 45, 47
Yellow-bellied marmot	Day	Sp, Su, F	Talus slopes and rock outcrops near and above treeline	Parkwide at higher elevations; hikes 6–10, 14, 15, 17, 24, 29–30, 34–43, 45, 47

Animal	Time	Season	Habitat	Likely Locations and Trails
Weasel (long-tailed weasel, short-tailed weasel)	Anytime	Year-round	Stream courses from forest to tundra, but generally under 10,000 feet	Parkwide; hikes 1, 2, 4, 6–24, 27, 28, 32, 42–44, 46, 47, 51–56
Bighorn sheep	Day	Year-round	Alpine meadows near rocky cliffs	Sheep Lakes at Horseshoe Park; hikes 24, 42, 43, 45
Moose	Anytime	Year-round	Willow thickets, lodgepole forests	Very few in park; Kawuneeche Valley; hikes 46–52
Mountain Lion	Anytime, especially dawn and dusk	Year-round	Rocky canyons and cliffs, forest meadows	Sighted more frequently on west side of park; hikes 44–56
Mallard	Day	Sp, Su, F	Lakes, streams, ponds	Parkwide at lower elevations; hikes 2, 5, 8, 9, 11–13, 16, 23, 46, 56
Hairy Woodpecker	Day	Year-round	Montane forests, river groves, and mixed forests	Abundant parkwide; hikes 1, 2, 18, 31–33
Red-tailed hawk	Day, especially midday	Sp, Su, F	Open country, areas with high rock ledges and adjacent woodland	Open meadows of lower and middle elevations, Lumpy Ridge; hikes 1–8, 21
White-tailed ptarmigan	Day	Year-round	Alpine tundra	Parkwide on tundra; hikes 17, 24, 34–43, 45

A young explorer at the lake at Alluvial Fan (Photo by Ned Strong)

PREFACE

Rocky Mountain National Park occupies a special place in my heart. It is where my writing adventures began, where I introduced my daughters to wilderness, and where I've gone on magical backpacking trips with my husband and best friends. The idea of writing outdoor guides came to me on a solo camping trip in the park when I was a mother of two young girls. Restless in my job at the U.S. Environmental Protection Agency, I wanted to spend more of my life in a place like Rocky Mountain National Park—a place so special and beautiful that I couldn't wait to get up in the morning just to breathe its air. I wanted my life to have a purpose, however, so I decided to try to share the joy I feel so deeply here and in other beautiful wilderness areas. Gazing at bright stars one night in Rocky Mountain National Park, I imagined a guidebook that not only would reveal special places in spectacular settings, but also would help parents share those places with their children.

I've always viewed our earth as an endangered place. My hope was that by introducing children to the wonders of nature and the joy of wilderness, wild animals, forest trails, and rocky climbs, they would be inspired to live lives caring about the earth in a deep, fundamental way. I imagined that families enjoying this spectacular park would build memories together that would last a lifetime and create the desire to preserve places like this around the world and to protect the air, water, and wildlife of our planet.

The wonderful nonprofit publisher, the Mountaineers Books, understood my vision and gave me the opportunity to write this guidebook. It has been nearly twenty years since the book's first edition. Two of my daughters have adopted the Rocky Mountains as their home, at least temporarily. The time they spent in the mountains' namesake park must have touched their hearts.

My last visit to Rocky Mountain National Park was, however, bittersweet. I introduced my youngest daughter to its splendor but, after years of absence, I was stunned by the changes. In just one generation of my own family, from my oldest daughter to my youngest, the park was dramatically different. Climate change has been devastating to the park's ecosystem—evidenced by dying forests and vanishing wildlife. To observe so much damage, in so short a time, was nothing short of frightening.

Thus, in this third edition of *Outdoor Family Guide: Rocky Mountain National Park,* I take the time to point out such changes—the dying pine forests, the diminishing of pika, the changing lakes. Be assured that Rocky Mountain National Park is still one of the most beautiful places in the world, and it always will be. The park's easy access to forests, meadows, lakes, and alpine regions; to abundant wildlife and birdlife; to views of towering ranges and dramatic peaks—all accessed by an amazing trail system—such experiences are unequaled among our nation's national parks. I am thrilled to point out improved trails, new visitor centers, and expanded shuttles. But, as you appreciate the great beauty that remains here, it is also important to understand the impact of climate change on Rocky Mountain National Park and elsewhere. My hope is that pointing out these changes will encourage readers and their families to take action to fight global warming in the many ways that we can.

ACKNOWLEDGMENTS

This book could not have been written without the encouragement and incredible support of my husband, Frank, and the cooperation and joyful participation of my daughters, Sarah, Grace, and Lilly. I also received invaluable help from my many wonderful, nature-loving friends: Ned, Julie, Peter, and Laura Strong; Mary Ann Fomunyoh; Richard Foote; Gennie Devaud; and Rick Ashley (for generously loaning me his marvelous camera). I also want to thank the former chief park naturalist of Rocky Mountain National Park, Jim Mack, and the park service staff, including Douglas Caldwell and Dr. D. Ferrel Atkins, for their helpful suggestions. In addition, I appreciate the assistance of the Rocky Mountain Nature Association, including Curt Buchholtz and Deanna Ochs. I thank the staff at the YMCA of the Rockies, Estes Park, for their help in finding near-perfect accommodations.

I also want to thank Kent and Donna Dannen for their fine and informative books, which helped me get started on this project. This book was inspired by the writing excellence of my brother, Jim, and made possible by the unwavering support of my mother and father.

Lastly, I want to send special thanks to Larry Frederick, Chief of Interpretation and Education, for help with this third edition.

Rybergia *(alpine sunflower)*

Fun picnics, amazing views, and family togetherness—the perfect vacation!.

INTRODUCTION

This book describes fifty-six hikes in Colorado's Rocky Mountain National Park. The hikes are divided into three groups—East Side, West Side, and Trail Ridge—according to their location within the park (see map within the Table of Contents). The "East Side Hikes" lie east of the Continental Divide, which bisects the park north and south. The "West Side Hikes" are west of the Divide. "Trail Ridge Hikes" occur on the high plateau of Trail Ridge, which spans the Divide.

HOW TO USE THIS BOOK

The hikes are classified as easy, moderate, or strenuous, according to their length, starting elevation, elevation gain, and terrain. Generally, easy hikes are 0.5 to 1.8 miles one way; moderate hikes are 1.8 to 3 miles; and strenuous hikes are over 3 miles. Because these ratings are both general and subjective, consult the detailed hike descriptions for specific information about trail conditions.

This guidebook also recognizes an additional category of trails, called "nature strolls." Nature strolls are short, easy, often surfaced trails, 0.25 to 1.25 miles one way, which can be hiked with strollers or wheelchairs (with assistance). Nature strolls that conform to federal standards of accessibility are so noted. Chapter 1 also lists picnic areas that are convenient to very short trails.

The trail descriptions do not provide estimates of walking time. Hikers, especially children, walk at such variable speeds that such approximations would not be reliable. To estimate roughly the time required for a hike, use the average walking rate of 2 miles per hour on level ground for adults carrying packs, plus one hour for each 1000 feet of elevation gained. Rough terrain and hiking children obviously increase the time needed. After a few hikes, you will find that you can work out estimates for your own family. Very broadly, strenuous hikes require a full day; moderate hikes, a half day; and easy hikes and nature strolls, one to three hours.

Many of the trail descriptions conclude with a section titled "Hiking Options," which contains suggested extensions to the featured hike. Often the section describes side trips of interest or tells how to link up with other trails to make longer hikes.

To help you quickly choose a hike that fits your needs, the "Hike Finder" at the beginning of this book contains a trip matrix for each hike that concisely lists information such as difficulty, distance, elevation gain, and attractions.

The "Wildlife Locator Chart" at the beginning of the book indicates what animals you are likely to see in Rocky Mountain National Park, on which trails

Fishing is a fun reward for reluctant hikers.

you can expect to find them, and the season and time of day they are most often seen.

This book also includes a recommended reading list that contains numerous books on nature for children and their parents.

HIKING TIPS

The following hiking tips will help you and your children make the most of your time on the trails.

Choosing the Right Hike

Hiking a trail that's too difficult for your children is sure to lead to frustration for all. Read trail descriptions carefully to find hikes that match your children's abilities. If you are uncertain how far they can walk, choose a hike that has intermediate points of interest so that you can shorten the hike if necessary. In addition, try to match a trail's attractions with your youngsters' interests, whether fishing, rock climbing, wildflowers, or wildlife.

The Right Time

The time of day you choose for your hike can determine the weather you encounter, how crowded the trail is, whether you see wildlife, and even the moods of your children. Take rhythms of the park, your youngsters, and yourself into account when planning a hike. Timing can be everything. For information on the park's weather and wildlife, see Chapter 1.

Snacks

Let hiking be a time when children can snack on their favorite foods. They will be working hard, and snacks high in carbohydrates and sugar are energy boosters. Offer salty snacks to replace salts lost through perspiration. Good-tasting treats can also be used as a motivating force for reaching the next rest stop. Also remember to bring plenty of water or juice, particularly in summer, when humidity is low and temperatures are high. Mild dehydration causes crankiness in children, and more severe cases can cause extreme discomfort.

Motivation

There are numerous ways to motivate children to reach a destination. The promise of a picnic or a treat is enough for some children. For others, encouraging good-natured competition with siblings or peers does the trick. You can also give your children trail patches as rewards for completing particular trails. These small patches, which can be sewn onto jackets or backpacks, exist for most trails and are available from souvenir and outdoor shops in Estes Park and Grand Lake.

When a child's motivation wears thin, distraction can be the best solution. Hiking songs, trail activities, games, and stories often invigorate sluggish youngsters. Your creative energy, of course, must be high to engage your children convincingly. For some suggestions to get you started, "Recommended Reading" at the end of this book.

Leaders

Allow the children to take turns leading your group. When the novelty wears off for one, assign the leadership role to another. Rotate the job among your children, and you'll be amazed at the distance you can cover. For safety's sake, however, be sure children do not advance too far ahead or out of your sight and reach.

The Pace

As much as possible, let your children determine the hiking pace. You'll progress more slowly than you'd like, but the hike will be much more enjoyable. Adults will also benefit from slowing down: you may cover only half the distance, but you'll experience twice as much.

Positive Attitude

Praise your children for all their hiking achievements. Positive reinforcement for beginning hikers is essential and will build a solid base of good feelings about hiking. Refrain from criticism if your children disappoint you. Nagging and criticizing a child will not make him or her a better hiker.

The Right Stuff

You can bring along a variety of items in your backpack to keep children happy on the trail. Magnifying glasses, binoculars, bug bottles, sketchbooks, gold pans, or materials for making rubbings may provide welcome diversions for youngsters who need a break. For additional suggestions for simple trail activities, see "Recommended Reading" at the end of this book.

Relax and Enjoy

When hiking with children, the joy is in the process of hiking, in the small achievements and discoveries of young hikers. Relax and enjoy. With children, you travel slowly enough to take joy in the sweet smell of the woods, the sweet taste of gorp, and the sweet squeals of delight from young, curious, and still-able-to-be-amazed children. With luck, you will find the child within you on the park's trails and be able to progress happily at "child speed."

WILDERNESS ETHICS

During your stay at Rocky Mountain National Park, it is important to use the park in a conscientious and ethical manner. If you abide by the following rules and teach them by example to your children, the park will be a more enjoyable, wild, and beautiful place.

Make a Positive Impact

The rule of Positive Impact goes beyond the oft-repeated "Take only pictures, leave only footprints." It asks that you consciously attempt to leave the park a better place. For example, by picking up a piece of litter you enhance the beauty of the trail for the next hiker. Give children a small bag that can be stuffed into pockets for their own litter as well as for stray wrappers left by others. Parents should also be sure to carry their own litterbags.

A second way to create a positive impact is to set a good example by hiking joyfully, attentively, and considerately. Your model will be contagious. Just as a crowd gathers to look at a sight in which others are showing interest, so other visitors may follow your lead if you find a hike interesting, fun, or exhilarating.

Respect Other Hikers

Hiking parties with children are likely to travel more slowly than other groups. As a courtesy, parents should be aware of other hikers who wish to pass and should see that their children move aside to let them do so. Also, picnics and rest stops should be conducted off the trail so as not to obstruct the path.

Leaders should discourage excessive noise. Youngsters may readily lower their voices when they learn that noise scares away birds and animals. Children, of course, should not be expected to march silently, but neither should they make unnecessary noise.

Do Not Feed the Animals

Do not feed the numerous chipmunks, squirrels, and birds who beg for handouts at the park. Feeding can be dangerous for both you and the animals. Human handouts are detrimental to wildlife for two main reasons. First, snack foods nutritionally cannot replace an animal's natural diet. Therefore, if handouts become its primary source of food, the animal may become malnourished and prey to disease and injury. Second, feeding an animal disrupts its natural foraging instincts. As a result, animals who depend on human feeding may not survive the winter. After all, the animal that relies on cheese doodles in July is likely to expect them in February as well.

Feeding park animals can also be hazardous to people. No matter how cute the chipmunks and deer may be, they are *wild* animals, and wild animals bite. The park's small mammals, like those in many other parts of the West, have been found to carry rabies. Rabies aside, a rodent's sharp incisors in your finger is painful. Second, fleas carrying bubonic plague have been found on the park's rodents. Although rare, instances of human contraction of bubonic plague from fleabites have occurred in national parks. Finally, remember that feeding wildlife is prohibited by park regulations.

Often, well-meaning park visitors feed wildlife in order to get a closer look at the animals. For safer and more ethical ways of viewing wildlife, see Chapter 1.

Let Wildflowers Flourish

From June through August, a dazzling display of wildflowers graces Rocky Mountain National Park. During these same months, more than 3 million visitors pass through the park. To ensure that all visitors have an opportunity to enjoy the flowers, it is essential everyone refrain from picking even one blossom. Above tree line, picking wildflowers poses a particularly critical problem because alpine plants may not bloom every year and, even when they do, they have little time in which to set seed. Removing plants from any part of the park means removing seeds, thus preventing annuals from reproducing.

Picking wildflowers can be expensive as well. The fine for picking the Colorado state flower, the Rocky Mountain columbine, is $500. Because most wildflowers wilt quickly after being plucked, the crime is ill rewarded in any event.

Stay on the Trail

The rule prohibiting shortcuts is essential for maintaining the integrity, beauty, and safety of the park's trails. Shortcuts are most tempting where a trail

Colorado blue columbine, the state flower

switchbacks down a steep slope. Yet these switchbacks have been cut in part to stabilize the trail. When hikers aim straight down a slope, they damage the vegetation between the switchbacks and contribute to the erosion of the slope. If shortcutting occurs frequently, a trail may wash away, leaving a scarred and barren hillside. In addition, leaving a trail on a precipitous slope is not only dangerous but may cause you to lose the trail altogether.

As a related matter, do not enter areas closed by the National Park Service for "revegetation." Such areas have usually been badly trampled and need years of protection to recover. Respecting trampled areas is especially critical on the alpine tundra, where plant life is particularly prone to damage and revegetation is extremely slow.

Observe Park Rules

Written copies of park regulations are available at the visitor centers. The rules are also frequently posted on trails. Please read and follow them. A few of the most important—and most commonly violated—are the following:

- Carry out all refuse. Nothing should be left on trails or in campsites. You should not attempt to burn or bury noncombustibles.
- Build campfires only in designated sites and in grates if provided. Use dead and downed wood only. Never cut down living trees, or portions thereof, for your own use—not even for cooking hot dogs.
- Dogs, cats, and other pets are not permitted on trails or away from roads or parking areas. Where permitted, all pets must be leashed. Although it may be tempting to allow the family pet to accompany you on the trail, it is potentially hazardous for your pet and for park wildlife.
- Do not cut, remove, deface, or disturb any tree, shrub, wildflower, or other natural object. Wild edibles, such as berries, can be gathered in small quantities for personal consumption. Carving on trees is a harmful and unfortunately widespread practice. Carving scars trees permanently and can even kill them.
- Do not tease, molest, or feed wild animals. All hunting is prohibited. Observe the park's wildlife from a safe and respectful distance. You can induce great stress in animals by approaching too closely. Such stress can leave the animal susceptible to disease or injury, or can provoke it to harm you.
- Fishing in the park requires a Colorado fishing license for all persons fifteen years of age or older. Check with a park ranger for areas of closure, possession limits, and restrictions on bait and tackle.

ENJOYING THE PARK SAFELY

This section summarizes the basic precautions to be taken when hiking in the park. Be alert to the dangers described below and be prepared with the appropriate gear to minimize hazardous situations. The checklist at the end of this section lists the essentials that you need to take on *every* outing.

There are three important caveats to this section. First, it cannot replace a good first-aid book, of which there are many on the market. Second, neither the following information nor a first-aid book can substitute for a firm base of practical knowledge and experience in safe hiking and first aid. One way to sharpen your skills is to enroll in a first-aid course. The knowledge and experience you'll gain will be invaluable. Finally, safe hiking requires the exercise of caution and common sense. Know the limitations of your group and read the warning signs of trouble, including fatigue, stress, and bad weather.

Hypothermia

Hypothermia is the lowering of the body's core temperature to a degree sufficient to cause illness. The condition is always serious and sometimes fatal. Signs of mild hypothermia include complaints of cold, shivering, loss of coordination, and apathy. More severe hypothermia causes mental confusion, uncontrollable shivering, slurred speech, and a core temperature low enough to potentially cause permanent damage or death.

Because small bodies lose heat more rapidly than large ones, children are more vulnerable to hypothermia than adults are. Early signs of hypothermia in children may be crankiness and fussiness, although these can also be caused by ordinary fatigue. A child may not even realize he or she is cold until serious shivering begins.

Hikers, especially children, can become hypothermic when temperatures are well above freezing. Wind chill is a critical, and often overlooked, cause of hypothermia.

Parents can guard against dangerous chills by observing the following precautions:

- Carry an adequate supply of warm clothing, including wool sweaters, socks, gloves, and hats to insulate against heat loss. Gloves, hats, and scarves are particularly effective because they protect hands, heads, and necks—areas that are especially sensitive to heat loss. Carry these items even when the weather looks warm and sunny, especially when at or above tree line. On cool, rainy days, avoid cotton clothing, which is not warm when wet and wicks warmth away from the body.
- Dress in layers and remove unneeded layers to prevent excessive sweating, which lowers body temperature through evaporation. Parents

must react quickly to temperature changes, whether occasioned by weather or changes in activity levels.

■ Avoid excessive exposure to wind and rain. Carry raingear on all hikes.

■ Carry food high in carbohydrates and sugar that the body can quickly convert to heat.

■ Carry warm liquids, such as hot cocoa, when hiking in cold weather.

■ Avoid resting against ice, snow, or cold rocks, which draw heat away from the body. Place an insulating barrier, such as a foam pad, between hikers and cold surfaces.

■ Cover the mouth with a wool scarf to warm air entering the lungs. If a member of your group shows signs of hypothermia, stop whatever you are doing and take immediate steps to warm the person up. Promptness is particularly important when treating hypothermia in children. Add layers of clothing. Replace wet clothes with dry ones. If possible, administer warm liquids or food. If necessary, build a small fire to warm the victim and dry out wet clothing. Holding a cold child close to your body while wrapping a parka or blanket around the two of you is particularly effective. Crawling into a sleeping bag with the victim is recommended for cases that do not respond readily to other treatment.

Heat-Related Illness

Hiking at high altitudes, in warm weather, or in the open sun can cause excessive loss of water and salts (electrolytes). Failure to replace water and electrolytes can lead to dehydration, heat exhaustion, or even heat stroke. To prevent heat-related illnesses, consume adequate amounts of water and electrolytes. Avoid salt tablets in favor of salted snacks and liquids, which you should always carry in amounts greater than you are likely to need. Flavored powders containing electrolytes may be added to water to replace those lost through perspiration. Remember that thirst is not a reliable indicator of the need for water. Schedule regular water stops to prevent dehydration.

Sun Exposure

At Rocky Mountain National Park, precautions against overexposure to the sun are necessary year-round. Harmful ultraviolet radiation increases with altitude. Therefore, the danger is greatest at or above tree line, where incoming solar radiation is twice that of sea level. To avoid sunburn, take the following precautions:

■ Protect exposed skin with sunscreen. Remember that children, especially babies, burn easily. Be particularly careful when carrying young children in back carriers, for their exposure may be prolonged and go undetected.

■ Bring brimmed hats, long-sleeved shirts, and sunglasses.

■ Don't be fooled by cool temperatures; you don't have to feel the sun on your skin to get a dangerous burn. Despite the frigid winds of the tundra, sunburns happen fast in the thin air.

Effects of High Altitude—Mountain Sickness

The decreased oxygen in the air at high altitudes can result in mountain sickness, whose symptoms include headaches, fatigue, loss of appetite, weakness and dull pain in muscles, shortness of breath, nausea, and rapid heartbeat. If ignored or left untreated, mountain sickness can be fatal. Consequently, do not overlook the early, easily treated symptoms of the disease. Mountain sickness strikes unpredictably. It affects both young and old, whether fit or not. Some members of a party may be affected while others are not. Some people may experience no symptoms on one day but quickly develop them on another. In any case, the cardinal rule when the early symptoms of mountain sickness strike is to descend at once to a lower elevation.

To reduce the likelihood of mountain sickness, acclimate your family to high altitudes gradually. The park ranges in elevation from 8000 feet at Moraine Park to 12,000 feet on Trail Ridge Road. At the beginning of your visit, choose hikes in the lower elevations or, at least, those in the high country that are not strenuous. Because children are often inarticulate about their physical condition, be attuned to crankiness as a sign of altitude discomfort. If suspected, rest and retreat to lower elevations as soon as possible. Hikers with a history of heart, circulatory, or lung ailments need to be especially cautious and should check with their physicians prior to visiting the park. To aid the family's acclimation, make sure everyone eats lightly, drinks plenty of fluids, gets plenty of rest, and limits physical activity for the first few days. Adults should limit their intake of alcohol at high elevations.

Lightning

Deep blue skies and low humidity are typical throughout the summer and fall. Fine summer weather is interrupted almost daily, however, by early afternoon thunderstorms, which begin around one or two in the afternoon and last approximately an hour. Because of the real danger posed by lightning, plan your hikes so that you are below tree line by early afternoon. Start ascents or high-country hikes early in the morning so that you can reach your destination before noon—even earlier if your hikers are slow or you want more time on the summit. To be above tree line during an electrical storm is particularly dangerous because lightning strikes at the highest object in a landscape, which could well be you or your family in a treeless area.

If you do get caught in a thunderstorm, take the following precautions:

- Do *not* seek shelter under natural features, such as lone or tall trees, rock overhangs, or large boulders, which project above their surroundings. Such large, exposed objects are more likely to be hit by lightning because of their height.
- Do *not* lie flat on the ground. To do so is to increase the body area exposed to electrical current in the event of a nearby lightning strike.
- Do *not* seek shelter in a tent, because its metal rods conduct electricity. For the same reason, do *not* wear a metal-frame backpack during a lightning storm.
- Do *not* remain on or next to a horse. Sitting on a horse increases your height; standing next to a horse gives the lightning a larger target.
- Keep away from puddles, streams, and other bodies of water, because water conducts electricity.
- Assume the safest position, which is to huddle on your knees with your head down. Crouch near medium-sized boulders, if available.
- If you are retreating to safety during a storm, stay as low as possible, remove children from back carriers, and walk with your legs wide apart.
- Safe places during thunderstorms include cars and large buildings (the larger, the better).

When hiking, be aware of the fickleness of mountain weather. Storms can approach extremely rapidly, turning blue skies to black in a matter of minutes. When hiking above tree line, continually check the skies for brewing storms. Although wind direction may be one indication of where a storm is heading, it is definitely not reliable. Mountains create their own wind pockets and weather systems. If you see a storm, the most prudent course is to retreat at once to a safe area.

Drinking Water

Always carry a lot of safe drinking water—at least a quart per person. It is *not* safe to drink from any of the lakes and streams in the park. The waters are often infested with *Giardia lamblia,* a parasite that wreaks havoc in the human digestive system. *Giardia* infestation is caused when mammals such as beavers and muskrats defecate in or near the water, or when water has been contaminated by careless disposal of human waste. Symptoms of giardiasis in humans include diarrhea, abdominal distention, gas, and cramps. The symptoms appear seven to ten days after infection. To purify water, boil it for ten

Use extreme caution with children near waterfalls and all rushing water in the park.

minutes. You may also disinfect the water chemically or by filtration, but these methods have not been proven as effective as heat. All water that might be swallowed must be treated, including water used for cooking, cleaning dishes, and brushing teeth.

To help prevent the spread of giardiasis and other harmful diseases, dig temporary latrines at least eight inches deep and 200 feet away from water sources, trails, and campsites. Of course, hikers should wash hands thoroughly after use of the latrine. Parents should teach children safe toileting practices to protect their health and to keep lakes and rivers clean.

Snowfields and Ice Fields

Be extremely cautious when hiking over snow or ice. Never venture near the edge of snow or ice slopes or cornices. These areas can be treacherous and unstable. Do not venture out onto glaciers or glissade (slide) down snowfields unless accompanied by park personnel who are familiar with both the hazards and the terrain.

Streams and Waterfalls

The park's streams can be extremely dangerous. The current of even small streams can be strong, especially in the spring and particularly for children. In all seasons, the park's waters are frigid and potentially hazardous. Flash flooding may occur during thunderstorms. If there is a storm upstream (even if it is not raining where you are), move away from a stream or canyon bottom to higher ground. Stream levels can rise extremely fast. Children fishing or playing on stream banks are particularly at risk. Sadly, there have been a number of recent drownings.

Waterfalls can also present significant hazards. Slick rocks and steep drop-offs warrant a close watch on children.

Ticks

Rocky Mountain wood ticks pose a danger because they transmit a viral disease called Colorado tick fever. The virus transmitted by the tick is serious but rarely life threatening. Symptoms include fever, headache, body aches, and, rarely, a skin rash. Rocky Mountain wood ticks are active in the park from February until mid-July. A Rocky Mountain wood tick is about one-sixteenth inch long, but may enlarge to one-half inch when engorged. To prevent contracting Colorado tick fever, take the following precautions:

■ Use an insect repellent containing DEET or permethrin; spray on shoes and clothing, especially socks, pant legs and cuffs, and shirtsleeves and cuffs. Avoid direct application of DEET to children's skin, for this potentially harmful chemical can be absorbed through the skin. DEET can also damage rayon, acetate, and spandex but is safe on nylon, cotton, and wool. When buying DEET, choose a formula containing approximately 35 percent DEET. Tests have shown that this amount provides as much protection as formulas containing higher concentrations.

■ Tuck pants into boots, and button cuffs and collars. Wear light-colored clothing to spot ticks more easily.

■ Check frequently for ticks on skin, scalp, and clothing. This may be done on rest breaks while hiking. Ticks often spend many hours on a body before they transmit the virus, so there is no need to panic if you find a tick. Infection can, nevertheless, be transmitted soon after the tick attaches, so it is prudent to check regularly.

■ Bathe after outings and inspect skin well.

■ Avoid areas of heavy tick infestation in April, May, and June. These areas include sunny south-facing slopes east of the Continental Divide, sagebrush clearings, and vegetation on the uphill side of trails.

If you should discover a tick, first cover the tick with oil or ointment to cut off its air supply. Then remove it using tweezers, as close to the skin as possible, pulling it straight out. It is important to remove all head and mouth parts to prevent infection. After removal, wash the area with soap and water.

Even though ticks are rare in late summer and fall, you should still check your family regularly.

Rocky Mountain spotted fever can also be transmitted by ticks in Colorado, but it is very rare. Symptoms of this serious disease include fever, a spotted rash beginning on the extremities, headache, nausea, and aches in abdomen and muscles. Spotted fever can be fatal if untreated. Unlike Colorado tick fever, Rocky Mountain spotted fever is treatable with antibiotics. Therefore, if a member of your group contracts a tick-related disease, see a physician so that the appropriate method of treatment can be determined. No cases of Lyme disease, another tick-borne illness, have ever been reported in Rocky Mountain National Park.

Bears

There are no grizzly bears remaining in the park. A few black bears do remain, but their population numbered only about thirty in 2010. They are most frequently seen in the Wild Basin area. Although you are unlikely to see a bear during your park visit, you should still take the following precautions:

- Never store food in your tent. Use a minimum of odorous food and seal it in clean wrapping material or airtight containers. Backcountry campers should hang their food in a tree, suspending it at least 10 feet above the ground and 4 horizontal feet from the trunk of the tree. Food, scented items, and garbage should be stored in commercially available bear-resistant portable canisters. Car campers should avoid storing food in their vehicles, but if necessary, they should carefully wrap their food and put it out of sight in the trunk of their vehicle. Ice chests are not bear-proof, and bears can peel open car doors like sardine cans if they spot a cooler inside. Pack out all garbage and dispose of it in bear-resistant dumpsters and trashcans. The National Park Service warns, "A fed bear is a dead bear."
- When hiking in bear habitat, especially in brushy areas where your sight lines are obscured, make sufficient noise so that you don't inadvertently surprise a bear.
- If you encounter a bear, do not approach it. Bears are not usually aggressive, but they are unpredictable. Be particularly cautious if you see a sow with cubs. Never approach bear cubs; an angry mother bear will seldom be far away. Report bear sightings to a park ranger.

Mountain Lions

Mountain lions have been observed in Rocky Mountain National Park, and attacks, although very rare, have occurred. Although the likelihood of encountering a lion is very low, it is prudent to be aware of these potentially dangerous animals. Talk with your children about what to do if they see a lion, do not let them play outside unsupervised, and always keep them within sight and reach when hiking. Lions may be active at any time of day or night. Thus, parents must be vigilant at all hours.

The Colorado Division of Wildlife suggests the following precautions:

- Hike in groups and make plenty of noise to reduce the chances of surprising a lion. Carry a walking stick; it can be used to ward off an attack. Make sure children are close to you and within your sight at all times.
- Do not approach a lion, especially one that is feeding or with kittens. Most mountain lions will try to avoid a confrontation. Give them a way to escape.
- Stay calm when you come upon a lion. Talk calmly yet firmly to it. Move slowly.
- If you encounter a lion, stop. Running may stimulate a lion's instinct to chase and attack. Face the lion and stand upright.
- Do all you can to appear larger. Raise your arms. Open your jacket. If you have small children, pick them up so they won't panic and run.
- If the lion behaves aggressively, throw stones, branches, or whatever you can get your hands on without crouching down or turning your back. Wave your arms slowly and speak firmly. What you want to do is convince the lion you are not prey and that you in fact may be a danger to the lion.
- Fight back if a lion attacks. Lions have been driven away by prey that fights back. Do not play dead!
- Contact a park ranger to report any lion activity.

Falling Trees

While falling trees are always a hazard when traveling in forested areas, the abundance of dead and dying lodgepole pines in the park significantly increases the risk of injury. Follow these guidelines to help avoid injury:

- Avoid dense patches of dead trees. They can fall without warning.
- Stay out of the forest when there are strong winds that could blow down trees. If you are already in the forest when the wind increases, go to a clearing that is out of reach of any trees that could potentially fall.
- Place tents and cars in areas where they will not be hit if trees fall.

Bubonic Plague

Bubonic plague is endemic to the park. This disease is transmitted by fleas from infected rodents, especially ground squirrels. Do not feed or approach ground squirrels or other small mammals. Symptoms of bubonic plague include swollen lymph nodes and fever, usually developing one to six days after exposure. Bubonic plague can be successfully treated by antibiotics, but untreated bubonic plague is fatal in about 50 percent of the cases.

Snakes

There are no poisonous snakes in Rocky Mountain National Park. The only snake inhabiting the park is the green garter snake, which is harmless.

Lost and Found

Carry current topographic maps for the areas in which you plan to hike. Visitor centers sell a variety of maps of the park. USGS maps are particularly useful because they show terrain features and elevations by means of contour lines. If you have old maps, make sure they are up-to-date before setting out. Finally, buy waterproof maps, or carry the maps in a waterproof pouch.

Also carry a reliable compass and know how to use it in conjunction with your topographic maps. If you don't feel confident, check with outing clubs in your area for instruction.

Children are particularly vulnerable to getting lost and less able to care for themselves if they do. On a hike, it is essential that children never stray from your sight. Take the following preventive measures to guard against potentially traumatic or dangerous situations:

- Teach children to stay with the group.
- Instruct children never to leave designated trails. Give children whistles, with strict instructions to use the whistles only when lost.
- Instruct children to remain in one place if they become lost. That way, they can be found more easily.
- If children must move while lost, teach them how to build "ducks" by placing a smaller stone on top of a larger stone. By leaving a trail of ducks, the children will be more easily found.

SPECIAL GEAR FOR CHILDREN

The following gear can make your outings safer and more enjoyable.

Carriers

Small infants ride in front carriers; those able to support their heads graduate to back carriers. The best carriers on the market are large enough so a child has room to grow. Choose a well-padded carrier that has a storage compartment attached. When hiking with a young child, it is good insurance to bring a back carrier, even though the child feels he has outgrown it. If the child becomes tired, the carrier will be invaluable. Carrying a child in a back carrier is much easier and safer than toting the child piggyback. Carriers can also be useful if quick evacuation from an area is required. For information on renting carriers, see Chapter 1.

Footwear

Lug-soled hiking boots, worn in and well fitting, are the best choice of footwear for children. These sturdy boots are essential for long hikes on rocky or steep terrain, or when children are carrying backpacks. The boots' stiff uppers and strong construction provide support and protect feet from injury. Before hiking, make sure waterproofing is fresh and effective.

Sturdy athletic shoes with good traction are a common substitute. Athletic shoes can be an adequate and comfortable substitute for boots on short outings and relatively easy, smooth trails. Athletic shoes give feet little support, however, on rough terrain. Also, if children are hiking in any type of sneakers, remember that the shoes are not waterproof and if soaked may result in cold, blistered feet.

Even the smallest children will enjoy hiking.

Children should wear wool or wool-blend socks. If wool socks get wet, they will still keep feet warm. When hiking in cool weather, you may be tempted to wear heavier socks for warmth. If possible, wear two thinner pairs of socks instead of one thick pair—the layers provide more warmth. Always bring an extra pair of socks for each child. Mud puddles and streams are too attractive to be passed up by most youngsters. Extra wool socks can also be used as mittens.

Clothing

Because of the changeable weather, always carry warm clothes and raingear. Hypothermia can occur even in midsummer, and children are more susceptible than adults are. Layers are the best for warmth. Carry extra wool sweaters and rain ponchos or waterproof jackets and rain pants. Before your trip, test all seams for watertight seals, and reseal if necessary. Sweatshirts are not recommended because they are useless when wet. In addition, carry hats and gloves for everyone.

Suggested First-Aid Kit

It is essential that you carry a first-aid kit on every outing. Once it is assembled, including the kit in your backpack will quickly become routine. Commercially packaged kits are available in convenient sizes, and some are quite good. If you wish to purchase one, check their contents against the following list and supplement when necessary. In addition, ask your family doctor to suggest medications that are specific to your family's needs. To make your own first-aid kit inexpensively, simply purchase the items listed below and place them in a nylon stuff bag, zippered container, or aluminum box. If size and weight are not problems, the box is recommended because it keeps supplies organized, so you can quickly tell when items need to be replenished. Your first-aid kit should include:

- Adhesive bandage strips. Bring many more than you actually need; their psychological value to children cannot be overestimated.
- Butterfly bandages for minor lacerations
- Sterile gauze pads (4 x 4 inches) for larger wounds
- Adhesive tape to attach dressings
- Roller gauze to attach dressings
- Antibiotic ointment to treat wounds and cuts
- Moleskin for blisters
- Triangle bandages for slings
- Athletic tape for multiple uses
- Children's pain reliever

- Adult pain reliever
- Betadine swabs (povidone iodine) for an antiseptic
- Alcohol pads to cleanse skin
- Elastic bandage for sprains
- Knife with scissors and tweezers. Tweezers are needed to remove ticks and splinters.
- Space blanket for emergency warmth
- First-aid instruction booklet

Remember that no matter how well stocked your first-aid kit is, the contents are worthless unless you know how to use them. A first-aid course will give you experience in using many of the above materials.

CHECKLIST FOR SAFE HIKING: THE "TEN PLUS" ESSENTIALS

Use the following checklist before departing on each of your hikes. It includes the list of "Ten Essentials" compiled by The Mountaineers and adds a few extra "essentials" specific to the needs of children and to the hazards of Rocky Mountain National Park. Bringing the following items prepares you for emergencies due to weather, injuries, or other unforeseen circumstances.

1. Extra clothing. The extra weight ensures against cold, cranky children and hypothermia.
2. Extra food and water. Extra food is useful as a hiking incentive and essential in emergencies or if a hike takes longer than anticipated.
3. Sunglasses. Hats with visors offer protection to youngsters too young to wear sunglasses.
4. Knife. A knife has multiple uses in emergency situations.
5. Firestarter candle or chemical fuel. In an emergency, you may need to make a fire for warmth or for signaling.
6. First-aid kit. See preceding list.
7. Matches in a waterproof container. The containers are available at most outdoor supply stores.
8. Flashlight. A flashlight will be needed to negotiate trails at night or prepare a camp at unexpected hours.
9. Map. Carry a current map in a waterproof case.
10. Compass. Know how to use it.
11. Protective sunscreen for adults and children. Test for skin sensitivity before the trip.
12. Whistles. These are to be used only in the event children become lost.
13. Water-purification tablets. The tablets ensure a source of emergency drinking water.

A NOTE ABOUT SAFETY

Safety is an important concern in all outdoor activities. No guidebook can alert you to every hazard or anticipate the limitations of every reader. Therefore, the descriptions of roads, trails, routes, and natural features in this book are not representations that a particular place or excursion will be safe for your party. When you follow any of the routes described in this book, you assume responsibility for your own safety. Under normal conditions, such excursions require the usual attention to traffic, road and trail conditions, weather, terrain, the capabilities of your party, and other factors. Keeping informed on current conditions and exercising common sense are the keys to a safe, enjoyable outing.

—*The Mountaineers Books*

Opposite: Bear Lake

CHAPTER I

ROCKY MOUNTAIN NATIONAL PARK

AN OVERVIEW

Rocky Mountain National Park covers more than 415 square miles and straddles 40 miles of the Continental Divide. Within the park, twenty peaks rise above 13,000 feet, including 14,255-foot Longs Peak, the highest summit in the park. More than 350 miles of trails for hikers of every age and ability explore montane meadows, lush forests, and treeless tundra. More than 150 lakes make fine hiking destinations. One of the park's most remarkable features is Trail Ridge Road, the highest continuous paved road in the United States, where one can drive above tree line for 11 breathtaking miles, offering easy access to vast expanses of spectacular alpine scenery.

Much of the park's dramatic topography was formed by alpine glaciers, which flowed down slope from accumulation basins high on the flanks of the mountains during the last ice age, about ten thousand years ago. By scouring canyon walls and carrying away the debris, massive tongues of ice widened narrow V-shaped river gorges into broad U-shaped valleys such as Forest Canyon, Spruce Canyon, and the Kawuneeche Valley. Glaciers in similar fashion steepened mountainsides, forming rugged precipitous peaks, like Longs Peak and the Keyboard of the Winds. Glaciers also scooped out the numerous depressions that now cradle the small lakes known as glacial tarns and transported the innumerable large boulders that litter the park. Known as glacial erratics, these boulders were carried miles by glaciers from their places of origin to their present resting places.

Rocky Mountain National Park is home to a large variety of plants, animals, and birds. Thousands of species of wildflowers bloom in the park each summer. More than 180 species of plants occur on the tundra alone. Over one-quarter of the park consists of alpine tundra, representing the largest area of protected tundra in the Lower 48 states. Among the fascinating large mammals inhabiting the park's diverse environments are mule deer, wapiti (elk), bighorn sheep, and moose. Other wildlife to be observed include the marmot, pika, coyote, red-tailed hawk, and beaver. Black bears and mountain lions occur in the park but are rare and seldom seen.

The park runs one of the finest ranger programs in the national park system. Lectures, hikes, demonstrations, and campfire programs present numerous opportunities for children and adults to learn about the park's history, geology, plants, and wildlife. Well-educated and experienced rangers staff all five of the park's visitor centers.

Rocky Mountain National Park's proximity to Denver and other population centers, and its wealth of natural assets, make it a very popular place. More than three million visitors enter the park each year. Six hundred thousand hikers use the trails annually. The park has five large campgrounds, and it issues use permits for its 267 backcountry campsites.

The official Rocky Mountain National Park website at www.nps.gov/romo is a rich source of up-to-date information about the park. The website contains more than two thousand pages of information about park activities, campgrounds, trails, road closures, and much more.

IMPORTANT CONTACT INFORMATION

Rocky Mountain National Park
   (970) 586-1206
   www.nps.gov/romo
Summer Campground Reservations
   1-800-365-CAMP (2267)
   www.recreation.gov/campgroundSearch.do
Publications (books, maps) on the park
   www.rmna.org/rmna.cfm
Weather and Road Conditions
   (970) 586-1206

HOW TO GET THERE

Rocky Mountain National Park has three entrances, two on the east side of the park near the town of Estes Park and one on the west side near the town of Grand Lake. The east and west entrances are separated by the high peaks of the Continental Divide but connected by the awesome Trail Ridge Road. Estes Park (population 6543) is the larger and more popular entrance, with more tourist accommodations and attractions. Grand Lake (population 500) is smaller, quieter, and more remote. The east side attracts more visitors, offering unparalleled views of the majestic Front Range Peaks as well as providing four of the park's five campgrounds. The west side also has superlative scenery, while lacking the east side's summer crowds.

By Car: Denver is located only 65 miles southeast of Estes Park, the east entrance of Rocky Mountain National Park. You have a choice of three possible routes to Estes Park:

1. The fastest and most direct route: From Denver, drive Interstate 25 north to US Highway 36, and then follow US 36 northwest through Boulder and Lyons to Estes Park. This route takes approximately 1.5 hours.
2. A slightly longer and more scenic alternative: Follow Route 1 to Lyons, and then take Colorado Highway 7 west through Allenspark to Estes Park. This route takes approximately 1.75 hours.

3. The longest of the three routes is through "The Gateway of the Rockies": Follow Interstate 25 north to US Highway 34, and then turn west and follow US 34 through the Big Thompson Canyon to Estes Park. The driving distance is approximately 80 miles.

Grand Lake and the west entrance of Rocky Mountain National Park are 98 miles from Denver. The drive takes approximately 2.25 hours. To get to Grand Lake, follow Interstate 70 west from Denver to where US Highway 40 branches north. Follow US 40 to Granby and the junction with US 34. Continue north on US 34 to Grand Lake.

By Van: For van service from Denver (including Denver International Airport [DIA]) to Estes Park, contact Estes Park Shuttle, 1805 Cherokee Drive, Estes Park, CO 80517, (970) 586-5151; www.estesparkshuttle.com or Emerald Taxi, reservations (970) 586-1991.

For transportation from Denver (including DIA) to Grand Lake, contact Home James Transportation Services, (800) 359-7503; www.homejamestrans portation.com.

Advance reservations are suggested.

WHEN TO GO

Rocky Mountain National Park has much to offer year-round. Hiking is best from late spring through early fall, when access to park trails is greatest. The following seasonal summaries will help you plan your visit:

Spring (April and May): In April, daytime temperatures (40 to 60 degrees Fahrenheit) permit comfortable hiking, but precipitation is high. Rain is likely at lower elevations, while snow still falls in the high country. All but the park's lowest trails are still snow-covered. Nighttime temperatures are cold, averaging 15 to 35 degrees. By late April, spring flowers begin to bloom at lower elevations.

In May the weather becomes a little warmer and much drier. Daytime temperatures range from 45 to 70 degrees. At night, temperatures fall to between 20 and 40 degrees. At lower elevations, there are generally brief daily showers in the late afternoon, which persist through August. May brings plentiful wildflowers, although snow generally continues to fall at the higher elevations. Usually in late May, Trail Ridge Road opens, making it possible to visit the tundra and the Alpine Visitor Center and to drive from one side of the park to the other. Depending upon the snow level, the Old Fall River Road occasionally also opens in late May, but heavy snows can delay its opening to early July.

Summer (June through August): June ushers in superb hiking weather. The days are warm (55 to 80 degrees), but the nights are still chilly (25 to 45 degrees). Wildflowers at lower elevations are magnificent. Brief afternoon thunderstorms are the norm.

Sprague Lake offers a handicapped-accessible backcountry campsite.

July is even warmer, with daytime temperatures of 70 to 85 degrees and nighttime temperatures between 35 and 55 degrees. Snow persists to mid-July on trails at the highest elevations. Wildflowers in the lower elevations are peaking in June to mid-July, while the tundra flowers bloom most spectacularly from late June to early July. Throughout July expect brief afternoon thunderstorms. In August the average temperatures are the same as in July, but rainfall is almost double. Cloudy skies often replace the clear blue skies of June and July. Temperatures may fall considerably in late August.

Summer's warm weather brings the greatest influx of visitors. Park attendance in June, July, and August accounts for more than 60 percent of the year's visitors.

Fall (September through November): Fall is a special time at the park. In mid-September the aspens turn gold and herds of elk descend to lower elevations for the mating season, which lasts into October. Clear blue skies prevail, and the hiking is excellent and uncrowded. The weather is brisk. Daytime temperatures average 55 to 75 degrees in September and 30 to 60 degrees in October. Nighttime temperatures average 30 to 40 degrees in September and 10 to 30 degrees in October.

In September, snow and rain may be mixed. The precipitation turns more consistently to snow in late October. Generally, the west side of the park receives more snow than the east side. Trail Ridge Road and Old Fall River Road may be closed intermittently in September because of snow. Both roads usually close for the entire season in October.

Winter (December through March): In winter the park offers cross-country skiing, ice fishing, and snowshoeing. In this season, hiking is generally limited to trails below 8700-foot elevation.

WHERE TO STAY

Your choice of lodging sets the tone for your park visit. Camping allows you to make the most of your wilderness experience. A rustic cabin also offers a close-to-nature adventure, while affording a minimum of modern conveniences. For all types of accommodations, it is wise to make reservations, especially during July and August.

Camping

Camping with children is both challenging and fun. Youngsters enjoy pitching a tent, gathering wood, and building a campfire. The tent may even be a focal point of play during the day, when a relaxing activity is needed. Camping in one of the park's campgrounds also gives you the opportunity to attend entertaining and educational evening campfire programs.

There are five drive-in campgrounds in the park: Aspen Glen, Longs Peak, Timber Creek, Moraine Park, and Glacier Basin. Aspen Glen, Longs Peak (tents only), and Timber Creek Campgrounds are first come, first served. For information on campgrounds, call the Information Office at Rocky Mountain National Park at (970) 586-1206. Reservations are required and highly advisable at Moraine Park and Glacier Basin from late June through Labor Day. To make a reservation, visit www.recreation.gov/campgroundSearch.do or call (800) 365-2267. During July and most of August, expect campgrounds to fill every day by early afternoon. In June and September, campgrounds are usually full on the weekends.

Park campgrounds are equipped with piped cold water and toilets, but there are no showers. Public showers are available in Estes Park. Recreational vehicles are allowed in all campgrounds except Longs Peak, but no hook-ups are available. Pets are allowed but must be kept leashed at all times. Moraine Park, Timber Creek, and Longs Peak Campgrounds are open year-round, but the water is turned off in the winter. For more information, go to www.nps.gov/romo/planyourvisit/brochures.htm and click on the link for camping.

To minimize driving, choose a campground near the area where you plan to hike:

- Glacier Basin Campground (150 sites): located on Bear Lake Road and offering easy access to the beautiful Bear Lake and Glacier Gorge hiking on the east side of the park. Bordered by Glacier Creek with views to the Continental Divide. Unfortunately, the mountain pine beetle outbreak has resulted in the removal of most trees, so there is little or no shade in the campground. Reservations advisable.
- Moraine Park Campground (245 sites): within easy driving distance of Estes Park, offers easy access to the popular Moraine Park trails, as well as to Bear Lake and Glacier Gorge. Reservations advisable.
- Aspen Glen Campground (54 sites): the closest campground to Estes Park, but not as convenient as other campgrounds to east-side trails.
- Longs Peak Campground (26 tent sites): at the southeast edge of the park; offers the easiest access to dramatic Longs Peak and secluded Wild Basin trails.
- Timber Creek Campground (98 sites): centrally located on the park's west side, 10 miles north of the town of Grand Lake on US Highway 34; offers convenient access to west side trails and is slightly closer than east-side campgrounds to the spectacular Trail Ridge hikes. Situated along the Colorado River in the Kawuneeche Valley with the Never Summer Mountains rising to the west. Unfortunately, the mountain pine beetle outbreak has resulted in the removal of most trees, so there is no shade in the campground.

Owing to the fragility of the tundra and the severity of the weather, there are no campgrounds on Trail Ridge.

Backcountry Camping

Rocky Mountain National Park offers 267 backcountry sites, including 35 sites less than 3 miles from the trailhead. Many of these campsites are identified in the hike descriptions. (For easy reference to backcountry sites, use the "Hike Finder," at the beginning of this book.) To plan a camping trip in the backcountry of Rocky Mountain National Park, download the "Backcountry Camping Guide" at www.nps.gov/romo/planyourvisit/brochures.htm.

All users of the park's backcountry **must** obtain a Backcountry Use Permit. Campers can pick up a permit at the Beaver Meadows Visitor Center Backcountry Office or at the Kawuneeche Visitor Center. Day-of-trip permits may be obtained in person year-round. Campers may also make reservations by mail or in person any time after March 1 for a permit for that calendar year.

You may also make reservations by phone from March 1 to May 15 and any time after October 1 for a permit for that calendar year. For permits, write Backcountry Permits, Rocky Mountain National Park, 1000 Highway 36, Estes Park, CO 80517 or call (970) 586-1242. For all reservations, include the following information: (1) name, address, zip code, and telephone number; (2) the dates you plan to enter and leave the backcountry; (3) the number of people in your party (limit of seven per party for individual campsites and limit of twelve for group campsites); and (4) an itinerary with dates corresponding to campsites where you plan to stay. Backcountry camping is limited to a total of seven nights between June 1 and September 30 and fourteen additional nights between October 1 and May 31, with an annual maximum of 21 nights.

During the summer, campers with reservations must pick up the permit by 10:00 AM on the first day of the planned backcountry stay or the permit will be canceled in its entirety and given to other backpackers. There is a twenty-dollar administrative fee for campsites during peak season.

Camping Outside Rocky Mountain National Park

Additional camping opportunities are available in Roosevelt National Forest, which borders Rocky Mountain National Park on the east; Arapaho National Forest, which borders the park on the west; and the Arapaho National Recreation Area, at Grand Lake. For information, contact the Arapaho and Roosevelt National Forests and Pawnee National Grassland, 2150 Centre Avenue, Building E, Fort Collins, CO 80526; 970-295-6600; www.fs.fed.us/r2/arnf or the Sulphur Ranger District, 9 Ten Mile Drive, Granby, CO 80446; (970) 887-4100.

Several private campgrounds are also located near Estes Park and Grand Lake. For information, contact the Estes Park Chamber of Commerce or Grand Lake Chamber of Commerce (see the following section for websites).

Nearby Lodging

A wide variety of lodging options can be found at both the east and west entrances of the park, from plush resorts to rustic cabins, dude ranches to motels. For information on lodging services and activities in Estes Park, call the Estes Park Chamber of Commerce at (800) 378-3708 or (800) 44-ESTES, or go to www.estesparkcvb.com. For information on Grand Lake lodging, activities, and services, call Grand Lake Chamber of Commerce Visitor Center at (970) 627-3402 or (800) 531-1019, or visit www.grandlakechamber.com. The visitor center is located at the corner of West Portal Road and US Highway 34.

Unique family-oriented lodging is available at the YMCA of the Rockies, which has one facility in Estes Park and a second in Winter Park, near Grand

Lake. Both YMCA facilities offer reasonably priced cabins and rooms, as well as a wide range of recreational and educational opportunities, including riding, swimming, youth camps, guided hikes, evening lectures, and concerts. For information, contact YMCA of the Rockies, 2515 Tunnel Road, Estes Park, CO 80511; (800) 777-9622; www.ymcarockies.org.

SERVICES
This section lists basic services available in and around Rocky Mountain National Park.

Books and Maps
For a superb selection of books, maps, and literature about the park, contact the Rocky Mountain Nature Association (RMNA), www.rmna.org, a non-profit organization serving Rocky Mountain National Park and other public land partners since 1931. RMNA runs the excellent bookstores at the park visitor centers and offers numerous educational, interpretive, and research programs. Their website offers an extensive online bookstore. All proceeds benefit the park.

Outdoor Supplies
Stores selling camping gear and other outdoor supplies are located in Estes Park and Grand Lake.

Rental Equipment
In Estes Park, several stores offer equipment rentals with children's needs in mind:
- Back carriers: Estes Park Mountain Shop, 2050 Big Thompson Avenue, (970) 586-6548, www.estesparkmountainshop.com; Estes Park Rent-All, 1120 Manford Avenue, (970) 586-2158; Traveling Babies, 184 E. Elkhorn, (970) 577-1277.
- Strollers and car seats: Estes Park Rent-All (see Back carriers, above)
- Bicycles: Estes Park Mountain Shop (see Back carriers, above); Colorado Bicycling Adventures (downhill bike tours in Rocky Mountain National Park), (970) 586-4241, www.coloradobicycling. com. (For more information on bicycling, see Mountain Biking later in this chapter.)

In Grand Lake, two stores offer rental equipment for children:
- Back carriers and baby strollers: Never Summer Mountain Products, 919 Grand Avenue, (970) 627-3642; http://neversummermtn.com.
- Bicycles: Grand Lake Sports, 900 Grand Avenue, (970) 627-3642.

EMERGENCY MEDICAL SERVICES

Emergency medical services are available in Rocky Mountain National Park, Estes Park, and Grand Lake.

Rocky Mountain National Park: In case of an emergency, dial 911 or (970) 596-1399. Emergency phones are located throughout the park, and 911 can be dialed free of charge from any phone. For other assistance, dial (970) 586-1206. Emergency phones are available at the following locations: Bear Lake parking area, Cow Creek Trailhead, Hidden Valley Ranger Station, Lawn Lake Trailhead, Longs Peak Ranger Station, and Wild Basin Ranger Station, as well as at all park visitor centers, including Beaver Meadows Visitor Center (Park Headquarters), Alpine Visitor Center, Kawuneeche Visitor Center, and Moraine Park Visitor Center.

Estes Park: The Estes Park Medical Center, 555 Prospect Avenue, (970) 586-2317, is a full-service hospital with a twenty-four hour, fully staffed emergency room; www.epmedcenter.com. Emergency transport by ambulance and helicopter is available. In an emergency, call 911.

Grand Lake: Grand Lake has emergency medical technicians on duty twenty-four hours a day. In an emergency, call 911.

PICNICKING

The park offers an infinite number of places to picnic. The following picnic areas are recommended because they offer parking, picnic tables, and uncrowded natural places for children to explore. All of the spots described below have minimal traffic noise and crowds, and all have paths leading to unique and lovely places. Areas accessible to the handicapped (with assistance) are noted, although access is usually not available to nearby trails. Additional information on picnic areas is available at www.nps.gov/romo/planyourvisit/picnicking.htm.

For other picnicking ideas, check the hikes designated as "nature strolls" (NS) in the "Hike Finder" at the beginning of this book. Nature strolls are very short wheelchair- or stroller-accessible trails, many of which lead to wonderful picnic spots.

Bear Lake Road

On the east side of Bear Lake Road, from Tuxedo Park to Prospect Canyon, there are many excellent places to picnic. Each spot offers access to sparkling Glacier Creek, a view of glacier-studded peaks, and a buffer zone between picnickers and busy Bear Lake Road.

■ Tuxedo Park: 2.8 miles south on Bear Lake Road from its junction with US Highway 36 (6.5 miles east of the Bear Lake parking area). Behind a quite ordinary picnic area, a trail leads down to five tables situated in a lovely, shady spot beside Glacier Creek. Flowered paths along the creek invite exploration.

- An A-Mazing Place: 4.7 miles south on Bear Lake Road from its junction with US Highway 36; 4.6 miles east of the Bear Lake parking area. This area offers a picnic table, fishing, ducks, and a maze of fishermen's trails.
- Glacier Creek #1: 5.4 miles south on Bear Lake Road from its junction with US Highway 36; 3.9 miles east of the Bear Lake parking area. This site features a shady table by a trail amid wildflowers and small boulders.
- Glacier Creek #2: 5.6 miles south on Bear Lake Road from its junction with US Highway 36; 3.7 miles east of the Bear Lake parking area. This large open picnic area has three tables under tall pines, with a soft carpet of pine needles and babbling Glacier Creek.
- Sprague Lake: 5.7 miles south on Bear Lake Road from its junction with US Highway 36. Lovely Sprague Lake (Hike 5) is a few steps away, as well as fishing from a wooden bridge at the lake's inlet. This large picnic area offers twenty-seven picnic tables and sixteen fire grates for an afternoon or evening of fun.
- Prospect Canyon: 7.9 miles south on Bear Lake Road from its junction with US Highway 36; 1.4 miles east of the Bear Lake parking area. From a table on the edge of scenic Prospect Canyon, paths descend steeply to a fast-flowing creek.

Hollowell Park

Hollowell Park's expansive meadow and level trail (Hike 4) are perfect for children who like to explore. It is also a great place to watch for red-tailed hawks.

- Hollowell Park: 3.6 miles south on Bear Lake Road from its junction with US Highway 36; 5.7 miles east of the Bear Lake parking area (see directions to Hike 4). Numerous picnic tables are situated in an open area of sagebrush bordered by glacial moraines and large boulders for climbing. The site offers handicapped access (with assistance) and toilet facilities.

Moraine Park

The following picnic places are all in Moraine Park, which is located 1.5 miles from the Beaver Meadows Entrance Station on Bear Lake Road. Moraine Park is an excellent spot for a summer picnic supper because it is a likely place to see deer and a wonderful place to view the sunset.

- Moraine Park View #1: 0.2 mile west on the road to Moraine Park Campground. A picnic table under a majestic ponderosa pine on the northern edge of Moraine Park provides good views of Longs Peak.

- Moraine Park View #2: 0.4 mile south of the Moraine Park Visitor Center on Bear Lake Road (turn right to a parking area). These two tables at the east end of Moraine Park are located at the trailhead to Hike 3. The area offers handicapped access and good views of the Front Range.
- Fern Lake Trailhead: 0.7 mile west of the Cub Lake Trailhead; 0.3 mile east of the Fern Lake Trailhead (see directions to Hike 2). This site offers handicapped access (with assistance) to two tables located in a pretty spot rimmed by moraines and graced with a variety of trees and wildflowers. A path leads to the Big Thompson River and beaver workings.

Upper Beaver Meadows

From the Beaver Meadows Entrance Station, drive 0.7 mile on US Highway 36, and then turn west on a dirt road to a series of fine picnic sites, all with tables, grills, and handicapped access (with assistance).

- Old Ute Trail Trailhead: at the end of the unpaved road, 1.5 miles from US Highway 36. This is the best picnic area in Upper Beaver Meadows. Explore a creek, expansive meadows, an elk enclosure, and the Old Ute Trail. Toilet facilities are nearby.

Horseshoe Park

Located near the Fall River Entrance Station, these picnic areas offer excellent sunsets over Endovalley and a good chance at dawn or dusk of sighting deer in the summer and elk in the fall. After picnicking at any of the places listed below, explore the pebbly beaches of winding Fall River as it meanders through Horseshoe Park. This area offers picnic areas perfect for larger groups and families as well as tables that are handicapped accessible.

- Convict's Cabin Site: 1 mile west on Endovalley Road from US Highway 34 to the historical marker on the left. This site housed the convicts who helped build Old Fall River Road in 1913. Tables are scenically situated between two aspen groves, with a path leading to a lake. The area is particularly beautiful in the fall.
- Endovalley Aspens: on Endovalley Road 0.1 mile east of the Convict's Cabin site. If the Convict's Cabin site is occupied, choose this one, which is similarly set among aspens.
- Endovalley Picnic Area: 2 miles from US Highway 34 on Endovalley Road. This very large picnic area offers toilets, handicapped access, and sixteen tables with fire grates. It also offers a stream and abundant birds and small mammals.

Deer Ridge Junction

This area makes a convenient stopping point when returning to the east side from a visit to Trail Ridge.

■ Hidden Valley Creek: 1.5 miles west on US Highway 34 from Deer Ridge Junction (Deer Ridge Junction is 2.9 miles west on US Highway 36 from the Beaver Meadows Entrance Station). Tables and grills are situated in a scenic and shady spot beneath tall pines. The site also has handicapped access (with assistance) and toilets.

Hidden Valley

The headquarters for the Junior Ranger program (see "Other Activities in the Park; Interpretive Programs") is located in this former ski area, which also offers numerous picnic tables (some under a pavilion) and short, creekside trails. Hidden Valley is west of Deer Ridge Junction, on Trail Ridge Road.

Lily Lake

Lakeside picnic tables offer opportunities for fishing and exploring the level shoreline trail (open all year). Good views of Longs Peak. A 0.25-mile trail from the lake leads to the Lily Lake group picnic area, a large twelve-table picnic site.

Lily Lake is located 6.1 miles south of Estes Park on Route 7.

WEST SIDE

The west side of the park has many beautiful picnic areas. The four listed here are particularly nice. Sunset at the Kawuneeche Valley is a spectacular sight, as the sun sets behind the Never Summer Range. Elk are plentiful in spring, early summer, and fall. There is also a good chance of seeing deer in the evening throughout the summer.

■ Lake Irene: 15.8 miles north of Grand Lake Entrance Station, or 5.2 miles southwest of Alpine Visitor Center on Trail Ridge Road. This site features a delightful high-country lake and a lovely easy path sprinkled with flowers and lined with spruce.

■ Upper Kawuneeche Valley: 8.9 miles north of the Grand Lake Entrance Station on US Highway 34; 12.1 miles southwest of the Alpine Visitor Center. The tables at this very pretty wayside are scenically arranged under pines overlooking a beaver pond. The area offers good views of the Kawuneeche Valley and access to the pond. The site also features handicapped access (with assistance) and toilets.

■ Coyote Valley Trail and Picnic Area: 5.3 miles north of the Grand Lake Entrance Station on US Highway 34. Adjacent to a handicapped-accessible trail (Hike 50), this lovely and fully accessible picnic area offers expansive valley views near the majestic peaks of Baker Mountain and Green Knoll. The Coyote Valley trail swings close to the Colorado River and provides river exploring and fishing opportunities. Interpretive signs along the trail provide commentary on the history and ecology of the area.

■ Harbison Picnic Area: 0.7 mile north of the Grand Lake Entrance Station on US Highway 34. From tables at the edge of the broad Kawuneeche Valley, enjoy good views of the Gore and Never Summer Mountains. This is a good place to see elk in spring and late fall.

VIEWING WILDLIFE

You will see more wildlife in Rocky Mountain National Park if you know where, when, and how to look for it. The following section offers general principles of observing park wildlife. More specific information on locating certain types of animals can be found in the "Wildlife Locator Chart" at the beginning of the book.

Where to Look

The best places to look for wildlife are where one type of habitat meets another, such as the transition area between forest and meadow. Such "edge environments" typically offer greater diversity of food and cover, and therefore support greater numbers and kinds of animals than either neighboring habitat by itself. The animal population of edge environments includes representatives of each bordering community, as well as species whose home is the edge environment itself. Areas that have a wealth of edge environments, such as patchy forests broken by meadows, or winding rivers with long shorelines, are productive areas for watching wildlife. Lush vegetation in these areas attracts large herbivores, such as deer, and small mammals, such as rabbits and mice, which in turn attract predators such as hawks, weasels, and coyotes.

To find a particular animal, you must know its habitat. In the course of a day, animals may use several different habitats for feeding, sleeping, hunting, and foraging. In addition, many animals change habitats seasonally. The more you know about a particular animal, the easier it will be to locate it.

When to Look

When looking for a specific animal, it is important to know when the animal is active. Animals may be diurnal (active during the day), nocturnal (active after dark), or crepuscular (active at sunrise and sunset), but in general the best time to observe wildlife is shortly after dawn or at dusk. At these times, diurnal, nocturnal, and crepuscular animals mingle in a transitional time zone. Furthermore, relatively few hikers are abroad at these hours, thereby increasing

Fall is an excellent time to spot elk in Moraine Park.

your chances of seeing wildlife. In contrast, at high noon in the summer, when human activity is at its peak, animals generally avoid the heat and activity, resting in day beds out of sight.

If you hike under the light of a bright moon, you may see the nocturnal animals of the park. Moonlit hikes can be magical and rewarding. Remember, however, that the use of artificial lights such as flashlights or headlights to view wildlife is disturbing to animals and is prohibited in the park.

Weather also affects animal behavior and, therefore, your opportunities to observe wildlife. Typically, animal activity increases immediately before or after a storm. Conversely, during periods of extreme weather, such as heat or cold, animals are likely to take cover. On windy days, when human scent is carried far, animals are more likely to be seen upwind than downwind.

How to Look

Anyone serious about viewing wildlife should invest in a pair of good binoculars. Decent binoculars are available for less than a hundred dollars, although the finest cost several times that much. Binoculars make it possible to view an animal while staying far enough away so as not to disturb it. After all, most animals have acute senses and are likely to smell, hear, or see human intruders long before the humans see them.

For best results, tread lightly and dress conservatively. Walking slowly and quietly lowers the likelihood of being detected. Although most mammals are color-blind, birds are very sensitive to color. Camouflaging your appearance by wearing colors found in nature, such as tan, green, brown, and gray, will make you less conspicuous.

To further increase your chances of seeing wildlife, keep your eyes moving. Forests have many layers where animals make their homes. Look at the ground, the grasses, the shrubbery, the tree trunks, the treetops, and the sky. Look close and look far; your varying gaze is likely to catch something interesting.

When searching for animals, be alert to signs of their presence. If you can read the signs animals leave—their tracks, scat, feeding debris, nests, and burrows—you can deduce their movements and activities without actually seeing them. With a little knowledge of scat, for instance, you can determine if elk have frequented an area. By studying tracks, you can identify a fleeing animal and its pursuer, even though the drama may have ended hours ago. From impressions in the mud, you can see where a doe and twin fawns drank by a subalpine lake.

Finally, observe wildlife safely. Never approach wild animals. This precaution is particularly true for large mammals such as deer, elk, and black bear, but it applies as well to small creatures such as chipmunks. All animals can be dangerous if they feel threatened. For precautions regarding particular animals, see "Enjoying the Park Safely" in the Introduction.

Viewing Ethics

Watch wildlife briefly, respectfully, and unobtrusively. Remember that animals usually feel anxious around humans. If an animal shows signs of agitation, leave immediately. Most animals live in a precarious balance between the demands of survival and the costs of obtaining enough fuel to survive. Even short interruptions of an animal's normal routine, when multiplied by a park full of curious visitors, may have harmful effects.

If you find young animals, leave them alone and do not linger. They were probably not abandoned. More likely the mother is nearby. Your presence may stop her from returning or, in the case of bears, for example, may anger her enough to precipitate an attack. Furthermore, your scent on or near a nest might permanently cause a mother to abandon her young. Fawns and elk calves are routinely left in the forest while their mothers feed. The odorless and camouflaged young usually go undetected by predators. If you happen to find one, or any other young animal, marvel at the wonderful sight and then quickly and silently leave.

Finally, never feed wildlife. Feeding wildlife is dangerous for you and for the animals. It is also prohibited by Park Service regulations.

Wildlife Habitats of the Park

The park contains three distinct life zones corresponding to altitude. The zones are discernible as bands of distinctive vegetation, which is the key factor determining what kinds of wildlife are likely to be found in a particular area.

The Montane Zone occurs at 6000 to 9500 feet elevation. On sunny and dry south-facing slopes, the montane forest is relatively open and dominated by ponderosa pine. On moister, less exposed north-facing slopes, Douglas-fir forms dense, dark green forests. Rivers and streams flow through montane parks that are carpeted with grasses and flowers. Their associated wetlands support willow and birch.

The ponderosa woodland, with its widely spaced trees and diverse cover of grasses, forbs, and shrubs, is home to a great variety of wildlife, including the most diverse bird population in the park. Mountain bluebirds, western tanagers, pygmy nuthatches, black-billed magpies, Steller's jays, and Clark's nutcrackers are typical. Mammals include Abert's squirrels, Nuttall's cottontails, porcupines, mountain lions, long-tailed weasels, and mule deer.

In contrast, the dense Douglas-fir forests of the montane zone choke out most understory plants and therefore support relatively little wildlife aside from the chickaree, a tree squirrel that thrives on fir cones.

In the open montane parks, coyotes and badgers find prime hunting ground for rodents such as the Wyoming ground squirrel and the western jumping mouse. In the meadows, elk and bighorn sheep find rich grazing and mineral deposits. Beaver and muskrat frequent riparian areas.

The Subalpine Zone occurs at approximately 9500 to 11,500 feet elevation. Its forests are dominated by subalpine fir and Engelmann spruce. In disturbed areas, lodgepole pine and aspen are plentiful. On exposed ridges, limber pine replaces the less hardy trees. In the upper reaches of the subalpine zone, near tree line, stunted trees grow in twisted islands called *krummholz* woodland. Interspersed through the subalpine forests are meadows covered by sedges, grasses, and flowers. Wetlands border subalpine streams, rivers, lakes, and ponds.

The floor of the subalpine forest is covered with a variety of shrubby and herbaceous plants, which support a wide variety of wildlife. Most of the animal inhabitants, with the exception of the snowshoe hare, are not specific to the subalpine forest and can be found in adjacent life zones as well. As in the montane zone, stream-bank communities support beaver, which feed on the willows, alders, and aspens near the water's edge.

Birds of the subalpine forest include Clark's nutcrackers, gray-headed juncos, and ruby-crowned kinglets. Chipmunks and chickarees are among the common mammals.

Particularly rich in variety of wildlife are the so-called edge environments, where subalpine forest meets meadows, wetlands, or riparian areas. Here predators such as coyotes, weasels, black bears, foxes, and martens enjoy a wide assortment of prey, including northern pocket gophers, yellow-bellied marmots, shrews, and voles. Elk and mule deer are found throughout the subalpine zone, including in the *krummholz* woodland.

The Alpine Zone lies above tree line, which occurs at about 11,500 feet. The alpine zone features grasslands, meadows, low shrubby areas, and rocky fellfields—a mosaic of communities collectively known as tundra. Vegetation on the tundra must survive hurricane force winds, arctic temperatures, and an extremely short growing season. Animals inhabiting the alpine zone include pikas, yellow-bellied marmots, white-tailed ptarmigans, white-tailed jackrabbits, and northern pocket gophers. In the summer, rosy finches, water pipits, and horned larks are found. A variety of low alpine grasses, sedges, forbs, and woody perennials provide summer range for elk, deer, and bighorn sheep. One-third of the park's elk herd (estimated at approximately 3500 parkwide) lives on the tundra year-round.

THE PARK'S CHANGING ENVIRONMENT

Global warming and air pollution have brought devastating changes to Rocky Mountain National Park. From the first edition of this book in 1991 to the third in 2011, the changes have been dramatic. Global warming is the cause of much of the damage. Over the past fifty years, the Western United States has warmed at twice the rate experienced in the eastern part of the country. Also, the scarcity of water in the West makes the region's ecosystems and wildlife especially vulnerable to changes in temperature, snowpack, and stream flows. The specific impacts to Rocky Mountain National Park are discussed below.

Global Warming and Dying Trees

Global warming is a powerful catalyst driving the park's severe epidemic of mountain pine beetles. Several species of bark beetles are presently killing forests of lodgepole, ponderosa, and limber pine, as well as Engelmann spruce, subalpine fir, and Colorado blue spruce. Because the average winter temperatures have been higher than normal over the past ten years, beetle eggs and larvae that would not ordinarily survive the cold winter have thrived. A prolonged period of low precipitation has further weakened trees, making them prime candidates for beetle infestation. This combination of milder temperatures and low precipitation has produced a vast outbreak of beetles, particularly on the park's west side. In fact, forestry officials estimate that all mature lodgepole pine forests in Colorado will be dead by 2013, according to the National Parks Conservation Association.

The park's once magnificent Glacier Basin Campground is a poster child for this devastation. This campground has seen half of its trees shorn to the ground, exposing once-sheltered campsites to full sunlight. Of course, the sweeping vistas of snow-clad peaks remain.

Pikas in Peril

Scientists are concerned that pikas—fuzzy little cousins of the rabbit—may be one of the first North American wildlife mammals to become a casualty of warming temperatures. Some wildlife advocates even warn that pikas, who need high-altitude homes and low temperatures, are at risk of extinction by the end of the century. (Temperatures above 78 degrees Fahrenheit can kill them.) In fact, pikas have already disappeared from over one-third of their previously known habitat in Oregon and Nevada. The situation is so dire that the U.S. Fish and Wildlife Service is considering the pika for protection under the Endangered Species Act.

In Rocky Mountain National Park, pikas were once easy to find on the slopes of the park's highest peaks. Their numbers are dropping, however. In fact, of the five populations of pika known in the park, two low-elevation populations disappeared in 2009, according to park officials. Researchers are studying the park's pika to better understand their changing populations.

Air Pollution Damaging Fish and Plants

Scientists are finding that airborne nitrogen pollution from car exhaust, agriculture, and industrial plants turns algae into "junk food" in the subalpine and alpine lakes of Rocky Mountain National Park. Air pollution from the east and southeast blows into the Front Range, where it is swept by winds into the mountains. When the pollution-tainted algae become less nutritious, the algae become unable to sustain the fragile populations of rare cutthroat trout and other aquatic life in the park. When this impact is added to the acidification of lakes also caused by nitrogen deposition, the effect can be the loss of aquatic organisms and entire fish populations.

Along with degradation of algae and water quality in the park's lakes, deposition of airborne nitrogen is being blamed by park biologists for an increase in sedges, compared to other grasses and flowering plants. A substantial increase in sedges may decrease habitat for some wildlife and diminish the park's famous wild-flower display. Scientists are also finding that the deposition of nitrogen and

A park ranger leads a "Meet the Wildlife" ranger program.

ammonia onto the fragile tundra is changing the basic chemical composition of the soil. In 2009, the National Park Service reported substantial increases in nitrogen-rich ammonium that could change ecosystems in this park, as well as in many other Western parks. Some researchers noted that nitrogen levels were twenty times higher than normal.

According to the National Park Service, high-elevation ecosystems in the park currently show subtle changes from nitrogen deposition, and studies indicate that damage will increase in severity if nitrogen continues to increase at the current rate. For more information on nitrogen loading, impaired water quality, haze, and soil acidification, see www.nature.nps.gov/air/Permits/ARIS/docs/romoNFact SheetV11200505Final.pdf.

Support Protection of Wilderness

Use your positive experience in Rocky Mountain National Park, as well as your awareness of the perilous threats to the park, to inspire actions at home to protect wilderness areas, fight pollution and global warming, and support the creation of additional wildlands. There is much you can do. Foremost, support the Rocky Mountain Nature Association—the organization that helps keep this park healthy and thriving (see www.rmna.org). Next, support an environmental nonprofit organization, such as Earthjustice or Sierra Club, whose missions are to protect the environment. These organizations will keep you informed, involved, and active in the national movement to preserve wilderness, slow global warming, and curb pollution. For more information, go to www .earthjustice.org or www.sierraclub.org.

OTHER ACTIVITIES IN THE PARK

Rocky Mountain National Park offers a wide variety of activities for children, each of which helps them to learn about the park's natural environment.

Interpretive Programs

From June through September, the National Park Service staff runs an extraordinary program of guided walks, slide shows, campfire talks, and skill demonstrations. For example, a July day may offer a daybreak campfire breakfast; fishing and rock-climbing demonstrations; bird, sketch, or photo walks; puppet shows; nature games; talks about mammals, tundra flowers, or Native American medicine; a twilight walk to see beaver; and a program of campfire songs and stories. The Park Service also offers half-day and full-day ranger-led hikes. A schedule of ranger programs is printed in the free park newspaper, *High Country Headlines*, which is available at all visitor centers.

The park also sponsors a Junior Ranger program. Requirements include attending a park program, completing an activity booklet, and picking up litter. Children are awarded a Junior Ranger badge upon completion. For more information about this program, inquire at a visitor center, at the Junior Ranger headquarters in Hidden Valley, or visit www.nps.gov/romo/forkids/beajuniorranger.htm.

Visitor Centers and Museums

The Park Service operates five visitor centers where friendly and well-informed rangers are available to answer questions regarding hiking, weather, directions, and other topics. The centers also offer an extensive array of books and maps for sale. Information on hours of operation can be found at www.nps .gov/romo/planyourvisit/visitor_centers.htm.

Beaver Meadows Visitor Center. Located at the east entrance to the park at Beaver Meadows, on US Highway 36, 3 miles west of Estes Park, this visitor center (and home to Park Headquarters) is open daily, year-round. The visitor center offers a short orientation film of the park. During the summer, evening programs are held nightly in its large indoor auditorium. For more information, write Park Headquarters, Rocky Mountain National Park, Estes Park, CO 80517 or call (970) 586-1206. Open daily year-round, 8:00 AM to 9:00 PM during peak season.

Moraine Park Visitor Center. Located at the east end of Moraine Park, on Bear Lake Road, 1.4 miles from the Beaver Meadows Entrance Station, this visitor center offers hands-on exhibits depicting the park's geology and natural history. In addition, a self-guided trail pointing out common park plants is adjacent to the center. Open daily from May 1 through Labor Day.

Alpine Visitor Center (AVC). Located on Trail Ridge Road, 20 miles from the Beaver Meadows Entrance Station, the AVC features exhibits on tundra plants and animals, a large observation deck over the Fall River Valley (where elk and deer may be seen with the aid of binoculars), and the world's highest puppet theater. Adjacent to the center is the paved Tundra Trail (Hike 40). The Fall River Store, also adjacent to the AVC, offers a variety of snacks and souvenirs. Open daily, late May through mid-October.

Kawuneeche Visitor Center. Located on US Highway 34 at the west entrance to the park, this center maintains natural history exhibits and dispenses information about the park's west side. The center is open daily year-round, (970) 627-3471.

Fall River Visitor Center. Located 4 miles west of Estes Park on US Highway 34, this visitor center opened in 2000. The center is dedicated to educating park visitors about wildlife and contains numerous wildlife exhibits as well as a Discovery Center with hands-on activities for children. Open all year, (970) 586-1415.

Junior Ranger Headquaters. Located at Hidden Valley along Trail Ridge Road. Youngsters ages six through twelve can join the Junior Ranger program. Junior Ranger books and programs are free and are offered every day during peak season. For more information on the Junior Ranger program, inquire at a visitor center or visit www.nps.gov/romo/forkids/beajuniorranger.htm.

Scenic Drives

Although the goal of this book is to get you and your children out of your car, there are two unique roads in the park that make fascinating and exciting scenic drives. Since both roads take you above tree line, be sure to bring warm clothes and sunscreen. Binoculars are also strongly recommended. Both roads lead to Fall River Pass, where you can visit the Alpine Visitor Center or get a snack at the Fall River Store (the only food concession in the park).

Trail Ridge Road. For spectacular alpine scenery, a drive on Trail Ridge Road is unsurpassed. The road climbs from montane parks through subalpine forest to above timberline, topping out at 12,183-foot Fall River Pass. Along the way, numerous overlooks reveal stunning views. The splendor of Trail Ridge Road culminates in 11 magnificent miles above tree line, offering expansive views over Forest Canyon and the Continental Divide. Before beginning the drive, stop at a visitor center for the "Trail Ridge Road Guide," a pamphlet that gives you a short history of the road and a brief description of each wayside. The round-trip distance from any park entrance is more than 40 miles. If you plan to stop at viewpoints, allow at least three hours for the drive. The best time for the trip is early in the morning or at dusk, when wildlife is likely to be more abundant than tour buses. Sunrises and sunsets are magnificent from Trail Ridge. Trail Ridge Road is usually open from late May until early October, although snow may close the road early and late in the season.

To reach Trail Ridge Road from the Beaver Meadows Entrance Station, drive 2.9 miles west on US Highway 36 to Deer Ridge Junction, and then bear left on US Highway 34, following the signs for Trail Ridge. From the Fall River Entrance Station, drive west on US Highway 34 to Deer Ridge Junction and turn right for Trail Ridge Road. From the Grand Lake Entrance Station, continue north on US Highway 34, which becomes Trail Ridge Road after Milner Pass. The Alpine Visitor Center is located roughly halfway along the route—20 miles from the Beaver Meadows Entrance Station and 21 miles from the Grand Lake Entrance Station.

Old Fall River Road. The unpaved Old Fall River Road goes from Horseshoe Park to Fall River Pass by a long series of steep and narrow switchbacks,

Preparing for a trail ride (helmet definitely recommended!)

rising 3200 feet in 9.4 miles. Built in 1913–14, Old Fall River Road was the first road to the pass and the only one until the completion of Trail Ridge Road in 1932. Old Fall River Road is now maintained as a one-way scenic attraction. It offers an intimacy and a sense of history that is lost on the finely engineered Trail Ridge Road. No buses or trailers can attempt this route. Steep hairpin turns make the climb laboriously slow, but there are rich rewards for the additional effort. Drive the road at dawn or near sunset, and you'll have it to yourself. Meadows in the upper sections are good places to see deer or elk at those hours. Be sure to pick up the booklet "The Old Fall River Road, Motor Nature Trail," which provides interesting information regarding the history of the road and its flora and fauna. The booklet is available at park visitor centers. Plan at least three hours for the round-trip drive, to allow time for stopping at scenic viewpoints.

To reach Old Fall River Road from the Beaver Meadows Entrance Station, drive 2.9 miles east on US Highway 36 to Deer Ridge Junction. At the junction, turn right onto US Highway 34, heading north to Horseshoe Park. At 1.7 miles from Deer Ridge Junction, turn left at the sign for Endovalley and Old Fall River Road. From the Fall River Entrance Station, drive west on US Highway 34 to the Endovalley Road. Old Fall River Road begins after 2 miles, at the end of the paved road. Since Old Fall River Road is one-way, the return will be via Trail Ridge Road. Old Fall River Road is open from July until September, weather permitting.

Horseback Riding

Horseback riding is permitted on many of the trails in Rocky Mountain National Park. Guided rides are available from the riding concessions located at Moraine Park and Glacier Creek. The concessions offer rides ranging in length from one hour to a full day. Children under six generally ride with an adult for a reduced price. For more information, call Sombrero Stables at Glacier Creek, (970) 586-3244, or Moraine Park, (970) 586-2327. Sombrero Stables are located inside the park during summer months; www.sombrero.com/locations.asp.

In addition, a number of stables located outside the park in Grand Lake and Estes Park offer rides within the park. For a list of these stables, see "Activities Outside the Park" later in this chapter.

Fishing

Fishing is permitted in many of the lakes and streams in the park. Four species of trout can be found in park waters: rainbow, brook, German brown, and cutthroat. Although the park's waters generally yield only small fish, children of all ages enjoy the pastime.

Anglers should acquaint themselves with the many important regulations that have been enacted to ensure the survival of the park's native species of trout. The park's indigenous greenback cutthroat trout is threatened with extinction and has been placed on the Threatened Species list. Some lakes and streams, including Bear Lake, are closed to fishing to protect the threatened trout. Be sure to stop at a park visitor center to obtain a copy of the regulations governing possession limits, methods of capture, prohibited waters, and designated catch-and-release areas. Colorado fishing licenses are required for anglers over the age of fifteen. Important information on fishing restrictions and the efforts to protect native species can be found at www.nps.gov/romo/planyour visit/fishing.htm.

The following lakes and their associated streams are among the better fishing spots in the park:

Sprague Lake (Hike 5)	Lake of Glass (Hike 10)
Mills Lake (Hike 8)	Sky Pond (Hike 10)
Jewel Lake (Hike 8)	Lake Haiyaha (Hike 15)
The Loch (Hike 9)	Lily Lake (Hike 26)

Guided fly-fishing excursions in Rocky Mountain National Park are offered by Scots Sporting Goods, 870 Moraine Avenue, Estes Park, CO 80517, (970) 586-2877 (May through September) or (970) 443-4932 (October through April); scots sportinggoods.com/; and Estes Park Mountain Shop, 2050 Big Thompson Avenue, Estes Park, CO 80517; (970) 586-6548; www.estesparkmountainshop.com. Both stores also rent equipment. Other area outfitters include: Kirks Flyshop, (970) 577-0790, (877) 669-1859, www.kirksflyshop.com; Rocky Mountain Adventures, (970) 493-4005, (800) 858-6808, www.shopRMA.com; and Estes Anglers, (970) 586-2110, www.estesangler.com. To guarantee success for your youngest anglers, visit Trout Haven Ranch, where they can catch rainbows in a stocked pond and have them cooked to order at the pond-side cafe. Located at 800 Moraine Avenue, Estes Park, CO 80517; (970) 577-0202 or (800) 794-7857, www.trouthavenranch.com. Peter's Pond also offers a guaranteed catch and grills on-site for picnics. Located at 510 Moraine Avenue, Estes Park, CO 80517, (970) 586-5171, www.etonnant.com/catch_wild_trout/.

Rock Climbing

The park's rock-walled mountains and cliffs provide excellent opportunities for rock climbing. The most popular climbing area in the park is the south-facing cliffs of Lumpy Ridge, along the park's northeastern boundary. Portions of Lumpy Ridge have been temporarily closed to climbers and hikers, however, to provide a sanctuary for birds of prey whose populations have recently suffered a decline. If you are planning to visit the Lumpy Ridge area, please contact a park ranger for information regarding closure.

For climbing instruction, the Colorado Mountain School offers a youth climbing program for children age seven and older. The school offers both half-day and full-day climbs, including instruction in rope climbing and rappelling. The Colorado Mountain School is conveniently located just outside the park's eastern entrance in Estes Park. For more information, contact the Colorado Mountain School Lodge, 341 Moraine Avenue, Estes Park, CO 80517, (970) 586-4677; www.totalclimbing.com. The Estes Park Mountain Shop also offers climbing instruction, equipment rental, and an indoor climbing gym. Special children's instruction is offered daily. Located at 2050 Big Thompson Avenue, Estes Park, CO, 80517, (970) 586-6548, (866) 303-6548, www.estesparkmountainshop.com.

Visitors interested in watching climbers can take the hike to Chasm Lake (Hike 29). Watching the climbers on the sheer east face of Longs Peak is amazing and inspiring. Be sure to bring binoculars; the intrepid climbers may be hanging 2000 vertical feet above you!

ACTIVITIES OUTSIDE THE PARK

Rocky Mountain National Park does not have a monopoly on beautiful scenery or recreational resources. To add variety to your vacation, you may want to engage in activities such as rafting, mountain biking, and horseback riding outside the park boundaries. Museums and historical sites in and around Estes Park and Grand Lake can also enrich your visit while providing a welcome change of pace.

Rafting

Rafting companies run trips on the Colorado and Cache la Poudre Rivers just outside Rocky Mountain National Park. The rafts are oar-powered and require riders to paddle. All trips require at least a half day. The minimum age allowed on the trips varies, depending on the class (degree of difficulty) of the river and on the policies of the particular rafting company. All age requirements noted below are subject to change. Parents must inquire specifically at the time of booking.

Colorado River Trips. Several companies offer trips down the Colorado River. The trip combines moderate rapids with stretches of peaceful floating. One- or two-day trips are available. The rafting site is about forty-five minutes from Grand Lake, and time on the river is estimated at five to six hours for each day of rafting. June and July are generally the best months to raft this river.

- ■ Mad Adventures, P.O. Box 650, Winter Park, CO 80482, (970) 726-5290 or (800) 451-4844, www.madadventures.com; shuttle provided from Grand Lake.

- RapidTransit Rafting, P.O. Box 4095, 161 Virginia Drive, Estes Park, CO 80517, (970) 577-7238 or (800) 367-8523, www.rapidtransitrafting .com; minimum age: seven years; minimum weight: fifty pounds; shuttle provided from Estes Park and Grand Lake.
- Rocky Mountain Adventures, 358 Elkhorn Avenue, Estes Park CO 80517, (970) 493-4005, (800) 858-6808, www.shoprma.com.

Poudre River Trips. Two trips are offered on the Cache la Poudre River: one a peaceful float trip with some moderate rapids; the second a more demanding trip with difficult rapids. Full- and half-day trips are available. The drive from Estes Park to the rafting site takes about one hour, and time on the river for both trips is two and a half to three hours. The concessionaires do not provide transportation to the rafting site. The best time to run the Poudre River is generally late May through June.

- A-1 Wildwater, Inc., 2801 North Shields Street, Fort Collins, CO 80524, (970) 224-3379, (800) 369-4165, www.a1wildwater.com; minimum age: seven and fifteen years, depending on trip and water level.
- Wanderlust, 3500 Bingham Hill, Fort Collins, CO 80521, (970) 482-1995, (800) 745-7238, www.awanderlustadventure.com; minimum age: seven years; minimum weight: fifty pounds.

Horseback Riding

The following stables offer rides both inside and outside Rocky Mountain National Park.

Estes Park and Vicinity

- Sombrero Ranch, US Highway 34 East, Estes Park, CO 80517, (970) 586-4577, www.sombrero.com.
- Elkhorn Stables, 600 West Elkhorn Avenue, Estes Park, CO 80517, (970) 586-5225, www.elkhornlodge.org.
- National Park Gateway Stables, 4600 Fall River Road, Estes Park, CO 80517, (970) 586-5269, nationalparkgatewaystables.com.
- Cowpoke Corner Corral, 2166 State Highway 66, Estes Park, CO 80517, (970) 586-5890, www.cowpokecornercorral.com.
- YMCA of the Rockies, Estes Park Center, 2515 Tunnel Road, Estes Park, CO 80517, (970) 586-3341, (800) 777-9622, www.ymcarockies.org.
- Allenspark Livery Stables, P.O. Box 102, Allenspark, CO 80510, (303) 747-2222, www.sombrero.com
- Wild Basin Livery, 1130 County Road 84 W, Allenspark, CO 80510, (303) 747-2222.
- Silver Lane Stables, 621 Big Thompson Avenue, Estes Park, CO 80517, (970) 586-4695.

Grand Lake and Vicinity

- Winding River Resort Village, 1447 County Road 491, Grand Lake, CO 80447, (970) 627-3215.
- Sombrero Ranch, Grand Lake, CO 80447, (970) 627-3514; www.sombrero.com.
- Sombrero at Snow Mountain Ranch, YMCA of the Rockies, just off Highway 40, Grandby, CO 80446, (970) 887-1999.

Mountain Biking and Road Cycling

Bicycling on trails is prohibited in Rocky Mountain National Park, as is off-trail mountain biking. Mountain biking is permitted outside wilderness areas within the adjacent Roosevelt and Arapaho National Forests. Be forewarned that this is a demanding sport, appropriate only for older children. For more information, contact the National Forest Service office in Estes Park, (970) 586-3440.

Cycling enthusiasts may also choose to ride the park's demanding roads. Extreme caution, however, must be exercised when biking park roads owing to heavy traffic, narrow shoulders, and steep inclines. Early morning cycling is best because of reduced vehicular traffic. Mountain bikes may be rented from the following:

- Colorado Bicycling Adventures, Estes Park, CO 80517, (970) 586-4241; www.coloradobicycling.com.
- New Venture Cycling (guided tours and rentals), Estes Park Mountain Shop, 2050 Big Thompson Avenue, Estes Park, CO 80517, (970) 231-2736, www.newventurecycling.com.
- Grand Lake Sports, 900 Grand Avenue, Grand Lake, CO 80447, (970) 627-8124 (also rents bikes with attached child's seat).
- Aspen Lodge Ranch Resort, 6120 State Highway 7, Estes Park, CO 80517, (970) 586-8133 or (800) 332-6867, www.aspenlodge.net.

All stores offer bikes suitable for youngsters and provide maps with suggested trails.

Rainy Day Activities

Inclement weather, illness, or injury might keep you off the trails temporarily, but don't despair. There are interesting places to visit in Estes Park and Grand Lake that will please your youngsters and create new opportunities to learn about the ecology, geology, and history of the region.

In and Around Estes Park

- Estes Park Museum, 200 Fourth Street at US Highway 36, Estes Park, CO 80517, (970) 586-6256, www.estesnet.com/museum/. This museum will appeal to older youngsters who have an interest in Western history. There are amusing artifacts from the pioneer days, old photographs, an antique car, a homestead cabin, and an interactive children's area. Open daily May through October; Friday through Sunday, November through April.

■ Dick's Rock Museum, 490 Moraine Avenue, Estes Park, CO 80517, (970) 586-4180, www.redroserockshop.com. With a lot of native treasures mixed with rocks, geodes, and crystals from all over the world, this "hands-on" museum/store is a rock lover's dream. Countless specimens are displayed at child level and can be inspected by curious hands. One room shows visitors how rocks are cut and polished. Open daily. Admission free.

■ MacGregor Ranch Museum, 180 MacGregor Lane, Estes Park, CO 80517, (970) 586-3749, www.macgregorranch.org. This museum is actually a homesteader's ranch that survives largely unchanged from the 1870s. Children may find the old ranch equipment interesting. Open Tuesday through Saturday, June through August.

■ Eagle Plume's Gallery and Museum of Native American Arts (10 miles south of Estes Park on Colorado State Highway 7), Box 447, Allenspark, CO 80510, (303) 747-2861, www.eagleplume.com. This museum and gallery houses a fascinating collection of Native American art and artifacts. Within the small store/museum are beautiful jewelry, rugs, pottery, and artifacts such as weapons, beaded infant carriers, robes, and headdresses. There is even a tepee, which may be entered and inspected by all. Open daily. Admission free.

■ Enos Mills Cabin Museum, (8 miles south of Estes Park from the junction of US Highway 36 and Colorado State Highway 7), 6760 Colorado State Highway 7, Estes Park, CO 80512, (970) 586-4706, www.enosmills .com/home.html. Enos Mills's log cabin, built in 1885, is lovingly preserved and filled with period photographs and artifacts. It is located at the end of a short nature trail. Mills was instrumental in the creation of Rocky Mountain National Park. Open Tuesday and Wednesday in summer and by appointment. Visitors are encouraged to call when they are in the area and see if the museum is open. Admission free.

■ Estes Valley Library, 335 East Elkhorn Avenue, Estes Park, CO 80517, (970) 586-8116, www.estesvalleylibrary.org. This small library has a pleasant staff and a fine children's room with games and art supplies as well as books. Children's videos may be watched on the premises. If you are a regular visitor to Estes Park, you may obtain a seasonal library card. Open daily and many evenings.

In Grand Lake

- Kauffman House, Pitkin and Lake Avenue, Grand Lake, CO 80447, (970) 627-9644, www.kauffmanhouse.org. This log hotel was built in 1892. Now restored, it hosts a museum of local pioneer memorabilia. Open afternoons daily from Memorial Day through August and Saturdays and Sundays in September.

Special Events

A variety of special events are held in Estes Park and Grand Lake throughout the summer and fall. Some of the notable happenings include music and art festivals, horse shows and rodeos, bike races, and July Fourth fireworks. Check local papers and the Chamber of Commerce for information. In general, there is more activity in Estes Park than in the considerably smaller and quieter Grand Lake. If you want the season's schedule of events, check the websites of the chambers of commerce in Estes Park and Grand Lake:

- Estes Park Chamber of Commerce, www.estesparkcvb.com.
- Grand Lake Chamber of Commerce, www.grandlakechamber.com.

Opposite: Lily Lake

CHAPTER 2

EAST SIDE HIKES

The east side of Rocky Mountain National Park is its busiest. It is home to the Park Headquarters, housed in the Beaver Meadows Visitor Center, two other visitor centers, Glacier Basin and Moraine Park Campgrounds (the park's largest), and the extremely popular Bear Lake, Glacier Gorge, and Cub Lake Trailheads. The region offers hikes of every length and difficulty, delivering some of the park's most dramatic scenery on some of its shortest trails. The east side is also an easy drive from Denver and neighboring cities. As a result, the east side draws many more visitors than the west. Consequently, to enjoy a measure of solitude amid this spectacular beauty, choose trails with low or moderate levels of use, hike early in the morning, and avoid weekends. Alternatively, arrive after Labor Day, when visitation drops dramatically.

Avoid parking hassles by using the park's free shuttle buses. During the summer, lots at the Bear Lake and Glacier Gorge Trailheads are usually full by midmorning. The bus is a convenient way to reach both trailheads, and it allows you to begin and end your hikes at different trailheads, thereby greatly expanding your hiking options. There are three shuttle buses:

• **Bear Lake Shuttle** runs daily between the Park & Ride on Bear Lake Road and Bear Lake, with stops at the Bierstadt Lake, Glacier Gorge, and Bear Lake Trailheads. The bus runs every ten to fifteen minutes from 7 AM to 7 PM during peak season. The Park & Ride is located on Bear Lake Road, 5.1 miles from its junction with US Highway 36.

• **Moraine Park Shuttle** runs between the Park & Ride on Bear Lake Road and Fern Lake Trailhead, leaving every thirty minutes from 7 AM to 7 PM during peak season. This shuttle services the Fern Lake and Cub Lake Trailheads, Moraine Park Campground, Moraine Park Visitor Center, Tuxedo Park, Hollowell Park, and Glacier Basin Campground.

• **Estes Park Hiker Shuttle** runs daily between Estes Park Visitor Center in the town of Estes Park and the Park & Ride on Bear Lake Road, making only one stop, at the Beaver Meadows Visitor Center. This bus requires the purchase of a park pass and runs on an hourly schedule early and late in the day, switching to a half-hour schedule between 10 AM and 6 PM.

Check with the Park Service for a current schedule or consult www.nps .gov/romo/planyourvisit/shuttle_bus_route.htm.

When choosing a hike in Moraine Park (Cub Lake and Fern Lake Trailheads), Hollowell Park (Mill Creek Basin Trailhead), Bierstadt Moraine, Glacier Gorge, or Bear Lake, consult the Bear Lake Hiking Map (Hike 6) for additional hiking options. The area offers many lovely one-way hikes, which are possible using two cars or the shuttle bus. By beginning at Bear Lake, large elevation gains can sometimes be avoided.

In addition, young families should note that several east-side hikes are accessible to strollers and wheelchairs. Stroller-accessible trails include Moraine Park (Hike 3), portions of the Bear Lake Trail (Hike 11), and the Alluvial Fan Trail (Hike 22). Wheelchair users can access three very lovely trails, the Beaver Boardwalk (Hike 23), Sprague Lake Trail (Hike 5), and Lily Lake Trail (Hike 26), all accessible according to uniform federal accessibility standards.

ARCH ROCKS AND THE POOL

Difficulty: easy
Distance: 1.5 miles one way to Arch Rocks, 1.7 miles one way to the Pool
Usage: high
Starting Elevation: 8155 feet; elevation gain, 45 feet to Arch Rocks, 245 feet to the Pool
Backcountry Campsite: 1.2 miles from the trailhead
Seasons: spring, summer, fall
Map: USGS 7.5-minute McHenrys Peak

The trail to the Pool is a fine hike, especially for children. It offers a level grade, great diversity of vegetation, climbable boulders, access to a clear river, fishing, and good picnic spots. In the early morning or at dusk, watch for deer in Moraine Park and near the trailhead. To avoid crowds on this popular trail, hike early or late in the day. Bring plenty of drinks; this hike can be hot and dry in summer.

Drive US Highway 36 to Bear Lake Road, located 0.2 mile west of Beaver Meadows Entrance Station and 2.7 miles from Deer Ridge Junction. Drive Bear Lake Road 1.2 miles to the first road on the right, which heads toward Moraine Park Campground. Take this road and drive 0.5 mile; turn left just before the campground entrance and follow signs for the Cub and Fern Lake Trailheads. Drive 0.7 mile to the Cub Lake Trailhead and then go 1 mile to the parking lot for the Fern Lake Trailhead.

The wide, smooth, sandy trail begins at the west end of the parking lot and parallels the Big Thompson River on the left. Bordering the trail are bracken ferns, Rocky Mountain maples, and aspens. By the river, narrowleaf cottonwood, water birch, and thinleaf alder shade the banks. All contribute gay reds and yellows to the fall landscape, making this trail an excellent autumn hike.

Arch Rocks

Small pebbly beaches invite exploration of the riverbank. This area is prime beaver habitat. Notice the conical stumps of aspens cut by beaver. A beaver can fell a three-inch-diameter tree in less than ten minutes. Beavers make good use of the aspen, eating its bark and using its branches to build their dams. Look carefully along the river for evidence of beaver activity.

Large boulders are common here. Some were deposited by the glacier that retreated from this valley 13,000 to 15,000 years ago. Other boulders—the more angular ones—are probably of more recent origin, having fallen from the high cliffs nearby. Youngsters will enjoy the safe climbing provided by the boulders. They can also search for ghoulish faces and creatures in the pattern of cracks and crevices on the rocks.

After 1.2 miles on this nearly level trail, come to Arch Rocks Campsite, an excellent backcountry destination for beginning campers. Around dusk look for beavers, which are primarily nocturnal, to emerge from their lodges and begin their work.

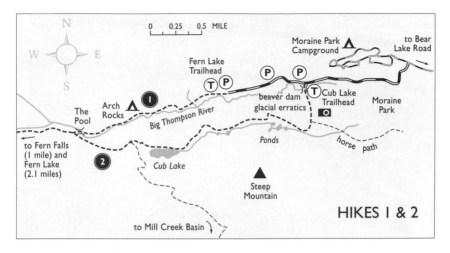

The stretch of trail between Arch Rocks Campsite and Arch Rocks (0.3 mile farther) offers a series of lovely, easily accessible picnic spots by the river. Anglers will want to try their luck trout fishing in the swiftly flowing water. Numerous flowers and large rocks enhance the scene.

At 1.5 miles from the trailhead, arrive at Arch Rocks, where several huge boulders form an arch over the trail. For the best view of the rocks, walk under them and turn around. Arch Rocks is a good turnaround point for hikers who wish to avoid uphill walking.

Just 0.2 mile beyond Arch Rocks is the Pool. As the Big Thompson River flows between steep rock walls, the water's motion has eroded a pool, whose calm contrasts with torrents crashing over rocks as the river rounds a bend. The sun-drenched flat rocks by the Pool are popular for picnicking. The substantial bridge over the Pool is also a good place to observe the powerful flow of the water.

Watch at the Pool for the curious dipper, or water ouzel. This brown bird, resembling a large wren, acrobatically flies in and out of the rushing water looking for small fish and aquatic insects. The dipper is able to walk on the bottom of streams, swim underwater, and fly behind waterfalls. Watch them disappear again and again in the rushing water. The dipper builds its nest on rocky ledges, often within the spray of a waterfall, where its eggs are safe from predators.

Hiking Options:

(1) At the Pool, the trail is joined by the path from Cub Lake, which lies 1 mile to the southeast. For a wonderful loop hike of 6 miles, start at the Cub Lake Trailhead, hike to Cub Lake, continue to the Pool, and then return along the

Fern Lake Trail. This loop is delightful from either direction, but beginning at the Cub Lake Trailhead affords fine views of the Front Range as you head west (see Hike 2). (2) Fern Falls is 1 mile west of the Pool on the Fern Lake Trail. The shady, steep trail switchbacks through thick subalpine forest and gains 480 feet elevation. The falls are perhaps unspectacular for the effort required. (3) Fern Lake is 2.1 miles from the Pool on the Fern Lake Trail and requires an additional 730-foot elevation gain from Fern Falls. The trail is strenuous. From the Fern Lake Trailhead, Fern Lake is 3.8 miles one way, with an elevation gain of 1375 feet.

2   CUB LAKE AND THE POOL LOOP

Difficulty: moderate
Distance: 2.3 miles one way to Cub Lake; 6-mile loop via the Pool
Usage: high
Starting Elevation: 8080 feet; elevation gain, 540 feet
Backcountry Campsite: 3.8 miles from trailhead
Seasons: spring, summer, fall
Maps: USGS 7.5-minute Longs Peak, McHenrys Peak

This hike is a jewel. Few trails in the park offer such diversity. The trail sparkles with wildflowers of innumerable variety. It is rich with birds and wildlife. Beautiful and interesting sights and sounds appear at every bend, including beaver dams, rushing streams, lily-filled ponds, and climbable boulders of all shapes and sizes. For bird watchers, wildlife enthusiasts, and flower lovers, this trail is a favorite. Hike in the early morning or late afternoon to avoid the midday crowds.

Drive to the Cub Lake Trailhead, as described in Hike 1. The trailhead is at the west end of the parking lot. If the lot is full, drive 0.3 mile farther to an additional parking area. From mid-June to mid-August, hikers may also use the park shuttle bus.

The trail begins by crossing a bridge over a branch of the Big Thompson River. The bridge provides a good view of a large beaver dam. Look for signs of recent beaver activity. Return at dusk for a chance to see these nocturnal rodents at work. In the fall, when beavers must gather food for the long winter to come, they may be out during the day. A family of nine beavers may consume a ton of bark over the winter.

The erratics at Cub Lake make for fun climbing.

Shortly after the first bridge, cross a second bridge. This is a good place for an early detour to explore the streamside environment. Willow and river birch are plentiful, as are numerous wildflowers, including yellow shrubby cinque-foil, blue chiming bells, and pink and violet shooting stars.

A maze of paths made by deer and fishermen leads along the river's edge, where pebbly beaches, cruising ducks, or trout anglers may interest your youngsters. The area between the bridges and along the river is also an excellent place to look for deer. Elk appear here in the fall.

For a closer look at the work of beavers, take the first path on the right, about 10 feet after the second bridge. There you find trees cut by beaver, evidenced by conical stumps and teeth marks.

For a beautiful flower-filled meadow with a backdrop of the majestic Front Range, take the second spur trail on the right after the bridge. Please be careful not to trample or pick the flowers.

Return to the main trail. From the second bridge, the main trail rolls gently through montane meadowlands. Even the youngest feet can negotiate this smooth trail. Early morning hikers find many types of animal tracks in the soft dirt. In summer look for the tracks of deer, marmots, rabbits, ground squirrels, and chipmunks. Elk tracks appear in the spring and fall.

The trail follows the western edge of Moraine Park. Lookouts to the east are tremendous places to watch for deer at sunset. To the right are a wealth of climbable rocks. Small mammals are plentiful here, including chipmunks and golden-mantled ground squirrels. Watch also for marmots, which are particularly easy to spot on sunny days, when they enjoy napping on the sun-warmed rocks.

The trail weaves through mature ponderosa pines, a conifer with reddish, deeply furrowed bark, needles five to eight inches long, and bark that smells like vanilla (truly!). Ponderosa pines are a favorite of the porcupine, which you may see napping on a limb. Never disturb one of these prickly rodents, each of which carries more than thirty thousand quills.

On the left, groves of aspens add brilliant color to the trail in the fall. One mature grove is home to a wide variety of cavity-dwelling birds. When aspens age and soften, they are often full of insects, which provide abundant food for birds such as woodpeckers, nuthatches, and chickadees. Listen for the tap-tap of the woodpecker. Once a hole is made, the bird probes for insects with its long tongue.

At 0.4 mile a horse path joins the trail from the east. Continue south on the main trail, which shortly turns west to follow a slow-moving stream. This portion of the hike is particularly fun for observant and imaginative children, who can see fantastic things in the giant, oddly shaped rocks—a whale with its snout on the trail, a leering dwarf with a pointed ear, and a giant dinosaur egg. On the left are abandoned beaver ponds, where leopard frogs, whirligig beetles, iridescent blue dragonflies, and water boatmen now thrive.

At 1.8 miles the trail begins to switchback to Cub Lake, becoming more rocky and shady in a mixed forest of conifers and aspens. After a relatively steep ascent (during which you may startle a deer in its daytime forest retreat), the trail levels out not far from the lake.

Cub Lake is wonderful. In summer, it is covered with yellow pond lilies. Its shady banks make a perfect picnic spot. Ducks on the banks join you, as will numerous small mammals. To the west, 12,922-foot Stones Peak rises majestically above the lake.

To hike the 6-mile loop by way of the Pool and Fern Lake Trail, continue on the trail along Cub Lake's north shore. At the west end of the lake, the trail enters lodgepole pines and in 0.2 mile meets the trail from Mill Creek Basin entering from the south. Keep right in a westerly direction, descending slightly along a partially exposed north-facing slope with very good views. Reach the Pool 1 mile from Cub Lake. To complete the loop, turn right on the Fern Lake Trail and descend slightly for 1.7 miles to the trailhead (see Hike 1). From the Fern Lake Trailhead, walk or ride 1 mile down the road (east) to the Cub Lake Trailhead.

Hiking Options:

(1) Combine the hike to Cub Lake with the hike from Hollowell Park to Mill Creek Basin for a one-way 5.4-mile trip (elevation gain 600 feet). A second

car or shuttle bus ride would be needed. See Hike 4 for a detailed description of the hike to Mill Creek Basin. (2) Hike mostly downhill from Bear Lake, via Bierstadt Lake and Mill Creek Basin, to Cub Lake and from there to the Cub Lake Trailhead, for a total distance of 6.5 miles. Again, the shuttle bus or a second car would be needed. See the Bear Lake Hiking Map (Hike 6).

3   MORAINE PARK

Difficulty: nature stroll, handicapped access with assistance
Distance: 0.25 mile one way
Usage: moderate
Starting Elevation: 8000 feet; elevation gain, none
Backcountry Campsite: none
Seasons: spring, summer, fall
Map: USGS 7.5-minute Longs Peak

This hike is a fine walk in a large, lovely meadow, brimming with wildflowers and dramatic sights of the glacial forces that formed Moraine Park thousands of years ago.

Moraine Park offers spacious meadows and beautiful mountain views.

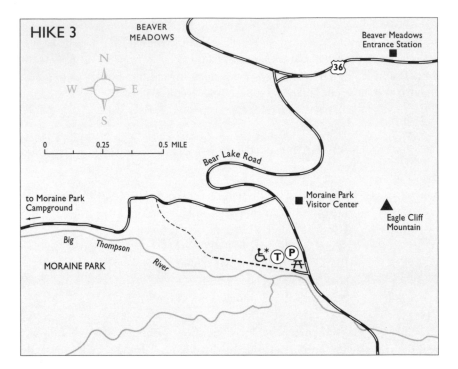

HIKE 3

BEAVER MEADOWS

Beaver Meadows
Entrance Station

N
W   E
S

0   0.25   0.5 MILE

Bear Lake Road

to Moraine Park
Campground

Moraine Park
Visitor Center

Eagle Cliff
Mountain

Big
Thompson
River

MORAINE PARK

Drive to Bear Lake Road, as described in Hike 1. Turn left on Bear Lake Road and drive 1.6 miles to a parking area on the right, at the eastern end of Moraine Park. The parking area is 0.4 mile south of the Moraine Park Visitor Center. The trail begins at the west end of the parking lot.

This hike at the eastern edge of Moraine Park starts on a paved road closed to traffic. The road begins at the picnic area near the parking lot and travels into Moraine Park along the Big Thompson River. To the west are excellent views of the Front Range. At dawn and dusk, willows by the river may hide feeding deer in the summer and elk in the colorful fall. In spring and summer, wildflowers are abundant in the meadow. After a short distance, the pavement ends, replaced by a wide, level path that is still accessible to wheelchairs and strollers. After 0.25 mile, the trail narrows. Visitors in wheelchairs must turn back. Hikers may proceed on the narrow path for another 0.5 mile to explore the meadow. This trail eventually leads to Upper Beaver Meadows, an uphill hike of approximately 1.75 miles. This portion of the trail is not recommended because of its heavy use by horseback riders and its proximity to US Highway 36. To return to the trailhead, turn around and retrace your steps.

The mammoth glacier that sculpted this area left its mark everywhere. The large boulders in the meadow are glacial erratics, which were torn from the mountains by the moving ice, which carried them downslope to be dropped far from where they originated. To the left is the glacier's south lateral moraine. This long pile of rock debris, now thickly forested, was gathered, pushed, and finally deposited here by the rivers of ice that flowed from Forest Canyon, Spruce Canyon, and Odessa Gorge. These ice streams united to form one massive glacier, whose depth as it entered Moraine Park ranged from 750 to 1500 feet.

More information on the history, geology, flora, and fauna of Moraine Park can be found in the booklet "Moraine Park Visitor Center and Interpretive Trail," published by the Rocky Mountain Nature Association and available at most park visitor centers. Visitors interested in geology should visit the Moraine Park Visitor Center, which offers ingenious interactive exhibits illustrating the geologic history of the park.

4 MILL CREEK BASIN

Difficulty: easy
Distance: 1.6 miles one way
Usage: moderate
Starting Elevation: 8339 feet; elevation gain, 600 feet
Backcountry Campsites: 1.6 and 1.8 miles from trailhead
Seasons: spring, summer, fall
Maps: USGS 7.5-minute Longs Peak, McHenrys Peak

Beginning in a dry meadow with expansive views and bordered by forested moraines, this easy hike offers big sky, sagebrush, and wildflowers on a dusty trail. A clear running stream with a beaver lodge adds interest to the latter part of the trail. Although this hike does not dazzle with dramatic scenery, it is un-crowded and excellent for spotting red-tailed hawks or hiking under the stars. The dusty trail has a typically Western feel, ideal for parents who can spin a tale or two about the Old West.

Drive to Bear Lake Road, as described in Hike 1. Follow the road 3.6 miles, and then turn right at Hollowell Park onto an unpaved road and continue to the parking area for the Mill Creek Basin Trailhead at the end of the road.

Head due west from the trailhead on the clearly marked trail through a large open meadow. The first 0.6 mile of sandy trail is smooth and level. Even your toddler can make good time along this section. Far to the south, Longs Peak, the highest peak in Rocky Mountain National Park, rises to 14,255 feet.

Examining (not picking!) wildflowers in Hollowell Park

The trail is fragrant with the scent of sagebrush, which covers the meadow in silvery green. Naturalists believe that the muted greens of dry meadow plants protect them from the intense heat and ultraviolet light of the sun. Look to the moister, shadier areas near Mill Creek to see darker, lusher greens.

The first half mile of this hike is filled with the sights, sounds, and smells of the Old West. Your "Wild West" tales will be effectively punctuated by the thundering of horses' hooves, for this trail is popular with the horse concessions. Mix in the facts below for an authentic Rocky Mountain tale.

Two hundred years ago, two Native American tribes, the Utes and Arapahos, used this area for seasonal hunting and foraging and fought frequently (perhaps on this site) to maintain their shares of the territory. Indian women probably gathered the plants of this meadow for medicine and food. Because plants comprised 80 percent of the Indians' total food supply, women were the backbone of their society. Notice, for example, the red Indian paintbrush beside the trail. The flower looks like a ragged brush dipped in red-orange paint. The Indians ate this flower and used its roots to make medicine to thin the blood, cure nervous disorders, and prevent fainting.

The trail heads south to meet Mill Creek, passing aspens that have been grazed by wintering herds of elk. When food is scarce, as it is each winter, the elk eat the inner bark of the aspen, leaving black scars on the yellowish bark. Although you will probably not see elk here in summer, notice how the twisted branches of the sagebrush look like fallen antlers, and how the dry, weathered wood by the path resembles bleached bones.

The meeting of the trail with Mill Creek at 0.6 mile makes a very pleasant rest stop. The coolness of the fast-flowing creek and the shade of the trees are welcome relief from the sunny, dry meadow. This spot may be a good final destination for your youngest hikers, for there is a lot to explore at the creek.

A little scouting nearby reveals a beaver dam and lodge. Farther up the trail, aspens have been cut by beavers for use in constructing their dams and lodges. Sharp eyes may spy brook trout in the pond.

White trappers came here for beaver in the 1800s, after eastern trappers had decimated the beaver population east of the Mississippi. Beaver were in great demand in the early nineteenth century for men's hats. The beaver hat was so popular in those days that the word *beaver* was used as slang for *hat*. Fortunately for the western beaver, fashion changed in the late 1800s, when the use of silk in top hats spelled salvation for the large rodent.

The trail continues west along Mill Creek, rising gradually, to Mill Creek Basin, 1.6 miles from the trailhead. Tall purple chiming bells appear, which, true to their name, resemble long stalks of bells. Look also for bedstraw, another tall plant with numerous small four-petaled white flowers. Early settlers used the stalks of bedstraw as mattress stuffing and its seeds as a coffee substitute.

Mill Creek Basin is a pretty meadow that lies between Mount Wuh (10,761 feet) to the west and Steep Mountain (9538 feet) to the northeast. A campsite at the basin provides a fine backpacking destination. From this point, trails lead north to Cub Lake and south to Bierstadt Lake. More scenic trails to these destinations are described in Hikes 2 and 16.

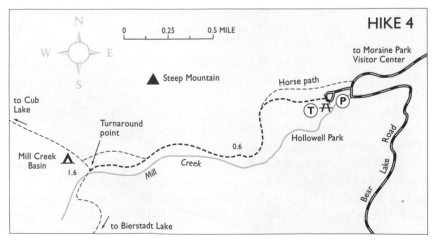

Return to the trailhead by retracing your steps. Walking back through Hollowell Park, notice the difference in the south- and north-facing slopes that flank the meadow. Large ponderosa pine, which require sunny, dry conditions, are widely spaced along the south-facing slopes, while dense, dark green forests of Douglas-firs, which prefer a cooler, moister environment, cover the mountainsides facing north. This pattern of growth occurs throughout the park. In fact, when Enos Mills, the "father" of Rocky Mountain National Park, was afflicted with temporary snow blindness, he determined his direction by using the type of tree growth as an indicator.

Hiking Options:

Using the park shuttle bus, hike a very scenic and varied trail from Bear Lake to Hollowell Park (with a visit to Bierstadt Lake), for a total distance of about 4.3 miles. To check the route of this lovely hike, see the Bear Lake Hiking Map (Hike 6).

5   SPRAGUE LAKE

Difficulty: nature stroll, handicapped access according
    to uniform federal accessibility standards
Distance: 0.5 mile around lake
Usage: high
Starting Elevation: 8710 feet; elevation gain, none
Backcountry Campsite: Handicamp (handicapped-
    accessible campsite) 0.3 mile from trailhead
Seasons: spring, summer, fall
Map: USGS 7.5-minute Longs Peak

This very easy, half-mile loop trail is a wonderful introduction to hiking for the park's youngest visitors. The trail offers children numerous natural attractions while providing parents with a level stroll, terrific views, abundant benches, and child-tested picnic spots. This beautiful trail is absolutely perfect for wheelchairs and strollers. Anglers in the family will enjoy trying for elusive cutthroat trout; children will rejoice in the many mallard ducklings.

Drive to Bear Lake Road, as described in Hike 1. Follow Bear Lake Road 5.7 miles to the well-marked turn for Sprague Lake. Turn left and drive to the parking lot and picnic area at the end of the road. The lake is at the northeast end of the parking area, reached after crossing a wide wooden bridge and turning left (north).

Begin the hike at the lake's edge and walk clockwise. Before you set out, be sure to purchase a guide to the Sprague Lake Nature Trail from the dispenser at the start of the trail (one dollar). The fourteen-page illustrated booklet provides information on the history, flora, and fauna of the lake and contains a useful schematic drawing of the peaks visible from the east side of the lake. The booklet is also available at park visitor centers.

Two hikers enjoy the views at Sprague Lake.

The stroll around the lake offers many opportunities for youngsters to view birds, insects, and small mammals. The air is rich with chirping, quacking, and chattering. Children can enjoy watching mallards paddling with their ducklings in tow. Chipmunks and golden-mantled ground squirrels are also abundant near the lake. At the southwest end of the lake is a deserted beaver lodge, and you may spot a trespassing muskrat, if you're lucky.

Also fascinating to the youngsters is the thriving insect life. Diving beetles, water scavengers, whirligig beetles, caddisflies, dragonflies, water boatmen, and midges appear by the thousands. It would be wise to bring along insect repellent for mosquitoes and fun to tote a small jar for bug hunting. (Be sure to free all insects unharmed after observing them.) Less obvious but also present are leopard frogs, chorus frogs, and western toads.

Numerous benches along the shore provide majestic views of the lake and surrounding mountains. Also located at intervals around the lake are small wooden platforms with railings. Built over the water, these platforms allow children to observe the water safely without the danger of a steep fall.

Sprague Lake, like all lakes in the park, is too cold for swimming. Except in the lake's shallowest places, the water rarely exceeds 60 degrees Fahrenheit. Fishing is possible here, as early settlers of the area stocked the lake with trout. The chance of catching one is slim, but this does not discourage the ever-present anglers in their small boats or hip boots.

The best picnic spot is exactly halfway around the lake. It offers benches and large rocks where parents can rest and set out lunch while the children play. A pebbly beach adds to the fun. The spot boasts a superb view of many high peaks. The best views are those of Hallett Peak (12,713 feet) and adjacent Flattop Mountain (12,324 feet).

On the east side of the lake, a spur trail heading left leads to the Sprague Lake Accessible Campsite, a backcountry campsite accessible to wheelchair campers. It is a lovely spot among quaking aspens, only a short half-mile hike along a level trail. For more information on this backcountry campsite, inquire at the Beaver Meadows Visitor Center.

Continuing clockwise around the lake, the trail enters the shade of lodgepole pines. The trail eventually emerges via bridges and boardwalks at the northwest edge of the lake, where the trail began.

Hiking Options:

For an additional short hike in this area, find the Glacier Creek Trailhead on the southeast side of the Sprague Lake parking lot. A short walk of 0.6 mile along sparkling Glacier Creek is a pleasant and effortless stroll. The scenic banks of the creek invite exploration and offer quiet places for lovely picnics. Children will love to dip their toes in the icy water. Aspen and willow provide high color in autumn.

6　BOULDER BROOK / ALBERTA FALLS LOOP

> **Difficulty:** strenuous
> **Distance:** 5.8 miles one way
> **Usage:** mostly low, high at end
> **Starting Elevation:** 8840 feet; elevation gain, 1,450 feet
> **Backcountry Campsite:** 1.9 miles from the trailhead
> **Seasons:** summer, fall
> **Maps:** USGS 7.5-minute Longs Peak, McHenrys Peak

This fine, demanding hike is enjoyable in any season but is especially magnificent in the fall. The trail leads steeply up a mountainside covered with aspens, then levels out amid panoramic views of Glacier Gorge and the Bear Lake area. The last part of the hike takes you down through Glacier Gorge and by the popular and beautiful Alberta Falls.

Drive to Bear Lake Road, as described in Hike 1. Turn left and follow Bear Lake Road 6.5 miles to the parking area for the well-marked Bierstadt Lake Trailhead, which is on the right side of the road. Your trailhead, Storm Pass, is across the road, just 0.1 mile east of the Bierstadt Lake Trailhead. If all the

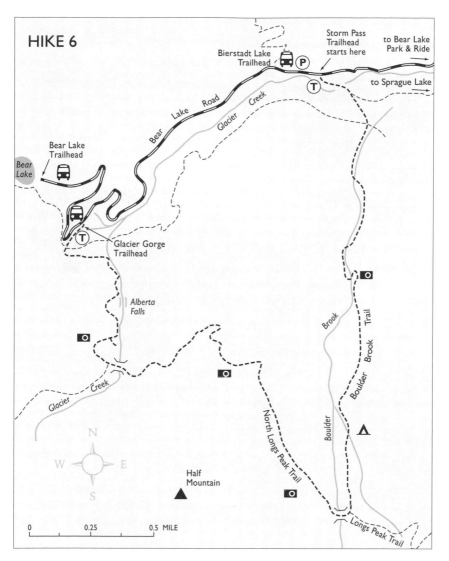

HIKE 6

Storm Pass Trailhead starts here

to Bear Lake Park & Ride

Bierstadt Lake Trailhead

P

to Sprague Lake

Bear Lake Road

Glacier Creek

Bear Lake Trailhead

Bear Lake

Glacier Gorge Trailhead

Alberta Falls

Boulder Brook Trail

Glacier Creek

N

W E

S

North Longs Peak Trail

Boulder Brook

Half Mountain

Longs Peak Trail

0   0.25   0.5 MILE

roadside parking places are full, backtrack 1.4 miles on Bear Lake Road and park in the Park & Ride shuttle bus parking area. The shuttle bus will take you to the trailhead. Note that this hike ends at the Glacier Gorge Trailhead, 1.8 miles farther west on Bear Lake Road. Use the Bear Lake shuttle bus to return to your car. If you'd like a longer hike or a complete loop, see the hiking options described below.

The trail begins at a large sign for the Storm Pass Trailhead. Follow the trail, heading east along the willow-lined bank of Glacier Creek. To the west,

Hallett Peak, Flattop Mountain, and Chiefs Head Peak rise dramatically above the creek.

Shortly cross a bridge over the creek and head into a forest of lodgepole pines. When the trail forks, stay to the right, on the main trail. Continue to a junction with trails to Bear Lake (right) and Wind River and Storm Pass (left). Continue straight ahead as indicated by the sign for the Boulder Brook Trail.

Boulder Brook runs parallel to the trail. The brook's banks are carpeted with pine needles and shaded by aspens and pines. Unfortunately, many aspens have been scarred by vandals. Please discourage this practice, because if cuts girdle the tree, the aspen may die.

Aspens are a valuable food source for many of the park's animals. Deer, elk, and moose browse the aspen's twigs, bark, and foliage; beavers and rabbits eat its bark, foliage, and buds; and the hardy ptarmigan feeds on its winter buds.

Boulder Brook offers many pleasant spots where hikers can sit on large rocks, watch the cascading water, and listen to the musical brook. The ground cover by the brook is wild blueberry, and in late summer it provides a delicious snack. As the trail continues to climb, small cascading waterfalls appear. Gray rocks, white rapids, streamside flowers, and flickering aspen leaves create a lovely scene.

At 0.7 mile from the trailhead, cross the brook. After two more crossings, the trail becomes less steep and more open. Wind, rocks, and the sounds of water predominate. A forest fire in 1900 cleared this area of trees, and new growth has come slowly. Enjoy good views of the Mummy Range to the north, Hallett Peak and Flattop Mountain to the west, and Half Mountain close by to the northwest.

A fourth crossing of the stream at 1.9 miles brings you to two backcountry campsites, Boulder Brook #1 and #2. Continue past the campsites to the junction with the North Longs Peak Trail, 2.3 miles from the trailhead. Turn right and follow the North Longs Peak Trail toward Glacier Gorge Trailhead.

The trail is now considerably easier. Relax and enjoy the superlative views, again made possible by the forest fire. Walk west along the north-facing slope for 2.2 miles (the Park Service sign indicates 3 miles). Happily, the trail heads downhill for most of the remaining distance. Dramatically shaped limber pines line the path, framing views of the surrounding mountains. Andrews Glacier can be seen clearly ahead, hanging majestically between Otis and Taylor Peaks.

Larger boulders and more aspens appear as the trail nears Glacier Gorge. Rock-strewn Half Mountain is on the left. After 2.1 miles on the North Longs Peak Trail (4.4 miles from the trailhead), come to a substantial bridge over Glacier Creek. The orange rock walls rise steeply to create a deep narrow

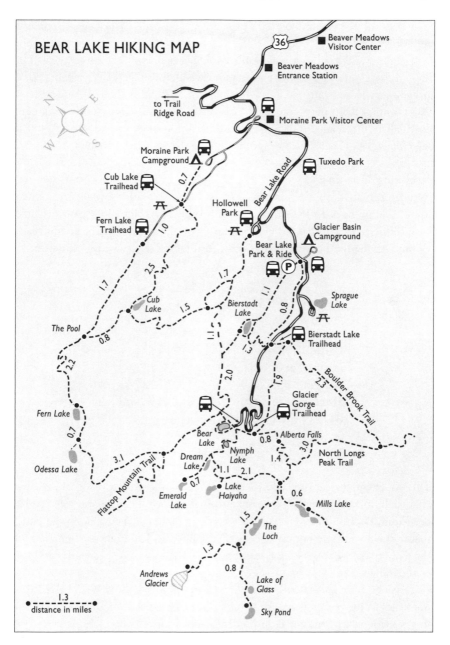

BEAR LAKE HIKING MAP

canyon. In autumn the aspens in this area are stunning. After the bridge, the trail heads uphill a short distance to the junction with the Glacier Gorge Trail.

Take the trail that heads downhill to the north, toward Glacier Gorge Trailhead and Alberta Falls.

The dry rocky trail to Alberta Falls switchbacks down the mountainside. On these rocky slopes look for marmots and pikas. Before you reach the falls, there are good overlooks into the gorge to the right. Listen for the falls below.

At 5 miles from the trailhead, arrive at Alberta Falls. Only 0.8 mile of easy downhill trail remains. (For a detailed description of this portion of the trail, see Hike 7.) At Glacier Gorge Trailhead, take the shuttle bus back to your car.

Hiking Options:

As an alternative to the shuttle bus, a 2.3-mile trail parallels Bear Lake Road, leading back to the Boulder Brook Trail. The total round-trip distance with this extension is 8.1 miles. Pick up this trail at Glacier Gorge Trailhead. Upon reaching the Boulder Brook Trail, turn left to return to the trailhead.

7   ALBERTA FALLS

Difficulty: easy
Distance: 0.8 mile one way
Usage: high
Starting Elevation: 9240 feet; elevation gain, 160 feet
Backcountry Campsite: none
Seasons: summer, fall
Map: USGS 7.5-minute McHenrys Peak

This short but rewarding hike leads to one of the park's most impressive waterfalls. You can hear the powerful falls before you take even one step on this brief trail. Because the waterfall is also among the most accessible in the park, this trail is extremely popular. To avoid the crowds, hike very early or late in the day, or reserve this hike for autumn, when the foliage is spectacular and the traffic is lighter.

Drive to Bear Lake Road, as described in Hike 1. Follow Bear Lake Road 8.4 miles to the parking area for Glacier Gorge Trailhead, on the south side of the road. Because parking is limited, the very convenient, free park shuttle bus is highly recommended. Parking for the shuttle bus is at the Park & Ride on Bear Lake Road, 5.1 miles from its junction with US Highway 36. The bus runs about every ten to fifteen minutes during the summer. Check at

Alberta Falls

a park visitor center for details or consult www.nps.gov/romo/planyourvisit /shuttle_bus_route.htm.

The beginning of the trail to Alberta Falls is wide, smooth, and fairly level. Wooden bridges that cross Glacier Creek provide interest from the start for the youngest hikers. The trail follows the creek through stands of aspen, fir, and spruce. Spur trails to your left access Glacier Creek for a streamside view of the rushing water. Note that some aspens have been scarred by vandals. Sadly, this phenomenon is common along the more popular trails in the park. Carving not only permanently disfigures the trees but can be detrimental to their health. Please point this out to your youngsters and heartily discourage the practice.

The wealth of aspens on this trail makes it an excellent hike in the fall, when the leaves turn brilliant shades of yellow-gold and provide a stunning contrast to the dark green of the conifers and the deep blue of the western sky.

At about 0.2 mile from the trailhead, reach a trail junction. Continue straight for Alberta Falls. To your left is the trail that parallels Glacier Creek and then goes to Sprague Lake (2.8 miles); to the right is the trail that reaches Bear Lake in 0.5 mile.

After a quarter mile, the trail becomes steeper and rockier. Wild blueberry covers the ground along the trail. This stretch is hot in summer because the young aspens that line the path provide little shade. The mountainside was burned by a forest fire in 1900 and has not fully rcovered. Consequently, hikers have fine views of the Glacier Gorge area and surrounding peaks. To the north, look for the distinctive peaks of the Mummy Range, including Mount Chapin (12,454 feet), Mount Chiquita (13,069 feet), and Ypsilon Mountain (13,514 feet), with its permanent snowfield in the shape of a Y. To the west, Flattop Mountain (12,324 feet) and the dramatic angular profile of Hallett Peak (12,713 feet) are visible. As you near the falls, the aspen's delicate leaves create a beautiful arch over the trail.

Over much of this short trail, hikers hear the rushing water of Glacier Creek as it crashes through Alberta Falls. The sound of the falls teases, growing louder with each bend in the trail, then fading with each switchback. The sound entices you to travel a little faster up the last steep sections of the trail.

Alberta Falls is truly impressive. The falls and narrow gorge reveal dramatically the power of running water to sculpt and erode. Welcome spray cools and refreshes after the warm ascent. For an even better view of Alberta Falls, climb (with supervision of children and *extreme* caution) on the rocks above the trail toward the head of the falls. There, the power of the water rushing over the rocks is felt and heard with a thrilling intensity.

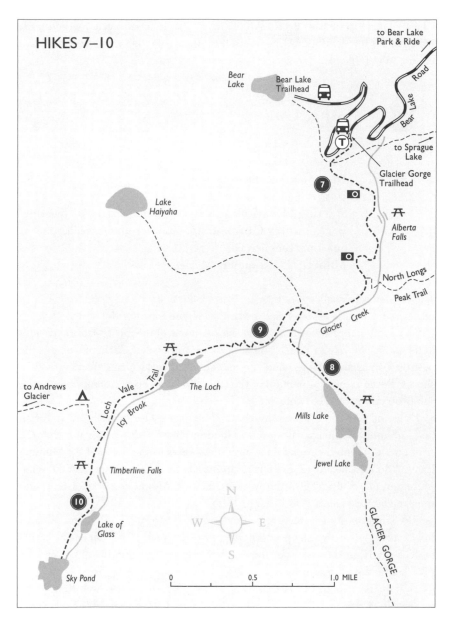

HIKES 7–10

to Bear Lake
Park & Ride

Bear
Lake

Bear Lake
Trailhead

to Sprague
Lake

Glacier Gorge
Trailhead

Lake
Haiyaha

Alberta
Falls

North Longs
Peak Trail

Glacier Creek

to Andrews
Glacier

Vale Trail

The Loch

Loch

Icy Brook

Mills Lake

Timberline Falls

Jewel Lake

Lake of
Glass

GLACIER GORGE

Sky Pond

N
W — E
S

0   0.5   1.0 MILE

Hiking Options:
(1) Continue 2.0 miles and climb 540 feet to Mills Lake (see Hike 8). (2) Continue 2.3 miles and climb 780 feet to the Loch (see Hike 9). (3) Continue 3.5 miles and climb 820 feet to Lake Haiyaha (see Hike 15). (4) From the

Glacier Gorge Trailhead, Bear Lake is only 0.7 mile by a clearly marked trail, which heads northwest. For information on Bear Lake hikes, see the Bear Lake Hiking Map (Hike 6).

8   MILLS LAKE

Difficulty: moderate
Distance: 2.8 miles one way
Usage: high
Starting Elevation: 9240 feet; elevation gain, 750 feet
Backcountry Campsite: 3.8 miles from the trailhead
Seasons: summer, fall
Map: USGS 7.5-minute McHenrys Peak

The moderately challenging hike to Mills Lake is extremely scenic. The trail offers sweeping alpine views and verdant subalpine forest with fine wildflowers. Upon reaching the lake, you are rewarded with one of the most beautiful cirques in the park. The lake's dramatic reflections are unequaled. Early morning is the best time to arrive, before wind ripples the lake's surface and hikers crowd its shores. Because the first portion of the trail climbs an open, sunny slope, bring sun protection and plenty of water.

Drive or take the free bus shuttle to the Glacier Gorge Trailhead and then hike 0.8 mile to Alberta Falls, as described in Hike 7. Above the falls, the trail continues to climb the rocky slope amid fine views to the north of the Mummy Range, Mount Chapin (12,454 feet), Mount Chiquita (13,069 feet), and Ypsilon Mountain (13,514 feet); to the west are Flattop Mountain (12,324 feet) and the precipitous Hallett Peak (12,713 feet).

The trail follows Glacier Creek. For good views of the rushing water, carefully approach the edge and peer into the gorge just before the trail heads sharply west, away from the creek. In these rocky environs, watch for quick-moving pikas and indolent marmots.

Shortly, the North Longs Peak Trail enters from the left (east). Keep right on the Glacier Gorge Trail, following the signs for Loch Vale and Mills Lake. A welcome stretch of trail descends into a pretty subalpine forest. Notice the conical aspen stumps with teeth marks—sure signs of beavers at work.

At 2.2 miles arrive at a junction with the trails to Loch Vale (Hike 9) and to Lake Haiyaha (Hike 15). Take the trail to the left, which leads to Glacier Gorge. The sign indicates Mills Lake and Black Lake.

The dramatic landscape of Mills Lake makes it worth the hike.

A short, shady walk leads to the crossing of a charming stream named Icy Brook. The trail then briefly enters denser woods, passing an area littered with glacial erratics, large boulders dropped by the glacier that flowed through this gorge. Soon the trail completely disappears on bedrock, but the way is clearly marked by rock cairns.

Limber pines grow seemingly straight out of bedrock. These hardy conifers thrive at timberline and on rocky ledges, where most other trees are unable to survive. Limber pines are magnificent both in life and in death. The sculptural, twisting shapes of long-dead limber pines give this rugged landscape an eerie beauty.

The trail briefly leaves the bedrock to cross Glacier Creek amid a variety of wildflowers. After another short segment over rock, the trail arrives at Mills Lake, 2.8 miles from the trailhead. Lying in a deep basin scooped out by a massive glacier, the lake is truly magnificent. Its rocky shore invites you to sit and appreciate the deep beauty of the place. In summer, vivid pink elephant-head flowers brighten the scene.

Arrive in the morning, when the lake is still, to enjoy its incomparable reflections of Longs Peak, Pagoda Peak, and the Keyboard of the Winds. The name *Keyboard of the Winds* derives from the strange organlike sounds that a rare wind makes as it blows across the rock spires. Even if you've missed this singular concert, there is always music at Mills Lake. The quiet sounds of the lake, the wind, and the birds overhead play their own delicate melodies. Mills Lake makes a superb picnic spot. In autumn, look for wild blueberries near the shore.

This special lake was named for Enos Mills (1870–1922), who was instrumental in creating Rocky Mountain National Park. Mills was a self-educated naturalist, avid mountaineer (he climbed Longs Peak more than 250 times), and pioneer in the conservation movement. He dedicated years of his life to creating Rocky Mountain National Park. It is fitting that such an outstanding lake bears his name. Mills wrote: "A climb up the Rockies will develop a love for nature, strengthen one's appreciation of the beautiful world outdoors, and put one in tune with the Infinite. The Rockies are . . . singularly rich in mountain scenes which stir one's blood and which strengthen and sweeten life." Hikers to his lake will agree.

Hiking Options:

(1) Hike to Jewel Lake, about 0.4 mile from the north end of Mills Lake on a trail that gains only 20 feet in elevation. To reach the small, marshy lake, continue on the trail along the eastern shore of Mills Lake. (2) Backpackers can find a fine campsite just 1 mile farther up the trail from Mills Lake. For details and a permit, contact the backcountry office at Park Headquarters. (3) The park shuttle bus enables a variety of loop hikes between Bear Lake and Glacier Gorge Trailheads. One excellent loop starts at Bear Lake, includes Lake Haiyaha and Mills Lake, and ends at Glacier Gorge Trailhead, for a total distance of 6.5 miles. See Hike 15 and the Bear Lake Hiking Map (Hike 6).

9 THE LOCH

Difficulty: moderate
Distance: 3.1 miles one way
Usage: high
Starting Elevation: 9240 feet; elevation gain, 990 feet
Backcountry Campsite: 3.3 miles from the trailhead
Seasons: summer, fall
Map: USGS 7.5-minute McHenrys Peak

This scenic trail takes you past Alberta Falls on a sunny, open slope to a beautiful mountain lake. The Loch is a fine destination, rimmed with limber pines and surrounded by distinctive peaks. The trail to the Loch is varied, offering both panoramic views and intimate forest paths. Start early to avoid the crowds on this deservedly popular hike. Be sure to bring sunscreen and an ample supply of water because the first part of the hike can be hot and sunny.

Begin this hike at Glacier Gorge Trailhead, as described in Hike 7. Hike the Glacier Gorge Trail past Alberta Falls to the Mills Lake Trail junction, as described in Hike 8. Keep straight ahead at the junction on the Loch Vale Trail.

The trail climbs gradually on an open slope with good views. After a quarter mile, as the trail swings closer to Icy Brook, aspens and yellow-flowered shrubby cinquefoil appear. The path next steeply switchbacks up a forested slope. Just before the lake are patches of snow, which last for most of the summer. Most youngsters cannot resist the novelty of throwing a few snowballs in July.

The Loch is just ahead, its rocky shore punctuated by beautiful limber pines. Limber pines are distinguished by their needles, which come in bunches of five, by their graceful, twisting contours, and by their ability to grow seemingly straight out of bedrock. The trunks of limber pines stand statuesque long after their death, resembling human torsos, their branches like arms outstretched.

High mountain walls surround the lake. To the west is the precipitous rock climber's playground known as Cathedral Wall. Taylor Glacier looms high above the Loch to the southwest. Standing at the northeastern end of the Loch, look southwest to the tiered cascade of Timberline Falls, 1.3 miles away (see Hike 10).

Ducks swim and dive in the water. The sounds of birds fill the air. Loudest is the cackle of the Clark's nutcracker, a large gray bird with handsome black and white wings. Unlike most male birds, the male Clark's nutcracker develops a brood patch, a bald area on his underside that swells with blood vessels shortly

The Loch's shoreline offers infinite delights to curious young hikers.

before his mate lays her eggs. The male shares the duty of sitting on the eggs, using this patch to warm them.

Anglers frequent the Loch to cast across its surface, enjoying the scenery and hoping for trout. If you plan to fish, check with the Park Service for current regulations.

The lake's rocky northern shore is an excellent place for a picnic but may be crowded. A pleasant trail leads around the lake, where many private spots can be found. The path is lovely, shady, and flower-filled. Purple mountain harebells, blue chiming bells, and purple composites attract bright green butterflies. The weathered trunks of downed trees and the sun-dappled stones combine to give the trail the feeling of a Japanese garden, where all elements are in their intended place. In such a spot, you cannot help but feel that you too are in your intended place.

Hiking Options:

(1) From the Loch, hike to Timberline Falls in 1.2 miles, Lake of Glass in 1.4 miles, and Sky Pond in 1.5 miles. Additional elevation gain for these destinations are, respectively, 270 feet, 640 feet, and 720 feet (see Hike 10). (2) Backpackers

can find a campsite 0.6 mile farther up the trail from the Loch at Andrews Creek (see Hike 10). (3) If the park shuttle is operating, a variety of loop hikes are possible between Bear Lake and Glacier Gorge Trailhead. See the Bear Lake Hiking Map (Hike 6).

10 TIMBERLINE FALLS, LAKE OF GLASS, AND SKY POND

Difficulty: strenuous

Distance: 4.3 miles to Timberline Falls, 4.5 miles to Lake of Glass, 4.9 miles to Sky Pond—all one way

Usage: moderate

Starting Elevation: 9240 feet; elevation gain, 1210 feet to Timberline Falls, 1580 feet to Lake of Glass, 1710 feet to Sky Pond

Backcountry Campsite: 3.5 miles from the trailhead

Seasons: summer, fall

Map: USGS 7.5-minute McHenrys Peak

This scenic trail leads to impressive Timberline Falls and to two starkly beautiful lakes high above Glacier Gorge. Along the way, you pass Alberta Falls and the Loch. The trail is varied and always interesting, offering both panoramic views and intimate forest settings. Reaching Lake of Glass and Sky Pond is a challenge because both lie above tree line. Nevertheless, this trail is a good one for strong young hikers, because it offers many fine intermediate destinations where you can turn back without feeling defeated. Bring sunscreen and an ample supply of water; the first portion of the hike is often hot and sunny.

Begin at Glacier Gorge Trailhead, as described in Hike 7. Hike 3 miles to the Loch, as described in Hike 9. From the northeast end of the lake, look southwest to the tiered cascade of Timberline Falls, your next destination.

The trail continues around the lake's northwest side. The path is lovely, shady, and lined with flowers. After the lake, the trail runs along Icy Brook. At 0.9 mile from the eastern edge of the lake, the way splits; take the trail to the left heading toward Timberline Falls, Lake of Glass, and Sky Pond. The trail to the right leads to Andrews Glacier and backcountry campsites at Andrews Creek. Backpackers should turn right and follow the trail 0.2 mile from the junction to find the sites.

Day hikers follow the left fork. A quarter mile after the fork, arrive at the

The view over Loch Vale

basin of Timberline Falls, an exquisite open area with the spectacular falls at its southern end. Large boulders in the basin make good perches on which to rest and watch the cascading water.

The trail leads across the basin and up alongside the waterfall. Climb with the utmost care, for the rocks are slippery. In early summer, snow or ice may make the steep climb treacherous. Depending upon conditions and the strength of your hikers, you may want to end your hike at the falls.

Above the waterfall lies a treeless, rocky landscape, for Timberline Falls was aptly named. Travel 0.2 mile over bedrock to arrive at Lake of Glass. The views to Loch Vale, and beyond to the far peaks of the north, are fabulous. The lake itself has a desolate beauty, surrounded by rocks and tundra and dark, towering peaks. To the west, massive Taylor Peak (13,153 feet) and Taylor Glacier loom high above the lake.

The watershed you've entered—including Sky Pond, Lake of Glass, the Loch, and the adjoining mountainsides—is one of the most studied watersheds in the world. For twenty years, scientists have monitored chemical inputs from wind and precipitation and found that winds from the south and east sweep nitrates and ammonium from car exhaust, factories, and agricultural activity up into these mountains. As a result, nitrate concentrations in precipitation have increased significantly. Eventually, chronic acidification of the lakes can lead to the loss of aquatic organisms and entire fish populations. Unfortunately, these changes can be almost impossible to reverse. However, Colorado state officials and Front Range communities are becoming increasingly aware of the harm caused by this pollution and are seeking solutions to save the park's lakes.

The easy 0.4-mile walk to Sky Pond follows the path around the lake. Sky Pond is twice as large as Lake of Glass and seems twice as desolate. The cliffs that nearly surround it are at once beautiful and menacing. Imaginative young minds may find mysterious cliff dwellings in the jagged spires or threatening faces in the rocks. The impression is that this lake is guarded. The scene has a forbidding, untamed quality. The bare, cold rocks and chilling wind at the lake are reminders that people are but visitors in this wilderness.

Along the shore of Sky Pond, the winds blow hard and cold, so picnickers may want to retreat to the protected cove of the Timberline Falls basin. But don't hurry off the mountain. The trip back to the trailhead is a pleasant down-hill hike with abundant panoramic views

BEAR LAKE

Difficulty: nature stroll, handicapped access to lake according to uniform federal accessibility standards, handicapped access with assistance 300 feet in either direction on loop trail

Distance: 0.5-mile loop

Usage: high

Starting Elevation: 9475 feet; elevation gain, 20 feet

Backcountry Campsite: none

Seasons: summer, fall

Map: USGS 7.5-minute McHenrys Peak

Bear Lake is one of the park's most visited lakes. Its level trail and large parking lot attract huge crowds in the summer. To avoid noise and congestion, hike early. At daybreak, the reflection of peaks on still water is unforgettable, bird songs are uninterrupted by chatter, and the self-guided nature trail can be experienced at a leisurely pace. Spy dew glistening on a web or a hare eating breakfast amid the grass, and Bear Lake will seem a long way from its multi-acre parking lot.

Drive to Bear Lake Road, as described in Hike 1. Follow Bear Lake Road for 9.3 miles to the large parking area at its end. Because this lot is often full by midmorning during the summer, the free park shuttle bus is highly recom-mended. Parking for the bus is at the Park & Ride on Bear Lake Road, 5.1 miles from its junction with US Highway 36. Schedules are available at visitor centers and at www.nps.gov/romo/planyourvisit/shuttle_bus_route.htm.

Two booklets enhance the stroll around Bear Lake. The "Bear Lake Nature Trail" pamphlet, published by the Park Service, is an informative guide to plants, wildlife, and geologic features. *The Grandpa Tree,* by Mike Donahue, is a brief, sensitive, and beautifully illustrated account of the life of a fir tree. Both publications are available at the visitor centers.

Bear Lake is also a good trail to learn about the park's small mammals and birds. To help children identify Bear Lake inhabitants, several inexpensive guides are available (see "Recommended Reading"). Watch for chipmunks, golden-mantled ground squirrels, snowshoe hares, Steller's jays, Clark's

HIKES 11–15

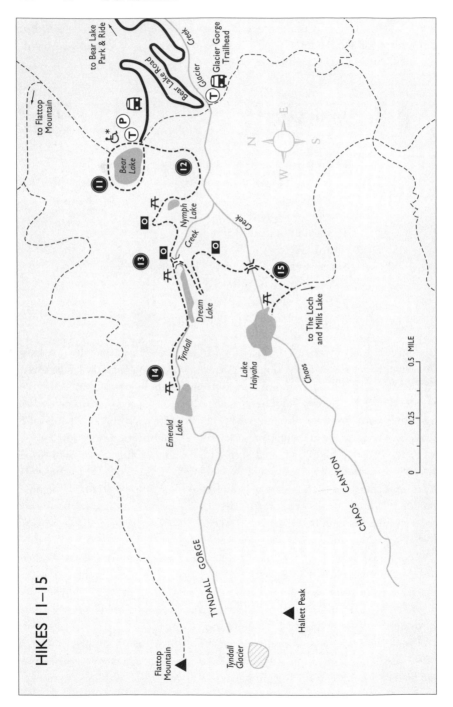

Contemplating Longs Peak, Keyboard of the Wind, and Pagoda Peak while enjoying Bear Lake.

nutcrackers, gray jays, blackbilled magpies, chickadees, and hairy woodpeckers. You may even see a harmless green garter snake, the park's only snake.

The Bear Lake Trail is level and very easy to walk. A changing panorama of dramatic peaks rises behind the lake. From the east side, where the hike begins, the sheer north side of Hallett Peak (12,713 feet) is most striking. From the north side of the lake, Longs Peak (14,255 feet), the highest mountain in the park; the spires of the Keyboard of the Winds (west of Longs Peak); and aptly named Pagoda Peak (13,497 feet) dominate. Visible from many trails within the park, these three distinctive peaks are prominent fixtures in the landscape. Getting to know them is like learning the faces of new friends. If you learn their countenances, they greet you on every visit to the park.

On the south side of Bear Lake, pass a marshy area where a creek deposits sand and silt that is slowly filling the lake. Each year new soil and new invading plants create a progressively drier environment.

Peer into the lake's waters to catch a glimpse of a greenback cutthroat trout. Overfishing and the introduction of non-native fish almost drove this native trout to extinction. In an effort to save the greenback, the Park Service removed all non-native fish from Bear Lake. As a result, the greenback is making a comeback. To hasten its recovery, fishing is prohibited in Bear Lake. Furthermore, in certain waters in the park, the greenback is protected by a catch-and-release policy, whereby the trout must be returned to the water unharmed. The Park Service hopes that these efforts will restore the greenback to its former numbers.

Despite its name, there are probably no bears in the immediate vicinity of Bear Lake. The lake was named for a black bear sighted during the nineteenth century, when the bear population in the region was still vigorous. Rocky Mountain National Park is home now to only a few black bears, perhaps thirty to forty. Hunting and loss of habitat have greatly diminished their numbers.

Loss of bear habitat was accelerated by the Park Service's former fire-suppression policy, which dictated that all forest fires be promptly extinguished. Lack of naturally occurring fires resulted in loss of meadows, mountain shrub communities, and young forests—habitats where bears find their favorite forage. Without periodic fires, the mosaic of plant communities gave way to expanses of thick forest, which don't support the berries, nutritious forbs, nuts, and grasses that constitute the bulk of a bear's diet. A greater awareness of the positive effects of fire, however, is changing the park's policies to allow most naturally occurring fires to burn themselves out. In addition, recent prescribed burns by the Park Service have increased the variety of habitats. Perhaps with the opening of meadows and shrub lands by these fires, the black bear population will rebound.

Hiking Options:

Bear Lake is the departure point for numerous hikes of every level of difficulty. Use of the free park shuttle bus greatly increases your options. See the Bear Lake Hiking Map (Hike 6).

 NYMPH LAKE

Difficulty: easy
Distance: 0.5 mile one way
Usage: high
Starting Elevation: 9475 feet; elevation gain, 225 feet
Backcountry Campsite: none
Seasons: summer, fall
Map: USGS 7.5-minute McHenrys Peak

Nymph Lake is a lovely, lily-covered lake set beneath high peaks. The views from the lake are varied and awe-inspiring, yet its shoreline offers intimate and accessible exploring. Because of its beauty and nearness to the trailhead, Nymph Lake is often crowded. Hike early in the day to have this jewel to yourself.

Hike early in the day to enjoy the peace at Nymph Lake.

Another benefit of early morning hikes is a near-perfect reflection of towering peaks in the lake's still water.

Begin at the Bear Lake Trailhead (see Hike 11). Before the trail arrives at Bear Lake, turn left (south) at the well-marked trail junction. Shortly the trail forks again; keep right, heading uphill. Fir and spruce give way to a towering stand of lodgepole pines along the steep half mile up to Nymph Lake.

The trail meets Nymph Lake at the south end and travels around the eastern shore to the north side of the lake. From the northeastern shore, enjoy an excellent view of precipitous Hallett Peak (12,713 feet), towering more than 3000 feet above the lake. Looking south from the north side of the lake, Longs Peak, the Keyboard of the Winds, and Pagoda Peak dominate the scene.

Nymph Lake was named for the yellow pond lilies that cover much of this small lake. The lily's scientific name was originally *Nymphaea polysepala*—hence Nymph Lake. The plant's botanical name, though not the lake's, was subsequently changed. From late June through August, large bright yellow blossoms adorn the lily pads. Native Americans once gathered the large seeds of the pond lilies; when roasted, they taste remarkably like popcorn. Today, ducks enjoy the seeds with little competition.

Hiking Options:

(1) Dream Lake is only 0.6 mile farther and 200 feet higher than Nymph Lake (see Hike 13). (2) Emerald Lake is 1.3 miles farther and 380 feet higher (see Hike 14). (3) Lake Haiyaha is 1.6 miles farther and 520 feet higher (see Hike 15). For more Bear Lake hikes, see the Bear Lake Hiking Map (Hike 6).

13   DREAM LAKE

> **Difficulty:** easy
> **Distance:** 1.1 miles one way
> **Usage:** high
> **Starting Elevation:** 9475 feet; elevation gain, 425 feet
> **Backcountry Campsite:** none
> **Seasons:** summer, fall
> **Map:** USGS 7.5-minute McHenrys Peak

Dream Lake is the second in a series of pretty lakes above Bear Lake. The trail is scenic, affording panoramic views as it climbs above Nymph Lake. Dream Lake is well worth a visit in fall, when aspens grace the trail with gold. In summer, hike very early to avoid the crowds who have discovered this trail to be one of the easiest and most pleasing in the park.

The hike begins at the Bear Lake Trailhead (see Hike 11). Hike to Nymph Lake, as described in Hike 12. The trail, which ends just before Nymph Lake, begins again on the west side of the lake. A view to the right, over a rocky ledge, reveals Bear Lake and the ridge of Bierstadt Moraine. The trail soon climbs to an overlook above Nymph Lake. Ahead, Hallett Peak presents a very imposing profile.

In the fall, this section of trail is ablaze with brilliant aspens, whose delicate leaves turn a bright yellow or red. The small rounded leaves flicker in the breeze, creating lively patterns of light on the trail. Because of the way the leaf

Hallett Peak rises prominently above the trail.

is attached to the stem, it quakes or trembles, true to the tree's botanical name, *Populus tremuloides,* or trembling aspen.

In the summer, wildflowers are particularly colorful along this slope. Look for Indian paintbrush, which looks like a shaggy brush dipped in vivid vermillion, and purple larkspur, a lovely wild relative of the garden delphinium that is highly poisonous to cattle.

The trail levels a bit and soon presents breathtaking views of Longs Peak and Glacier Basin. Enjoy the view for a quarter mile as the trail traverses the sunny south-facing slope—a magnificent stretch of trail in any season.

Listen for the sound of Tyndall Creek, which flows below, just out of sight. The trail meets this clear running creek, generated in part by glacial runoff from Tyndall Glacier, just before Dream Lake. At the creek the trail divides; the left branch heads over a bridge to Lake Haiyaha (see Hike 15). Keep right for Dream Lake.

Dream Lake is long and narrow, with outstanding reflections of Hallett Peak and the spires of Flattop Mountain. Anglers may be trying for cutthroat trout in its cold waters. Large rocks and logs along the shore make good picnic and viewing spots. Arrive in the morning, when the water is still and hikers are few, for breakfast in a magnificent setting.

Following a lush and beautifully flowered trail, be sure to walk along the north side of the lake to its western end to see where Tyndall Creek flows into the lake.

Hiking Options:
(1) Emerald Lake is 0.7 mile from and 180 feet higher than Dream Lake (see Hike 14). (2) Lake Haiyaha is 1 mile from and 320 feet above Dream Lake (see Hike 15). For an overview of Bear Lake hikes, see the Bear Lake Hiking Map (Hike 6).

14 EMERALD LAKE

Difficulty: moderate
Distance: 1.8 miles one way
Usage: high
Starting Elevation: 9475 feet; elevation gain, 605 feet
Backcountry Campsite: none
Seasons: summer, fall
Map: USGS 7.5-minute McHenrys Peak

Emerald Lake is third in the string of beautiful tarns above Bear Lake. All the lakes are very accessible and, consequently, show signs of overuse. The trail to Emerald Lake, however, is lovely and varied, and crowds can be avoided by starting early in the day. The early morning hiker is richly rewarded with panoramic views and first-rate reflections of glacier-studded mountains in three very different lakes—Nymph, Dream, and Emerald. It is worthwhile to follow the trail to its conclusion, for Emerald Lake is perhaps the wildest, most dramatic, and most beautifully desolate of the three.

Hike to Dream Lake, as described in Hike 13. Continue on the trail along the north side of Dream Lake. Bright pink elephanthead thrives along this moist section of trail. This plant resembles a totem pole of elephant heads, each with an upturned trunk. At the lake's end, the trail heads steeply up through mature subalpine forest, keeping within sight of Tyndall Creek on the left. Subalpine fir and Engelmann spruce border the trail, with a colorful undergrowth of flowers such as white mountain figwort and blue chiming bells. The climb is steep, gaining over 200 feet in a quarter mile.

Finally, the trail levels and then descends slightly to Emerald Lake. The steep rock walls of Hallett Peak and Flattop Mountain rise directly from the water. Emerald Lake is a tarn, a small lake lying in a basin carved by a glacier that scooped out rocks and carried them down the mountain. Melting snow and glacial runoff then filled the resulting hole with water, thereby creating the lake. The chill winds that blow across the water serve as reminders that this lake is glacier-created and glacier-fed.

Not surprisingly, Emerald Lake is barren. The gray rock that surrounds the lake is broken only by weather-beaten, wind-sculpted limber pines and, occasionally, by hardy firs and spruce. The twisted forms of the pines seem to grow straight from the rock.

Emerald Lake was named for its intense, radiant green waters. On a cloudless day (the best chances are in the morning) the combination of the intensely blue Colorado sky and the luminous green water are strikingly beautiful.

The wildlife is friendly at Emerald Lake. On the rocky slopes, look for yellow-bellied marmots, which are especially abundant on sunny summer days. Picnickers will undoubtedly be visited by golden-mantled ground squirrels, chipmunks, Clark's nutcrackers, Steller's jays, and mountain chickadees. Please do not feed them.

Explore the rocky lakeshore with care, following it all the way around to the far (west) side of the lake. At the far side of the lake is a waterfall where water flows down from Tyndall Glacier into Emerald Lake. Use extreme caution, for slippery, unstable snowfields remain throughout the summer on the western shore.

Hiking Options:

Back at Dream Lake, a trail leads south 1 mile to Lake Haiyaha (elevation gain, 320 feet; see Hike 15). For an overview of Bear Lake hikes, see the Bear Lake Hiking Map (Hike 6).

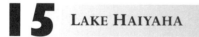

15 LAKE HAIYAHA

Difficulty: moderate
Distance: 2.1 miles one way
Usage: high
Starting Elevation: 9475 feet; elevation gain, 745 feet
Backcountry Campsite: none
Seasons: summer, fall
Map: USGS 7.5-minute McHenrys Peak

Lake Haiyaha is a distinctive lake with stark, boulder-strewn shores. The trail to the lake is very scenic, with wildflowers in the summer, bright foliage in autumn, and a wealth of panoramic vistas in all seasons.

Begin this hike at the Bear Lake Trailhead (see Hike 11). Hike to Dream Lake, as described in Hike 13. At 1 mile from the trailhead, just before arriving at Dream Lake, the trail to Lake Haiyaha heads left. Before continuing, however, walk a short distance up the Emerald Lake Trail, on the right, to visit lovely Dream Lake. After visiting the lake and taking in the bright wildflowers on the path around its north side, backtrack to the Lake Haiyaha junction. The trail heads southwest and crosses a bridge over Tyndall Creek. Lake Haiyaha is 1 mile away.

Wear sturdy shoes if you want to explore the shore of Lake Haiyaha.

After the bridge, the trail curves to the right and switchbacks up a shady ridge with a good view of Dream Lake. Snow lasts here into midsummer under the subalpine firs and Engelmann spruce. If there are other hikers at Dream Lake, you may notice how easily voices carry up the mountain. In consideration of other visitors, be aware of the excellent acoustics of natural amphitheaters and control the noise level of your youngsters accordingly.

The trail is moderately steep, but excellent vistas appear as it rounds a bend and climbs an east-facing slope. From the mountainside, Estes Park is visible in the distance. Nearby are good views of Nymph and Bear Lakes. Looking farther down Bear Lake Road, Sprague Lake is also visible. There are also magnificent views to the southeast of Longs Peak, with Mills Lake at its base.

The trail then descends to a forest of fir and spruce, crossing a bridge over Chaos Creek, which flows out of Lake Haiyaha. Approximately 0.2 mile before reaching the lake, the trail from the Loch (Hike 9) and Mills Lake (Hike 8) enters from the south. After this junction, the trail to Lake Haiyaha turns west and leads to a small pond with a beach at its eastern end. The clear, still pond is a lovely place to pause. Large boulders punctuate the shore, looking like moored ships whose "helms" can be seized by nimble youngsters.

The trail continues to the right of the pond over a very rocky landscape, soon disappearing among the boulders. As you head toward a large, handsome limber pine whose twisting limbs reveal its struggle, Lake Haiyaha comes into view.

Large, clear, and beautiful, the lake is wholly surrounded by boulders. The name *haiyaha,* in fact, comes from an Indian word meaning "rock." The large rocks make exploration of the shoreline difficult, but with a little effort, you can travel around the edge of the lake. The other side of the lake offers good views to Longs Peak.

Above the lake to the left is Chaos Canyon, between the high peaks of Otis (to the south) and Hallett (to the north). The impassable jumble of rocks leaves no question as to the origin of this canyon's name.

Hiking Options:

A hike to Lake Haiyaha can be combined with Glacier Gorge hikes, such as to the Loch and Mills Lake, to create a wonderful, but lengthy scenic loop of about 7.5 miles. The free park shuttle can be used to return to the Bear Lake Trailhead. See the Bear Lake Hiking Map (Hike 6).

 ## BIERSTADT LAKE

Difficulty: easy
Distance: 3 miles one way
Usage: moderate
Starting Elevation: 9475 feet; elevation gain, 255 feet
Backcountry Campsite: none
Seasons: summer, fall
Map: USGS 7.5-minute Longs Peak, McHenrys Peak

This easy hike offers exquisite hiking in three very different environments: shady forest, a pristine lake basin, and the side of a steep glacial moraine. The scenery runs from intimate to expansive. The lake, conveniently located at the midpoint of the trail, makes a wonderful picnic spot.

This hike begins at the Bear Lake Trailhead and ends at the Bierstadt Lake Trailhead. Use two cars or the shuttle bus to connect the trailheads. You can park at the shuttle parking area or at the smaller lots at either trailhead. All three are on Bear Lake Road. To reach these lots, drive to Bear Lake Road, as described in Hike 11. The shuttle parking area is 5.1 miles from the junction with US Highway 36. Limited parking is available at the Bierstadt Lake and Bear Lake Trailheads, at 6.6 miles and 9.3 miles from the junction.

Head right (north) on the Bear Lake Trail (Hike 11) and shortly come to the Flattop Mountain Trail on the right. Take this trail and begin a fairly steep ascent through pines and aspens. As you climb, observe the tenacity of the trailside trees, which appear to rise right out of the boulders beside the trail.

Bierstadt Lake is a refreshing destination on summer days.

At 0.4 mile, arrive at a second fork and again bear right. The trail now travels along the top of Bierstadt Moraine, which leads toward Bierstadt Lake. Numerous ground squirrels accompany you on this part of the hike; resist the temptation to feed these bold beggars.

The ascent is quickly rewarded by outstanding views of impressive peaks, including the dramatic profiles of Hallett Peak (12,713 feet) and Flattop Mountain (12,324 feet). After 0.75 mile, the Bierstadt Lake Trail forks. Take the right fork, which descends gently into the cool, shady tranquility of a mature forest of Engelmann spruce and subalpine fir, where sufficient light filters through the branches to dispel any gloom. At this point, the trail improves, becoming wider, smoother, and more level.

Within this magnificent subalpine forest, you can sense the passing of generations—the millennium of trees that have lived and died here. Weathered trunks of tremendous lodgepole pines lying on the forest floor are mute reminders of the trees that once dominated the area but were long ago shaded out by the firs and spruce. Now the fallen pines tell of the natural succession of trees in the forest. The downed trees provide natural benches for a snack stop, places to play "King of the Limb," or balance beams on which children can test their skills.

Don't rush through this area too quickly. Rest on a great trunk or boulder, watch the acrobatic chipmunks, or browse the sculpture garden of giant gnarled upturned roots. Shortly, there is another fork in the trail. As the sign indicates, take the trail to the left.

At 1.5 miles from Bear Lake, come to the Bierstadt Lake fork. A spur trail on the right leads to the water, where mallards provide a noisy welcome. The large rocks scattered along the shoreline invite resting, reading, or playing. Take time to gaze upon the profiles of Longs Peak, Hallett Peak, and Flattop Mountain, which create the exquisite backdrop for the 1.4-acre lake.

This is a perfect picnic spot. The lake has several pebbly beaches where tiny waves lap teasingly. Explore the shoreline on an overgrown footpath. The most difficult part of the hike is over; the trail is literally all downhill from here.

A short section of trail at the lake's southwest end leads to the main trail, where you head left. (Or, if you wish to retrace your steps to Bear Lake, return to the main trail the way you came, turn left at the main trail, and keep to the left, heading south.) Travel on a straight path through a tremendous stand of lodgepole pines, whose slim, straight trunks rise row after row. Indians once used the tall pines as tepee poles—hence the tree's name. The forest rapidly thins as the trail approaches the edge of the Bierstadt Moraine, where you are suddenly greeted with a wide view of the mountains to the south and east, as well as of the valley below. The transformation in scenery is dramatic and renewing. The views of the Front Range are truly magnificent. Below, Glacier Creek winds through the green valley.

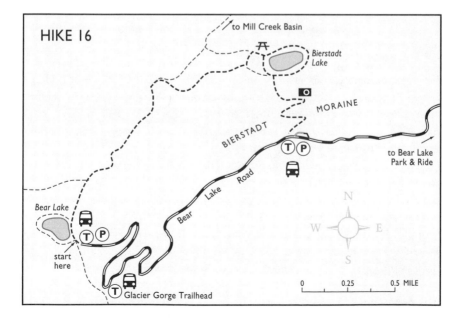

The hillside is pleasant as well. In midsummer, wildflowers are abundant, and in fall the golden foliage of the aspens is spectacular. Ponderosa pines grow on the moraine in open parklike stands. The pines are trees out of a child's magination, perfectly formed giants with huge cones and bark that smells like vanilla.

The trail down the moraine is hot and sunny on most summer days. You will be glad to be descending as you pass many hot and grumbling hikers struggling up the path. Following the descent of the moraine, return briefly to a level, shady path, after a short distance arriving at Bierstadt Lake Trailhead and the completion of your hike.

Hiking Options:
See the Bear Lake Hiking Map (Hike 6).

17 FLATTOP MOUNTAIN

Difficulty: strenuous
Distance: 4.4 miles one way
Usage: high
Starting Elevation: 9475 feet; elevation gain, 2,849 feet
Backcountry Campsite: none
Seasons: summer, fall
Map: USGS 7.5-minute McHenrys Peak

Flattop Mountain is a superb hike, strenuous but rewarding in a multitude of ways. The views from the trail and summit are outstanding. Wildlife is frequently seen, and wildflowers in midsummer are spectacular. Best of all, the well-trod path is so smooth that you can spend most of your time watching the wonders around you instead of watching your feet.

Begin at the Bear Lake Trailhead (see Hike 11). Head right (north) on the Bear Lake Trail and, after a short distance, turn right and head uphill on an unpaved path marked by a trail sign for Flattop Mountain. The trail climbs steeply and quickly above Bear Lake among aspens, which are particularly beautiful in the fall. After 0.4 mile, the trail divides. The right fork leads to Bierstadt Lake (Hike 16). Keep left and continue to climb. After a few switchbacks, enjoy good views of Longs Peak to the south and Bear Lake below.

After another 0.4 mile, the trail divides again. Take the left fork. The Flattop Mountain Trail rises steeply through fir and spruce. Beginning here, enjoy

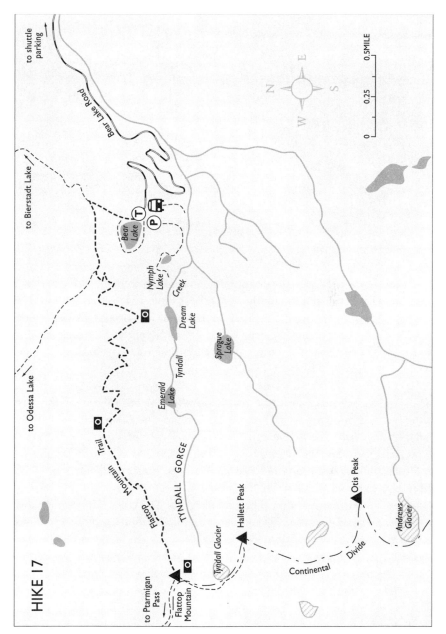

good views through breaks in the trees. Dream Lake Overlook, on the left, is a good place to see how far you've come. There are also excellent views to the southeast of Longs Peak with lovely Mills Lake below it. Angular Hallett Peak looms overhead to the west.

A ranger-led hike is a great way to learn about the flora and fauna on Flattop Mountain.

As tree line approaches, the trees become sparse and stunted. "Banner trees," with branches growing on only the east side of the trunk, reveal the force of the prevailing westerly winds. Only the limbs on the leeward side have escaped the wind's destructive and scouring blasts. At tree line, the gnarled islands of *krummholz* (a German word meaning "crooked wood") struggle against the high winds, intense cold, and short growing season.

Above tree line, the views are stupendous. There are also marvelous sights on the tundra beneath your feet. A multitude of minute but vibrant wildflowers stand out like jewels against the gray rock. Look for the Colorado blue columbine, a showy flower with blue sepals and white petals. It is the Colorado state flower and was once abundant throughout these mountains, before acquisitive and selfish hikers drastically reduced its numbers. Park regulations now prohibit the picking of wildflowers.

Look also among the rocks for pikas and marmots. The elusive and industrious pika, a round-eared relative of the rabbit, resembles a guinea pig. During the summer, it busily scurries over the rocks, gathering flowers and grasses. The pika lays its harvest of herbs on rocks to dry and then gathers and piles the hay in little stacks. The pika assaults this chore with unceasing energy, for these piles will be its food during the long alpine winter. The animal's ability to scamper with speed and precision is due to the "nonskid" fur on the soles of its feet. Recently, as a result of warming temperatures, the population of pikas in the park has dropped precipitously. Treasure your sighting of these adorable creatures.

Watch also for the larger and more easily observed yellow-bellied marmot. On sunny days, this relative of the woodchuck can usually be found sunning itself on the rocks. Like the pika, the marmot also dens on talus slopes and

114

boulder-covered mountainsides. Unlike the hard-working pika, the objective of the indolent marmot is to acquire a sufficient amount of body fat to see it through its winter's hibernation. By summer's end, most marmots have sleek coats and pleasingly plump figures.

Watch closely also for the well-camouflaged ptarmigan, a grouse that inhabits the alpine tundra. In summer you may see a mottled brown hen with chicks.

The trail steadily climbs to the top of aptly named Flattop Mountain, whose summit is a spacious, uplifted plateau. Extending from Bighorn Flats to Andrews Glacier, this high plain was once continuous with the broad plateau of Trail Ridge, which is visible to the north and now separated from Flattop Mountain by Forest Canyon.

The summit, though not dramatic, is a fine place to be. The broad expanse of Flattop allows hikers to spread out in every direction, and the views are spectacular.

Hiking Options:

(1) An easy 0.3-mile trail leads south from Flattop Mountain to the top of Tyndall Glacier. The trail is clearly marked by cairns and signs. (2) A very challenging trail that gains 389 feet in 0.6 mile leads to Hallett Peak, one of the most dramatic summits in the park. Follow the trail leading south across the summit of Flattop, past Tyndall Glacier. The path periodically disappears among rocks, but cairns point the way. The way is steep and the rocks unstable, so climb slowly and carefully. The views from the summit at 12,713 feet are spectacular.

18 GEM LAKE

Difficulty: moderate
Distance: 1.8 miles one way
Usage: high
Starting Elevation: 7840 feet (Lumpy Ridge/Gem Lake Trailhead); elevation gain, 1090 feet
Backcountry Campsite: none
Seasons: summer, fall
Map: USGS 7.5-minute Estes Park

This delightful hike among the weird and wonderful rock formations of Lumpy Ridge—a popular spot for rock climbers—offers beautiful views, diverse vegetation, and a child-sized lake. In summer, however, the trail can be hot and

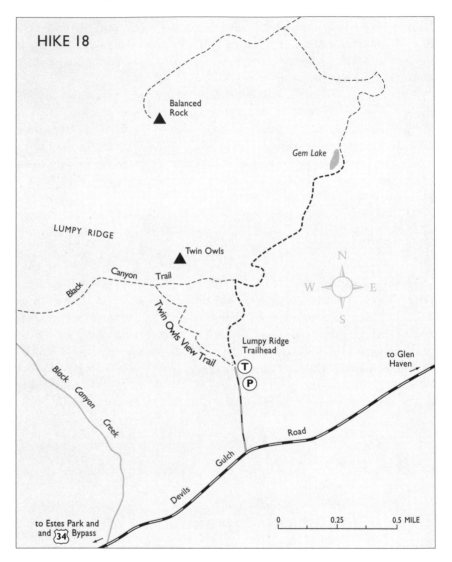

HIKE 18

Balanced Rock

Gem Lake

LUMPY RIDGE

Twin Owls

Canyon   Trail

Black

Twin Owls View Trail

Lumpy Ridge
Trailhead

T

P

to Glen Haven

Black   Canyon   Creek

Road

Gulch

Devils

to Estes Park and
and 34 Bypass

N

W   E

S

0   0.25   0.5 MILE

tiring and a real challenge for youngsters. To combat fatigue on this worthwhile hike, start early in the morning; bring plenty of drinks, hats, and sunscreen; and proceed slowly.

From the intersection of US 34 Bypass and MacGregor Avenue on the north side of Estes Park, turn right (north) onto MacGregor Avenue, which becomes Devils Gulch Road north of this intersection. At 0.8 mile, pass the well-marked MacGregor Ranch. After the ranch, drive another 0.5 mile to the Lumpy Ridge Trailhead and parking lot, on your left.

Cool your toes at tiny Gem Lake.

The trail to Gem Lake starts near Twin Owls, a prominent rock formation that, especially from a distance, looks like two owls.

From the trailhead, bear right and hike through a stand of young aspens and then begin the climb up the ridge. Cross briefly though private property. Above you to your right, catch a glimpse of the amazing rock formations—strangely eroded to resemble heads on narrow necks. Ponderosa pines dot the slopes, framing but not obscuring the excellent views of Longs Peak and Estes Park. These pines are home to Abert's squirrels. These beautiful and distinctive squirrels are dark gray or black, with conspicuous ear tufts and a long, full tail fringed with white hairs.

Notice the many dead ponderosa pines. They have been invaded and killed by the mountain pine beetle. Most of the trees have numerous holes made by woodpeckers. These holes provide homes for swallows, chickadees, bluebirds, nuthatches, and other cavity-dwelling birds.

Also along the trail are sun-loving wildflowers and an abundance of prickly pear cactus. Local Indians used this cactus in a variety of ways, one of which was to treat the mumps by removing the spines, roasting the stems, and tying the cactus to the patient's neck.

As the trail turns left to climb a gulch between Lumpy Ridge and a second, smaller ridge, it suddenly enters a cooler, moister environment where Douglas-fir thrives among flowers and shrubs. As the trail climbs up and over the ridge, sun and wind return, and Douglas-fir gives way to limber pine, which survives tremendous adversity. At tree line, high winds often twist limber pine into beautiful gnarled shapes. The limber pine is the only conifer in Rocky Mountain National Park whose needles grow in bunches of five.

At approximately 0.5 mile, the trail meets the Black Canyon Trail. The sign indicates the many colorfully named climbing destinations that dot the cliffs of Lumpy Ridge to the west (left): Batman and Checkerboard, the Book Area, Pear. If these curious names entice you to take a closer look at Lumpy Ridge, turn left onto the Black Canyon Trail. Follow it for 0.4 mile, to where it intersects the Twin Owls View Trail. You can then return to your vehicle via a loop route by turning left onto the Twin Owls View Trail. It will lose and then regain several hundred feet of elevation before reaching the trailhead in 0.6 mile.

If your glimpses of rock climbing in Lumpy Ridge inspire you to try this exciting sport, you can make plans to return later with a climbing class. Several outfitters in Estes Park offer lessons, including instruction for youngsters. See Chapter 1 for more information about rock climbing.

To reach Gem Lake, 1.3 miles away, head right at the intersection with Black Canyon Trail. Immediately after this junction, good views are abundant and the picnicking and rock-scrambling spots are too attractive to resist. If the group is weary of hiking, this area makes a satisfying turnaround point. In several places, spur trails lead to overlooks or to more climbing destinations. The steep trails that lead to climbing destinations may be closed to protect raptors during nesting season (March through July). Please respect these closures.

Farther up the trail are more unusual rock formations, in which imaginative children (and adults) can see Gila monsters, chickens, snakes, and, in one amusing pile, two turtles lying on a whale. The rock faces of numerous ghoulish unnameables watch from the ridge top or emerge from the surfaces of fallen boulders. The rocks also can be forts, lookouts, ancient beached ships, and trolls' caves. Only your imagination limits what you see on Lumpy Ridge.

Good views continue after an aspen grove until the trail turns into a cool, moist canyon. Enjoy the sudden wealth of flowers thriving there. In autumn there is an abundance of wild raspberries and bitter golden currants. Native Americans mixed the currants with dried buffalo meat and fat and poured the mixture into bags to form loaves. Closer to our modern tastes, settlers made a tasty currant jam with the addition of much sugar and spice.

Shortly after leaving the canyon, hike up a series of switchbacks to Paul Bunyan's Boot, one of the more famous of Lumpy Ridge's rock formations. The hole in the sole of the boot was created naturally by chemical weathering. Look for other interesting rock formations in this area and on the ridges above you.

Leaving this natural sculpture garden, climb another series of switchbacks to tiny Gem Lake, which is only 5 feet deep and covers about 0.2 acre. Gem Lake is truly a gem, a lovely place to picnic, play, and rest. Sit on its small sandy beach and contemplate the high rock walls that rise dramatically behind it. When the wind is still, they are reflected perfectly in the clear water. The beach will beckon the child in you to remove your shoes and cool your hot, tired feet.

Hiking Options:

Two miles beyond Gem Lake is a fascinating rock formation called Balanced Rock, 3.8 miles from the Lumpy Ridge Trailhead. To reach this destination, continue traveling north from the north end of the lake. After 1.25 miles, reach a fork in the trail. Turn left. This trail leads into a gully containing many interesting formations. It reaches the unmistakable Balanced Rock in 0.75 mile. From Gem Lake, there is no elevation gain.

 DESERTED VILLAGE

Difficulty: moderate
Distance: 3 miles one way
Usage: low
Starting Elevation: 7960 feet; elevation gain, 200 feet
Backcountry Campsite: none
Seasons: spring, summer, fall
Maps: USGS 7.5-minute Glen Haven, Estes Park

This gentle, unassuming trail descends to a canyon and follows the North Fork of the Big Thompson River along a cool and shady path to a meadow that was

The North Fork of the Big Thompson River

once the site of a nineteenth-century resort. Today only one cabin remains. The flowers along the path are plentiful, and in late summer ripe berries are abundant. Adventurous children can find spots for swimming in the North Fork on hot summer days. The trail begins in the Roosevelt National Forest, at the park's northeastern boundary. The long drive to the trailhead goes through Devils Gulch, where the winding road drops 600 feet in 1 mile. On the way, you pass tiny Glen Haven, a picturesque Western town that is a perfect place to stop for a snack.

From Estes Park, find Devils Gulch Road (see Hike 18 for directions). Drive north for 4.2 miles on Devils Gulch Road/Route 43. At 7.5 miles from Estes Park, pass the small town of Glen Haven. At 9.4 miles from Estes Park (1.9 miles past Glen Haven), turn left on Dunraven Glade Road (County Road 51B). Look for a sign for Dunraven Trailhead. Follow Road 51B 2.2 miles to the parking lot at the road's end. Dunraven Trailhead is at the southwest end of the parking lot. (There are two trailheads here—one for Dunraven, along the North Fork Trail, and another that leads to Signal Mountain—make sure you start your hike at the Dunraven Trailhead.) Heavily used by horse riders, the trail may be littered with manure.

Head over a small rise and then descend quickly into a cool gulch. Just before reaching the North Fork, the trail divides. Head right for Deserted Village. The trail follows the river, providing plenty of access to the water. Wildflowers and berry bushes line the way for the entire distance. Watch particularly for delicious wild raspberries.

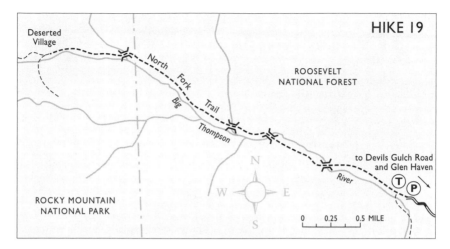

The trail is almost level. A variety of trees including aspen, willow, blue spruce, and Douglas-fir appear. Numerous aspens make this a fine hike in the fall, when their leaves turn brilliant gold. Cross and recross the river on a series of bridges as the canyon cliffs rise in interesting formations above you.

After approximately 1 mile, the trail passes through private property, complete with barbed wire and many buildings, including a large stable. The feeling of wildness is lost, if only temporarily.

After crossing another bridge, follow an old, wide, level road for a short distance before the trail reappears. The trail temporarily narrows, then widens again at the national park boundary.

After crossing three more large bridges, arrive at the meadow that was the site of a popular hunting resort founded by the infamous Lord Dunraven in the 1870s. Today a lone cabin is all that remains.

Lord Dunraven was an Irish lord who visited Estes Park in 1872 and was impressed by its magnificent scenery and fine hunting. The wealthy Dunraven made up his mind to buy the entire area for a private hunting preserve. By using and abusing the homestead laws, he accumulated 15,000 acres, mostly under fraudulent claims. Honest and indignant homesteaders eventually discovered his scheme and challenged his claims. Frustrated by the litigation, the aspiring Rocky Mountain lord surrendered his holdings in 1880 and returned to Ireland. His legacy continues in the names of mountains, lakes, and meadows within Rocky Mountain National Park.

Others succeeded Lord Dunraven in running the fashionable hunting resort at this site. Its popularity might have continued, but a dysentery epidemic in 1909 significantly lessened public enthusiasm. By 1914, the resort was abandoned.

20 BRIDAL VEIL FALLS

Difficulty: moderate
Distance: 3.2 miles one way
Usage: low
Starting Elevation: 7840 feet; elevation gain 1,060 feet
Backcountry Campsite: 1.4 miles from the trailhead
Seasons: spring, summer, fall
Map: USGS 7.5-minute Estes Park

Escape the crowds for a long but undemanding walk to Bridal Veil Falls. A gentle trail rolls through montane meadows and follows Cow Creek to the tallest falls in the park. Along the way, the anthropomorphic rock formations of Lumpy Ridge loom high above the hiker. Only 1.4 miles from the trailhead, backpackers can find a quiet campsite on Cow Creek. This dry, sunny hike can get quite warm in midsummer, so bring plenty of liquids. Plentiful aspen display excellent color in autumn.

From the intersection of US 34 Bypass and MacGregor Avenue on the north side of Estes Park, turn right (north) onto MacGregor Avenue, which becomes Devils Gulch Road. Drive 3.5 miles on Devils Gulch Road to a dirt road on the left signed for McGraw Ranch. (This is a private road, but the landowners permit the public to use the road to reach the ranch.) Turn left onto the dirt road and drive 2.1 miles to its termination at McGraw Ranch where you'll find the Cow Creek Trailhead. Park along the side of the road, after the cattle grate but before the ranch gate. Enter the ranch on foot.

This hike begins at the historic Indian Head Ranch, which originally operated as a cattle ranch and later as a dude ranch in the late 1800s. Today the ranch

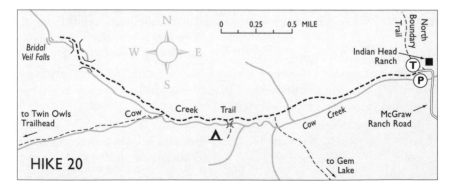

Bring your camera to scenic Bridal Veil Falls.

no longer hosts dudes, but provides critical winter grazing for elk and bighorn sheep. Follow a dirt road past the historic cabins to the Cow Creek Trailhead.

At the trailhead, the North Boundary Trail heads right (north) while the Cow Creek Trail follows an old road west. Take the Cow Creek Trail down the old road that parallels the willow-lined creek. Broad, flowered meadows flank the trail, rising to high green slopes on either side. Summer flowers include orange Indian paintbrush, white cut-leaf daisy, yellow blanket flower, and bright pink locoweed.

Locoweed graces the surrounding meadow with beautiful color, but the pretty plant can cause great harm to cattle. The plant absorbs barium from the soil, and if cattle consume a great quantity, the animals may actually suffer poisoning and act crazy. Thus the name *loco,* which in Spanish means "crazy."

After about 0.6 mile, the road narrows to a trail and gently climbs. Cow Creek drops away to the left down a steep ravine. Pass through a wet area where wild roses thrive, and then arrive at a trail junction 1.2 miles from the trailhead. To the left lie Gem Lake and Balanced Rock. Take the right fork and continue straight ahead (west). Fragrant ponderosa pines flank the trail. Their cinnamon-colored bark, broken into platelets, resembles a thick giraffe's neck. If you're melting in the hot sun, find a pine and sniff a whiff of vanilla from its bark. It smells as if cookies are baking inside!

At 1.4 miles from the trailhead, arrive at a turnoff on the left for Rabbit Ears backcountry campsite. High above the trail a rock formation illustrates the source of this colorful name. The campsite is located in a shady area near Cow Creek and is a good site for family backpacking.

The trail continues west, once again traveling beside Cow Creek. Pass many aspen, grazed and scarred by elk, beside the trail. Measure your progress by the rock formations to the right (north) of the trail. Youngsters can find faces and other recognizable shapes in the outcroppings.

At approximately 1.9 miles from the trailhead, arrive at another junction. The trail to the left heads for the Twin Owls Trailhead. Stay right and begin to climb gently. Rise into the shade of a lodgepole forest. The trail levels and then dodges numerous large and amusing trailside boulders, including a cabin-sized boulder to your right and a shark with a gaping mouth to your left.

Finally arrive at the banks of Cow Creek and some welcome shade and moisture. The remainder of the trail hops along the creek bank, crossing and recrossing the creek, following it upstream to the falls. Just below the falls, hikers must ascend a smooth and steep rock face. The ascent is short, but children might need assistance.

After climbing up a set of stone steps, hikers arrive at Bridal Veil Falls. The impressive falls glides powerfully over rock and bounces upon impact, sending out a lacy veil of spray to onlookers. The cool spot at the falls is excellent for a picnic, a "photo op," or simply a rest stop before you retrace your steps to the trailhead.

21 | DEER MOUNTAIN

Difficulty: strenuous
Distance: 3 miles one way
Usage: high
Starting Elevation: 8930 feet; elevation gain, 1,083 feet
Backcountry Campsite: none
Seasons: summer, fall
Map: USGS 7.5-minute Estes Park

The trail up Deer Mountain offers wonderful views from sunny, open slopes. From the summit, the whole eastern side of the park is visible. The disadvantage of this hike is that the first section is within sight and sound of busy Deer Ridge Junction and its connecting highways. In addition, horse riders heavily use this trail. An early start on this popular hike will bring you up to the summit before the crowds, traffic, and heat and will spare you the thunderstorms that arrive most summer afternoons.

The trailhead is located at Deer Ridge Junction, where US Highways 34 and 36 intersect. The junction is 2.9 miles northwest of the Beaver Meadows

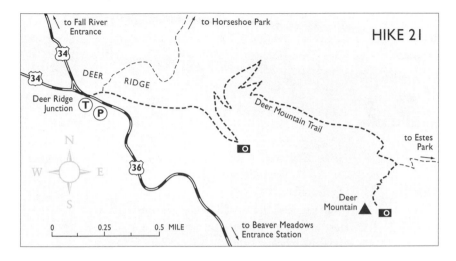

Entrance Station. Park along the shoulder of US Highway 36, just east of the junction, at a trail sign for Deer Mountain.

The trail starts on a sunny slope amid ponderosa pines. Bring plenty to drink on this hike, for much of the trail traverses these bright, dry slopes. At the first junction, bear right. The trail to the left descends into Horseshoe Park.

Ascend the sunny slope amid a variety of sun-loving flowers. There are fine views of the Mummy Range to the northwest and the Front Range and Longs Peak to the south and southwest. After reaching a grove of aspens that has been heavily grazed by elk, the trail begins to switchback up the mountain.

The trail traverses to the west side of the mountain, where there is often a cooling wind. The path becomes shadier as it climbs among conifers. The switchbacks are tiring, but the changing views keep the trip interesting. Views alternate between the sheer east face of Ypsilon Mountain (13,514 feet) and the massive square summit of Longs Peak (14,255 feet), the highest in the park.

After a little more than 1 mile, the trail heads to the north side of the mountain. The switchbacks continue, finally leveling off on a broad, flat shoulder of the mountain. Enter an area studded with the dramatic corpses of lightning-struck limber pines. Because of its location, Deer Mountain is a magnet for thunderstorms, which are very frequent in this part of the Rockies. The mountain is struck often, and the resulting fires have created the strange forest of charred statuesque pines that adorns it. If the skies look threatening, retreat to a lower elevation. See precautions set forth in Chapter 1.

Continue on this broad plateau for 0.6 mile to a spur trail on the right. Take this trail, which leads directly to the summit. Do not continue straight ahead because that trail descends steeply to Estes Park.

Once on the spur trail, it is a short hike to the summit. The trail becomes tough at the end, but the summit is soon attained. The summit offers good views and an excellent spot to picnic.

22 ALLUVIAL FAN TRAIL

Difficulty: nature stroll, handicapped access with assistance
Distance: 0.8 mile one way
Usage: high
Starting Elevation: 8540 feet; elevation gain, 60 feet
Backcountry Campsite: none
Seasons: spring, summer, fall
Map: USGS 7.5-minute Trail Ridge

The Alluvial Fan Trail tours the dramatic changes wrought by the violent Lawn Lake flood of 1982. When the earthen dam burst at Lawn Lake, 14 miles away, a wall of water thirty feet high crashed down the narrow Roaring River Valley, dislodging hundreds of tons of boulders and uprooting trees. The resulting mass of boulders and debris, which fans out from Horseshoe Falls, creates an eerie and strangely beautiful place. Imagine the force with which the boulders and uprooted trees were hurled through the valley above. Now a gentle paved path winds through the debris fan and across a bridge over the cascading river. The boulders that once embodied the terrifying force of the flood now form a giant playground for rock-hopping youngsters. Try visiting the fan at dusk, when the sun is setting over beautiful Endovalley, and the sky above Horseshoe Park glows in lovely pastels.

Drive to Deer Ridge Junction, as described in Hike 21. At the junction, turn right toward Horseshoe Park on US Highway 34. Drive 1.8 miles to the road to the Endovalley picnic area and turn left. (From the Fall River Entrance Station, the road to Endovalley is 2.1 miles west on US Highway 34.) After the turn for Endovalley, the Alluvial Fan Trail is 0.5 mile on your right. Parking is at the trailhead.

The immense volume of water and debris unleashed by the dam redesigned Horseshoe Park. The lake across the road was created when flood material dammed the Fall River. The destructive force of the flood was immense; three campers lost their lives, $31 million in property was destroyed, and muddy floodwater stood 6 feet deep in the streets of Estes Park. For more information on the flood, pick up the Park Service brochure "The Flood of '82," which is available at park visitor centers.

Notice the numerous dead trees standing amid the fan's boulders. Debris carried by the flood choked the trees' root systems. During the summer, these trees are home to a population of birds, including swallows, sapsuckers, flickers, and hairy woodpeckers.

The lake across the road is an excellent place for children to explore. Its wide gravel shores are especially inviting for walking and picnicking. Unfortunately, the lake is not accessible to wheelchairs or strollers.

An intrepid young climber on the Alluvial Fan Trail

23 BEAVER BOARDWALK

Difficulty: nature stroll, handicapped access according to uniform federal accessibility standards
Distance: 0.15-mile boardwalk
Usage: high
Starting Elevation: 8600 feet; elevation gain, none
Backcountry Campsite: none
Seasons: spring, summer, fall
Map: USGS 7.5-minute Trail Ridge

Stroll along the Beaver Boardwalk to see how beavers can change a landscape and create new and fertile environments for diverse plants and animals. The wide wooden boardwalk provides access to a marsh and old beaver ponds. Although most of the beavers have left the site, this stroll above the water is tranquil and lovely, and children love looking down into the clear ponds to see trout, ducks, and aquatic insects. Benches built into the walkway encourage visitors to linger.

Beaver Boardwalk is an accessible nature trail.

Drive to Deer Ridge Junction, as described in Hike 21. Turn left on US Highway 34 and drive 1.9 miles to the Beaver Boardwalk parking area, on the right (north) side of the road.

The wooden boardwalk is accessible to strollers and wheelchairs, although the ramp to the walkway is moderately steep. The boardwalk leads over a marshy area to ponds created by beaver dams. Informative signs along the way, telling the story of the beavers, help you to interpret what you see. Watch for the mallards and other ducks that make their nests in these ponds.

The ponds at the Beaver Boardwalk were created by numerous beaver dams along the Hidden Valley Creek. Before the beavers arrived, Hidden Valley Creek probably coursed through a grassy meadow. A series of beaver dams along the creek inhibited the flow and caused it to overflow its banks, creating shallow ponds. Beavers build dams in order to provide quiet water for food gathering and safe haven for their lodges. The dams raise and stabilize the creek level so that the lodges, and especially their underwater entrances, are surrounded by enough water to discourage most predators from invading the beavers' homes. The living quarters of the lodges are built above the water level, making them cozy and dry. Dusk and dawn are the best times to look for beaver and other wildlife at the ponds.

24 MUMMY RANGE

Difficulty: strenuous
Distance: Mount Chapin, 1.5 miles; Mount Chiquita,
    2.4 miles; Ypsilon Mountain, 3.5 miles—all one way
Usage: low
Starting Elevation: 10,640 feet; elevation gain, 1814 feet
    to Mount Chapin; 2429 feet to Mount Chiquita;
    2874 feet to Ypsilon Mountain
Backcountry Campsite: none
Seasons: summer, fall
Map: USGS 7.5-minute Trail Ridge

The peaks of the Mummy Range make memorable, though very demanding, destinations. The summit views from all three peaks are unforgettable, and the hikes have a wildness that is rare in this well-visited park. There are, however, no trails up the steep and rocky slopes. To add to the difficulty, the starting elevation is high and the elevation gain significant. Yet hiking on the flower-filled slopes of the Mummies is an adventure, and a hike of any length is worthwhile. The Chapin Creek drainage is filled with deer and elk, and the scenery is filled with grandeur. Hikers of all ages and abilities can walk this hike to the flowered meadows near Chapin Pass, but only experienced young hikers, with their parents, should attempt to reach the peaks.

Drive to Deer Ridge Junction, as described in Hike 21. Turn right at the junction and proceed 1.8 miles to Endovalley Road. Turn left at Endovalley Road and drive 2 miles until the pavement ends. Old Fall River Road starts here. Drive up Old Fall River Road for 6.3 miles to the sign for the Chapin Creek Trailhead (Marker 20), on the right side of the road. Parking is available along the road. (From the Fall River Entrance Station, Endovalley Road is 2.1 miles west on US Highway 34.) Because Old Fall River Road is one-way, you must return via Trail Ridge Road, which is 2.4 miles from the trailhead.

The trail begins on a wide path ascending through subalpine fir and spruce. Follow this path uphill for 200 yards to Chapin Pass, where a narrow signed trail heads right (east) toward Mount Chapin.

The trail leads through a wet area filled in the summer with wildflowers. Look for red Indian paintbrush, white mountain bistort, and purple and yellow composites. Pass a small pond that may have deer and elk tracks on its shore. Although similar, elk tracks are approximately 4½ by 3 inches, while deer tracks are only 3 by 2¾ inches and are more heart-shaped.

The trail heads steeply up a ridge. Among the rocks, watch for beautiful Colorado blue columbine, a striking flower of white petals and sky blue sepals. Pause on this ridge to look down to the verdant valleys of Chapin Creek and Cache la Poudre River. The valleys are excellent deer and elk habitat. Arrive in the early morning to see them.

The faint trail winds around the southern side of a bulge on the ridge and leads to tree line. Before the trees completely disappear, the trail passes sprawling islands of *krummholz,* also known as elfinwood. These shrublike trees struggle to survive in the face of severe temperatures, gale winds, and destructive snow and ice. Dead trees on the windward sides of the gnarled tree islands protect the living growth in the center and on the leeward side. Look carefully for deer and elk in this area.

Above tree line, pick up the faint trail that traverses the west-facing slope

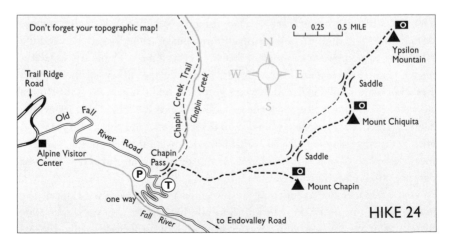

Tundra hiking on Mount Chiquita

of Mount Chapin, the mountain farthest to the right. At 12,454 feet, Mount Chapin is the nearest and the smallest of the three peaks. If it is your goal, simply head upslope toward the summit. Mount Chapin offers a view down its precipitous south-facing wall to dramatic rock spires. The best view, however, is from the higher, eastern summit.

If Mount Chiquita (13,069 feet) is your destination, traverse Mount Chapin on a faint trail, crossing its west slope, heading north to the saddle between the two peaks. Unstable talus slopes and deep tundra turf impede progress. From the saddle, at 12,000 feet, pick a route northeast to the top of Mount Chiquita. The 1000-foot climb to the summit is demanding and requires more time than you might suspect. Unstable rocks again slow progress. From Mount Chiquita's summit, however, a truly spectacular panoramic view opens up, including a breathtaking peek down Chiquita's sheer east face. A good map will help you to identify the universe of mountains, lakes, and valleys spread before you.

To climb Ypsilon Mountain (13,514 feet), descend Chiquita to the saddle and then ascend to Ypsilon's summit. Alternatively, skip the summit of Chiquita altogether. Instead, traverse its western side for 1 mile to reach the afore-mentioned saddle. Both routes are very demanding. Traversing these mountains is much harder than it looks. The slopes are steep, and travel across the trailless tundra is tiring. From the lofty summit of Ypsilon Mountain, the 360-degree view is sensational. Look down the sheer east face for a striking view of Spectacle Lakes, more than 2000 feet below.

The variety of tundra wildflowers on all these slopes is astounding. From early to midsummer, watch for the alpine forget-me-not, a minute flower of the most intense blue. Larger and more common throughout the summer are the rydbergia, or old-man-of-the-mountain. These yellow flowers always face east, away from the prevailing westerly winds. Their peculiar name derives from the whitish hairs that cover leaves and stems to protect against cold and dehydration. The flowers of the alpine tundra have adapted to what is among the severest terrestrial habitats for plants. Their size reflects the limitations of plant growth at these altitudes.

Return to the trailhead by traversing back across the mountain slopes. Or descend a few hundred feet into the green valley above Chapin Creek and hike south to Chapin Pass. The walk below tree line is easier, and the chance of seeing deer is excellent. Be sure not to descend too far into the valley, thus adding unnecessary climbing to your already strenuous hike.

25 LILY MOUNTAIN

Difficulty: moderate
Distance: 1.5 miles one way
Usage: moderate
Starting Elevation: 8780 feet; elevation gain, 1,006 feet
Backcountry Campsite: none
Seasons: summer, fall
Map: USGS 7.5-minute Longs Peak

At 9786 feet, Lily Mountain is hardly monumental, but its summit provides impressive and memorable views. Because the trail is relatively short and only moderately difficult, an ascent of Lily Mountain is an excellent first climb for young and aspiring mountaineers. Its trailhead is also convenient to Estes Park. The only drawback to this trail is that, owing to its proximity to Colorado State Highway 7, vehicular noise can clearly be heard during parts of the hike. Be sure to bring a generous supply of water, for the morning sun can be quite intense.

To reach the trailhead, drive south from Estes Park on Colorado State Highway 7 for 5.7 miles to the trailhead on the west side of the road. Watch for the sign on the highway designating Lily Mountain. Limited parking is available on both sides of the highway.

The trail begins on a dry, east-facing slope of ponderosa pines. Wide, soft, and easy to walk, the trail traverses the mountain, slowly gaining altitude. Early in the morning, deer tracks may be seen in the sandy soil. In summer you hear the constant clicking of flying grasshoppers.

At 0.8 mile, the path loses a little altitude and comes to a junction. Follow the left fork, which heads up the mountain to the northwest. The right fork continues to descend.

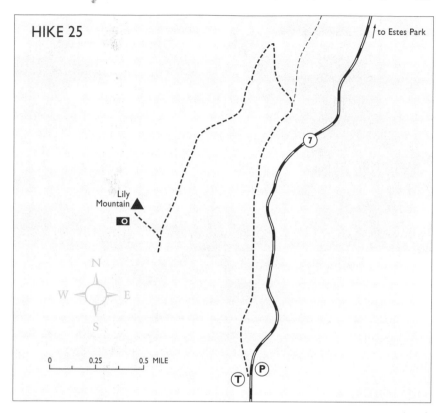

HIKE 25

to Estes Park

Lily Mountain

7

N
W — E
S

0   0.25   0.5 MILE

T   P

From the fork, the trail climbs steeply up a series of short switchbacks. Large boulders dot the mountainside, providing resting places for weary climbers.

Views open to the southeast of Twin Sisters Peaks (11,428 feet), with its green slopes and lumpy rock summit. Enter an area with even larger boulders and good views northeast over Estes Park and Lake Estes. Finally the trail begins to gain altitude seriously amid dense lodgepole pines. Rock cairns mark the way.

The trail suddenly turns to the northwest for the final portion of the ascent. This last section is a scramble over boulders, the direction indicated clearly by cairns. The way is steep, but it is not treacherous.

Once on the summit, Lily Mountain's strategic position becomes apparent. Because the trail ascends the east side of the mountain, the view to the west is hidden until the summit, making the view all the more rewarding. From this lofty perch, the 360-degree view takes in the Mummy Range to the northwest with Mount Chapin (12,454 feet), Mount Chiquita (13,069 feet), and Ypsilon Mountain (13,514 feet); Hallett Peak (12,713 feet) and Flattop Mountain

Longs Peak and Mount Meeker from Lily Mountain

(12,324 feet) to the west; Longs Peak (14,255 feet), Mount Meeker (13,911 feet), and Estes Cone (11,006 feet) to the southwest; Estes Park and Lake Estes to the northeast; and Twin Sisters Peaks to the southeast. Lily Mountain's bare rock summit is a marvelous lunch spot, with a nearly unparalleled view for the altitude gained.

26 LILY LAKE

Difficulty: nature stroll, handicapped accessible according to uniform federal standards of accessibility
Distance: 1-mile loop
Usage: moderate
Starting Elevation: 8900 feet; elevation gain, 6 feet
Backcountry Campsite: none
Seasons: spring, summer, fall
Map: USGS 7.5-minute Longs Peak

Constructed in 1997, this delightful, handicapped-accessible trail takes hikers effortlessly around Lily Lake, providing terrific views of surrounding peaks, good fishing access, and close encounters with a lovely variety of wildflowers in spring and summer. At the lake's west side, a short spur trail, not accessible to wheelchairs, takes hikers to secluded picnic spots with gorgeous views.

Reach Lily Lake by driving south on Route 7, 6.1 miles from the intersection of Route 7 and Route 36 in Estes Park. Lily Lake is located directly across from the former Lily Lake Visitor Center (now closed) on Route 7. A small parking lot abuts the lake on the right side of the road.

Upon arrival at the shore of Lily Lake, you are greeted with tremendous views west to Trail Ridge and the Continental Divide. Begin your hike by walking north, following the lakeside path counterclockwise. On the lake's north side, pause to appreciate the impressive views of Longs Peak and Estes Cone across the lake to the south. The notched summit of Longs Peak (Hike 30) is easily recognized, for it is the highest peak in the park. Estes Cone (Hike 28) is the smaller pyramidal peak with the bare rock summit northeast of Longs Peak. The second-highest peak on the horizon, just east of Longs Peak, is Mount Meeker.

Anglers will find plenty of access and plenty of company at Lily Lake. Summer days attract a flotilla of waders and inflatable craft, as anglers of all ages cast for native cutthroat trout at this spring-fed lake. Despite its name, there are no lily pads to snare lines at Lily Lake, for all of its pond lilies died one winter in the 1930s.

The fully accessible, hard-packed gravel trail goes around the lake and wetlands for nearly 1 mile. Visitors will also find an accessible vault toilet, picnic tables, and small fishing pier at the lake.

Begin your walk by heading right (north) over a wooden bridge. Shortly after the bridge, the accessible trail continues to hug the lakeshore, while a spur trail to the right (not wheelchair accessible) climbs up the ridge above the lake. This spur trail is highly recommended. Climb rock stairs to a sandy trail through the forest where you parallel the lakeshore path. You escape the crowds, and pines artfully frame terrific views of Longs Peak and Mount Meeker. The trail is gorgeous and scented by the sweet vanilla of the ponderosa pines. Rock ledges form natural rest stops along the way. The spur trail ends too soon and you drop to meet the lakeshore trail at the west end of the lake. Bear left at trail junctions to regain the main trail.

All hikers can observe the five-needled limber pines that hug the rocky slopes above the lake. Limber pines are excellent rock climbers. Look for their dramatically gnarled shapes near timberline on ledges you'd think would never support a tree. At the lakeshore, keep your eyes peeled for a grand Douglas-fir. These magnificent trees are fun for youngsters to identify. Find the large, Christmas tree–shaped conifer whose cones are shaggy with three-pronged bracts. The papery bracts resemble the hind legs and tails of mice jumping for shelter between the scales. No other conifer in the park bears cones quite as interesting.

Lily Lake's calm waters reflect Mount Meeker and the distinctive notched summit of Longs Peak.

In summer, a wildflower book is an excellent companion on this hike (a variety are available at the visitor center). Trailside, hikers can readily find yellow blanket flower, wallflower, and golden banner; white cut-leaf daisy, yarrow, and mouse-ear; pink pussy toes, locoweed, and sticky geranium; and pale blue columbine, harebells, and wild flax. There's an especially beautiful field of flax at the west shore of the lake.

Three of these colorful flowers are especially fun to point out to your children. Delicate white mouse-ears are easy to identify because their small white petals come attached in pairs, like tiny mouse ears. Pale pink pussy toes are also true to their name. Their fuzzy, knoblike bracts hide bunches of tiny flowers. Children may like to *gently* touch the furry "toes." A rarer find are the bright pink shooting stars inhabiting the wetter areas of the meadow. These fragrant flowers resemble tiny, dartlike rockets caught in midflight. Native Americans roasted and then ate the roots and leaves of the shooting stars. A good place to find shooting stars is behind the picnic tables, amid the willows, near the end of this hike.

When you've walked to the far west end of the lake (exactly halfway around), look to the right for a wide trail entering from the west. For good views on a half-mile round-trip spur trail, turn right. (This trail is not handicapped accessible.) Almost immediately, turn right again on a wide, rising trail.

Walk up the trail for about a quarter mile to a quiet spot affording gorgeous views over a green valley to the impressive peaks of the Mummy Range. Rock outcrops supply great picnic perches from which to relax and contemplate the scenery. Then retrace your steps back to the Lily Lake Trail and continue your journey around the lake.

The trail continues along the lake's shady south shore. To the north, above the lake, is Lily Mountain (Hike 25), an easy peak for novice climbers. At the southeast edge of the lake, arrive at a marshy area. This is home to the inch-long, striped chorus frog. After a rain, you might be able to hear its call. To initiate a conversation with the frog, take out a pocket comb and run your thumb over the teeth. This sound mimics their call, and you just might get an answer back!

Just before you arrive back at the parking lot, at the southeast edge of the lake, find a small grassy "island." This was an old beaver lodge, now abandoned and grassed over. A few more steps bring you back to the parking area and visitor center.

Hiking Options:

The accessible trail continues south at the east end of the lake for about 0.2 mile, paralleling a service road and then bearing west (right) to shady picnic areas southwest of Lily Lake.

27 EUGENIA MINE

Difficulty: easy
Distance: 1.4 miles one way
Usage: moderate
Starting Elevation: 9400 feet; elevation gain, 508 feet
Backcountry Campsite: 1.8 miles from the trailhead
Seasons: summer, fall
Map: USGS 7.5-minute Longs Peak

This trail leads through pine forest to the ruins of a mine and cabin constructed at the turn of the century. There's not much remaining at the site, so your imagination must fill in what nature has erased. There is, nevertheless, an aura of mystery about the place, and you can send your youngsters searching for clues to the miners' lives amongst the flowers and trees that have grown in the clearing. The site is a good destination for a picnic.

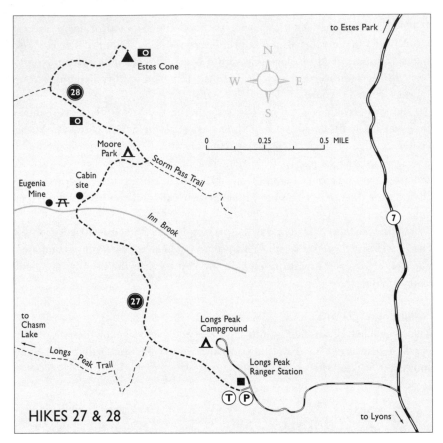

HIKES 27 & 28

From the junction of US Highway 36 and Colorado State Highway 7 in Estes Park, drive south on Colorado State Highway 7 for 9 miles to a road on the right (west) marked by a sign for the Longs Peak Ranger Station and Campground. Turn right and follow this road for 1 mile, and then turn left for the Longs Peak Ranger Station and parking area. The trailhead is next to the ranger station.

Begin on the Longs Peak Trail, which gains nearly 5000 feet in its 8-mile climb to the summit of Longs Peak. From the start, the trail steadily but gently gains altitude. After 0.5 mile, the trail to Eugenia Mine enters from the right (north). Take the right fork, which arrives at the mine in 0.9 mile.

The wide trail rolls gently through a forest of predominantly lodge-pole pine. In the summer the trail is dry and often warm because the tall, straight pines provide little shade. Watch for some old conifers of tremendous girth and unusual configuration to break the monotony. The trail is well used by horses, whose calling card is frequently encountered.

Crossing Inn Brook near the Eugenia Mine and cabin ruins

Watch for squirrel middens along the trail, places where red squirrels cache their pinecones. Occasionally successive generations of squirrels use the same burial place, resulting in enormous middens that can be as long as twenty feet. Evidence of a midden appears as a pile of pinecone cores and scales, sometimes in a hollow log or stump. Pinecone cores look like the remains of a miniature corncob, for squirrels remove the seeds of a pinecone just as people eat corn on the cob.

The mining site, located immediately after Inn Brook, is a good place to picnic. The shallow brook is perfect for children to explore, and the cool water is a welcome relief for hot toes. Along the water's edge, wildflowers flourish. The actual mine and tailing piles are a few hundred feet upstream and west (left) of the cabin. Climb steeply up the slope above the tailings to find several more digging sites.

The once sturdy cabin, whose walls now barely stand, was the property of Carl P. Norwall and his family, who lived at the site and worked the unproductive mine in the early 1900s. The Norwalls had two daughters and a very comfortable, well-furnished home, which included a piano. Reportedly, the piano and the Norwall daughters attracted many young miners and travelers from miles away. Despite the relative elegance by which the Norwalls lived in this pleasant forest clearing, the mine proved unsuccessful. The mine was dug more than 1000 feet into Battle Mountain but delivered no valuable lode. The last filing claim for the mine occurred in 1919. The Norwalls seem to have abandoned the site shortly thereafter.

Children enjoy "discovering" the mine tailings and old cabin and searching for scattered pieces of machinery. One curious piece of machinery hidden amid the trees resembles the Tin Woodsman in *The Wizard of Oz*. Even the setting is right. To a child, it might also look like an ancient space capsule. These types of ruins are not spectacular, but they are fun.

Be careful to leave the site exactly as found. Do not harm, alter, or remove any objects from the site. Children should not climb on the remains, which may be fragile. Finally, never let children enter an abandoned mine.

Hiking Options:

(1) The trail to the right of the cabin heads northeast 0.4 mile to Moore Park, a small, well-flowered meadow. This short and easy trip is highly recommended. Backpackers will find a nice campsite at Moore Park. (2) The same trail reaches Estes Cone (Hike 28) in 1.9 miles—a strenuous but rewarding climb.

28 ESTES CONE

Difficulty: strenuous
Distance: 3.3 miles one way
Usage: moderate
Starting Elevation: 9400 feet; elevation gain, 1,606 feet
Backcountry Campsite: 1.8 miles from the trailhead
Seasons: summer, fall
Map: USGS 7.5-minute Longs Peak

The climb to the summit of Estes Cone through steep forested slopes is not long, but it is very demanding. The summit is extremely satisfying, however, and has exceptional views. Along the way, visit the ruins of Eugenia Mine and the well-flowered meadow of Moore Park.

Drive to the Longs Peak Trailhead and hike to Eugenia Mine, as described in Hike 27. From the mine, the trail heads northeast, gently descending after 0.4 mile to Moore Park. This small meadow is a jewel in midsummer, sporting an abundance of multicolored wildflowers. The campsite at Moore Park would make an excellent destination for young backpackers because it lies only 1.8 miles from the trailhead, and the trail to it gains only 354 feet in elevation.

The trail leads through Moore Park, arriving in 0.1 mile at a junction with the Storm Pass Trail. Turn left (uphill). The trail rises up a sunny south-facing slope covered with lodgepole pines. The break in the trees on the left provides a good

Estes Cone is a prominent landmark.

view of Mount Meeker and Longs Peak. As the trail steepens, limber pines and wildflowers appear. Look for red Indian paintbrush and purple composites.

After 0.6 mile, come to the trail leading to the summit and turn right. The trail switchbacks very steeply up the slope. When the trail disappears, watch for cairns to show the way.

The last portion of the hike requires scrambling over large boulders. Though not particularly dangerous, this stretch is tiring and requires care, especially with young climbers. Very near the top, reach a false summit. Then descend slightly and rise over the last boulders to the peak.

The view from the summit is magnificent in all directions. To the east, you can see Twin Sisters Peaks (11,428 feet); to the northeast, Lily Mountain (9786 feet) (Hike 25); to the north, Lake Estes; to the northwest, Ypsilon Mountain (13,514 feet) and the Mummy Range (Hike 24); to the west, Hallett Peak (12,713 feet) (Hike 17); to the southwest, Battle Mountain (12,044 feet); and to the south, Mount Meeker (13,911 feet) and Longs Peak (14,255 feet) (Hike 30).

Estes Cone can be seen prominently on the west side of Colorado State Highway 7, as well as from various places in the park, including Trail Ridge Road. The peak stands out in the landscape because it is so perfectly cone-shaped. After this difficult climb, look with pride at the rocky summit, which, for one afternoon, was all yours.

29  CHASM LAKE

Difficulty: strenuous
Distance: 4.2 miles one way
Usage: high
Starting Elevation: 9400 feet; elevation gain, 2,360 feet
Backcountry Campsite: 1.2 miles from the trailhead
Seasons: summer, fall
Map: USGS 7.5-minute Longs Peak

This strenuous hike rises through thick forest to alpine tundra and climbs to a large lake dramatically set at the base of the park's tallest peak. The trail to Chasm Lake is one of the finest in the park. Scenic views, abundant wildflowers, and the exceptional beauty of the lake make it one of the park's most popular. To enjoy Chasm Lake to the fullest, start your hike as early as possible. And don't forget your binoculars.

Drive to the Longs Peak Trailhead, as described in Hike 27, and climb the Longs Peak Trail to the junction with the path to Eugenia Mine and Moore

The dramatic east face of Longs Peak from Chasm Lake

Park. Do not turn right; continue straight ahead, climbing amid firs and spruce. At approximately 1 mile, reach Alpine Brook, a cool and welcome rest stop. The trail continues to climb, following the brook. At 1.2 miles from the trailhead, arrive at the Goblins Camp backcountry campsite. If your young campers can carry their packs 1.2 miles and up 820 feet, this is a fine place to camp. The stand of strangely gnarled limber pines probably gave the campsite its name.

After numerous short switchbacks, cross a bridge over Alpine Brook and enter a riot of colorful flowers. A fine view momentarily opens up to the east, revealing the lumpy summit of Twin Sisters Peaks (11,428 feet).

As you climb, the trees get visibly shorter until, at timberline, you pass the last trees able to survive the severe temperatures, short growing season, and howling winds at 10,700 feet. Winds exceeding 200 miles per hour have been measured on Longs Peak in the winter. The strong winds create "banner trees," which have limbs only on their protected (leeward) side.

Switchback up Mills Moraine to a trail junction, about 3 miles from the trailhead. Climbers head to the right for the Boulder Field and the summit of Longs Peak. The left fork takes you to Chasm Lake. There is a toilet near the junction.

To the right at the junction is Jims Grove, which is currently closed for restoration. This area of picturesque limber pines is named for the infamous Estes Park mountain man, Jim Nugent. One of the most colorful characters in the history of this area, Jim lived in Estes Park from the 1860s until his murder in 1874. He was reputed to be a handsome man but only in profile, for a grizzly bear had severely mauled one side of his face. In 1873, Jim accompanied one of the first women to climb Longs Peak. Isabella Bird's fascinating account of the climb and of her travels in the area is memorialized in *A Lady's Life in the Rocky Mountains*.

In the morning the view to the east over the foothills reveals waves of purple resembling the shadowy mountains of a Japanese woodcut. To the west, the massive east face of Longs Peak inspires the mountain climber in everyone.

Follow cairns up Mills Moraine. The trail leads to the edge of the gorge of the Roaring Fork River, where there are views of Peacock Pool below, Columbine Falls spilling over the top of the gorge, and the face of Longs Peak towering above. The trail leading to the falls descends slightly. Walk carefully on the narrow ridge and, if snow remains on this narrow path, proceed with extreme caution.

From Columbine Falls, white rivulets fall over 100 feet to the dark pond of Peacock Pool, which resembles the intense blue "eye" of a peacock feather. Yellow cinquefoil profusely grace the mountainside. The real treat is the abundance of Colorado blue columbine near the head of the falls. With its intense blue sepals and white petals, the Colorado blue columbine is unmistakable.

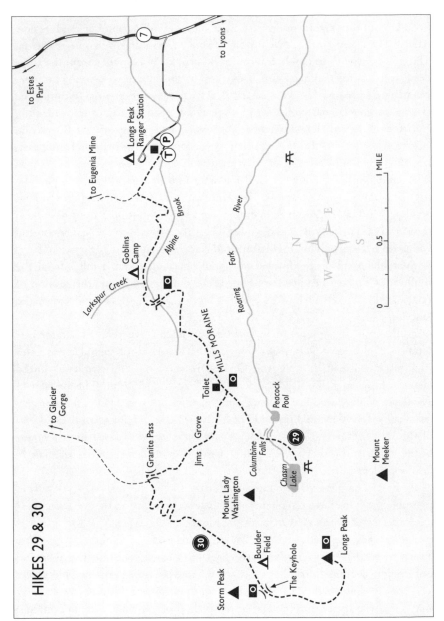

Above the falls, walk through a lushly flowered meadow beside sparkling Roaring Fork River. The intimacy of this wild garden forms a pleasing contrast to the sheer cliffs that loom overhead. Be careful not to stray from the path, for this beautiful meadow is just recovering from overuse.

The trail heads toward the Park Service rescue cabin at the end of the meadow. Travel past the cabin, following cairns marking the easiest route up a ledge. Youngsters might need assistance on this short but tricky ascent.

Chasm Lake is not visible until the top of the ledge is reached. This large tarn was carved by a glacier that flowed down from Longs Peak. When the ice pulled away from the peak, it took part of the mountain with it. The resulting cliffs form a dramatic amphitheater. The sheer east face of Longs Peak, the "Diamond," rises 2500 feet above the lake. The Diamond is a favorite playground for steel-nerved rock climbers. With binoculars, you can watch their rare and terrifying ballet.

The lake is a wonderful place for a well-deserved picnic. Marmots, who den in the rocky slopes, are certain to greet you. Watch also for the smaller and livelier—but rarer—pikas, which may be seen scurrying back and forth over the tundra rocks. Consider yourself very lucky to view these adorable relatives of the rabbit—warming temperatures in the park have decimated their numbers. Temperatures above 78 degrees can kill them. Lastly, for your health and theirs, please do not feed the wildlife.

30 LONGS PEAK

Difficulty: very strenuous
Distance: 8 miles one way
Usage: high
Starting Elevation: 9400 feet; elevation gain, 4,855 feet
Backcountry Campsites: 1.2, 2.8 (group site), and 6
    miles from the trailhead
Season: summer
Map: USGS 7.5-minute Longs Peak

Climbing Longs Peak is a thrilling, once-in-a-lifetime experience. It is also arduous, exhausting, sometimes scary, and potentially dangerous. The highest mountain in the park and the fifteenth highest in the state, Longs Peak is a magnificent mountain whose distinctive summit inspires dreams long after you leave its shadow. Though immensely difficult, the climb is also beautiful and diverse, continuously challenging the hiker with varying terrains. If weather, nerves, or weariness frustrates the climb, the hike to any of a number of milestones is still fun and worthwhile. All summit climbers should be comfortable with boulder-hopping, scrambling, steep drop-offs, and passages along narrow ledges.

Please heed the following precautions with the utmost seriousness. More than thirty-five people have died climbing Longs Peak since 1884. Your level of preparedness will help prevent serious accidents.

■ Start early. Because of the high risk of lightning strikes above tree line, you need to leave the summit by noon, at the latest. Even if the sky looks clear, abide by this time restriction. Storms develop very suddenly and without warning. Adult climbers should allow seven to eight hours for the ascent and five hours for the descent. Families must begin before the sun rises. Depending on the speed of your group, start between 2 AM and 4 AM.

■ Bring a minimum of one quart of liquid per person. Two quarts is better. All water sources on the mountain must be treated before drinking.

■ Prepare for stormy weather by carrying warm clothes and raingear.

■ Watch for symptoms of altitude sickness, and descend immediately if symptoms appear. Make sure all members of your group are acclimatized to high altitude before climbing.

■ Protect your skin by wearing a hat, sunscreen, and lip cream.

■ Do not push an exhausted climber of any age to reach the summit. Most accidents happen on the descent. Resist the urge to be overly goal-oriented. Make this a fun, safe climb.

■ The ascent may be made in two days by camping at one of the designated backcountry sites, but permits must be obtained beforehand. Reservations are often made months in advance for these popular sites.

■ Check snow conditions on the peak with a ranger at the Longs Peak Ranger Station. From October to June, snow usually remains on the summit, making this a *technical* climb, requiring rope, crampons, ice axes, and technical expertise.

■ Above all, turn back when common sense dictates, whether because of illness, weakness, injury, vertigo, time, or the weather. There is always another day!

To climb Longs Peak, follow the trail description for Hike 29 to the intersection atop Mills Moraine about 3 miles from the trailhead. At the junction, head right for the Boulder Field and Longs Peak. Most likely, Longs Peak climbers will be hiking in the pre-dawn darkness to this point. Bring flashlights, watch your footing, and rejoice in the knowledge that the trail will look new on the way down.

Enter a wind-sculpted forest of limber pine called Jims Grove. Climb, rising gently below the east face of Mount Lady Washington. About 0.7 mile from the trail junction at Mills Moraine, reach Granite Pass and the intersection with the North Longs Peak Trail. Granite Pass is a significant achievement. You've

Longs Peak

ascended above 12,000 feet and already climbed more than 2600 feet. (That's over half the vertical feet of the total climb.) Most hikers are likely to feel the thinness of the air at this altitude. Slow your pace, drink plenty of fluids, and apply ample sunscreen.

At the Granite Pass junction, head left (west) and ascend via demanding switchbacks. After the switchbacks, the grade moderates. From Granite Pass, it's about 2 miles to the Boulder Field, an immense moonscape of large rocks tucked dramatically below the sheer north face of Longs. Nine unique back-country campsites lie amid the boulders, hidden within circular stone walls. From these sites, moonlit views of the mountains are exceptional.

From the Boulder Field, it is only 2 miles to the summit, but it's a tough couple of miles. Pin your sights first on the Keyhole, an oval notch in the ridge between Longs and Storm Peaks, about 0.5 mile beyond the Boulder Field and a steep climb of about 500 feet. Shortly before the Keyhole, catch your breath at a stone hut, built in memory of two climbers who perished during a winter ascent in 1925.

Reaching the Keyhole (13,000 feet) is second best only to reaching the summit. Looking beyond the Keyhole to the west, an incredible panorama of magnificent peaks, valleys, lakes, and streams comes into view. Before you spreads an unparalleled view of Glacier Gorge, where three peaks over 13,000 feet form an amphitheater opening to the north. This view alone is well worth the climb.

Check your watch. From the Keyhole, the summit is 1.5 miles away with an elevation gain of about 1200 feet, a hike of at least two hours. If the sky looks stormy already (especially to the west), turn back.

Past the Keyhole, follow red and yellow bull's-eyes. Descend first along an exposed ledge traversing under the west face of Longs. After about 0.3 mile on the ledge, reach the Trough, a long gully filled with loose stones. Ascend the steep gully, taking care not to kick loose rocks that might injure climbers below. Snow often remains in the Trough long into the summer.

After a tiring half-mile climb, reach the Narrows, a ledge that exposes climbers to a steep drop-off. The ledge is wide enough for most (it is not steep and approaches sidewalk width in places), but it does narrow to a couple of feet in one section. Many will find this passage a bit terrifying. After several hundred feet of the Narrows, arrive at the Homestretch, wide slabs of granite lying at a steep incline all the way to the summit. Climbers must make their way up the smooth granite, about 450 vertical feet, to reach Longs' flat summit. The safest way is to use both hands and stay low to the rock, as the angle of incline is very steep.

Finally, arrive at the summit. For posterity, climbers will want to sign the summit register. Then relax and refresh yourself on the multi-acre summit. There are unforgettable views in *all* directions. You have earned the most awe-inspiring view in Rocky Mountain National Park.

Time and weather will pull you from the summit. To descend the Homestretch safely, try a slow fanny descent. Take extra care to reach the Keyhole safely. Descending these steep sections, especially the Trough, can be tricky, especially if you're fatigued.

It is important to keep the group moving to reach tree line before storms move in. Thus weary hikers must push on past the Boulder Field and Granite Pass. Upon descending past Jims Grove, you can relax and congratulate yourself on a climb to remember for a lifetime.

31 COPELAND FALLS

Difficulty: nature stroll, handicapped access with assistance
Distance: 0.3 mile one way
Usage: high
Starting Elevation: 8500 feet; elevation gain, 15 feet
Backcountry Campsite: none
Seasons: spring, summer, fall
Map: USGS 7.5-minute Allens Park

This is a delightful hike on a wide path through a well-flowered subalpine forest to a small waterfall. A great variety of trees, flowers, birds, and small mammals grace the area. In the fall, Rocky Mountain maples and quaking aspens light up the trail with red and yellow.

Drive 12.7 miles south from Estes Park on Colorado State Highway 7 to a signed road on the right (west) leading to the Wild Basin Ranger Station. Turn right on this road and take the first right fork after Wild Basin Lodge onto a narrow, unpaved road marked with signs for the ranger station and Copeland Lake. Follow the unpaved road for 2 miles, past Copeland Lake, to a parking lot at the Wild Basin Ranger Station. The trailhead is located at the south end of the lot.

The hike begins by crossing Hunters Creek on a wooden bridge. Flowers dot the forest floor with color, and aspens tremble in the breeze. The vanilla-like fragrance of the mature ponderosa pines fills the air. The variety of trees, flowering shrubs, and wildflowers creates a lovely, gentle, and immensely inviting setting.

Among the wildflowers, watch for the deep yellow wallflower, whose four-petaled flowers are arranged on its stem like miniature bouquets. The wall-flower got its name by its tendency to grow beside walls. Unpopular girls at

Copeland Falls is a perfect destination for tiny hikers.

HIKES 31, 32 & 33

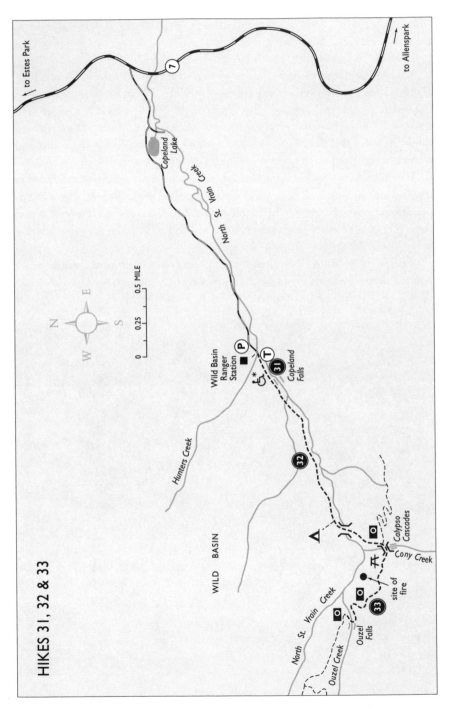

dances were called wallflowers because they also had a tendency to line the dancehall walls. Native Americans and settlers used the seeds of this member of the mustard family as a flavoring.

The abundant flowering shrub beside the trail is wild rose, which sports pink five-petaled blossoms from late May to mid-July. Red rose hips, a fruit savored by many varieties of wildlife, including black bear, replace the flowers in late summer. Native Americans found many medicinal uses for wild rose, including applying the stem, in powdered form, to wounds as a way of reducing scarring. The Indians also blew ground rose petals into sore throats.

The trail is level to Copeland Falls, but may be wet in several places. Puddles are easily dodged by hikers, but a wheelchair or stroller will need assistance.

After 0.3 mile, small Copeland Falls appears. The waterfall is pleasant but unspectacular. Nevertheless, the clearing by the falls makes an excellent picnic spot if the summer crowds have not yet arrived. If the falls are crowded, stroll a short distance up the trail to find a quiet place along the North St. Vrain Creek, where a wealth of gentle riverbank awaits exploration.

Hiking Options:
(1) Continue 1.5 miles and climb 685 feet to Calypso Cascades (see Hike 32).
(2) Continue 2.4 miles and climb 935 feet to Ouzel Falls (see Hike 33).

32 CALYPSO CASCADES

> **Difficulty:** easy
> **Distance:** 1.8 miles one way
> **Usage:** high
> **Starting Elevation:** 8500 feet; elevation gain, 700 feet
> **Backcountry Campsite:** 1.4 miles from the trailhead
> **Seasons:** spring, summer, fall
> **Map:** USGS 7.5-minute Allens Park

This short, scenic hike leads past Copeland Falls through lovely subalpine forest to roaring Calypso Cascades. Wildflowers, a multitude of birds, and the North St. Vrain Creek accompany the hiker. Walk just a little beyond Calypso Cascades to see the site of the 1978 Wild Basin fire, where fireweed blooms radiant pink against a mountainside of blackened trunks. Start early to avoid summer crowds and to secure a parking place at the trailhead.

As described in Hike 31, drive to the Wild Basin Ranger Station and hike

Calypso Cascades

to Copeland Falls. Continue past the falls. The trail becomes sunnier and drier, and to the left are many spur trails leading to North St. Vrain Creek, a couple of yards away.

Rocky Mountain maple appears by the trail, adding brilliant red color in the fall. Look also for the conical stumps of aspens that have been cut by beaver. At one time, this area was rich with this industrious and luxuriously furred rodent. The North St. Vrain Creek was named, in fact, for a nineteenth-century trading post located on this creek, where Indians and mountain men brought their beaver pelts.

Farther down the trail, enter a dense forest of lodgepole pines. Within this forest, just before a substantial wood bridge across the creek, a trail to the right leads to Pine Ridge backcountry campsite. Located only 1.4 miles from and 400 feet higher than the trailhead, this campsite would be a good destination for young backpackers.

At 1.4 miles from the trailhead, you reach the bridge across North St. Vrain Creek, which offers a nice view of the rushing water below. Take a moment to watch this spectacle before beginning the ascent to Calypso Cascades. After the bridge, the serious climb to the falls begins. The well-constructed trail gains 300 feet quickly, leaving North St. Vrain Creek to follow Cony Creek due south. Stairs help you rise rapidly above Cony Creek. Just before Calypso Cascades, there is a large flat boulder upon which to stand for good views over Wild Basin and to the mountains beyond. Soon after, the trail levels and arrives at the cascades.

You are well rewarded for your climb. Water rushes madly over the rocks. The water-chilled air rising from the cascades provides welcome coolness after the climb. In the falls, tree trunks washed bare by the water crisscross the rocks. Just beyond Calypso Cascades are large boulders for picnicking.

Through the month of June, search the ground near the falls in moist shady spots for the Calypso orchid, also known as the fairy slipper. Large patches of this delicate pink flower once blanketed the area. Greedy admirers, however, left few for today's hikers. Be sure you do not crush or pick these beauties; leave them to delight and multiply.

For a worthwhile side trip, walk the trail a short distance west, beyond the falls, to the area burned by the Ouzel Lake fire of August 9, 1978. This area features wildflowers, a graveyard of charred stumps, and good views to the north and east. For more information on this fire, see Hike 33.

Hiking Options:

To visit beautiful Ouzel Falls from Calypso Cascades, continue on the trail to the west for 0.9 mile and an elevation gain of 250 feet (see Hike 33).

33   OUZEL FALLS

Difficulty: moderate
Distance: 2.7 miles one way
Usage: high
Starting Elevation: 8500 feet; elevation gain, 950 feet
Backcountry Campsite: 1.4 miles from the trailhead
Seasons: summer, fall
Map: USGS 7.5-minute Allens Park

This wonderful hike offers great diversity: two fine waterfalls, a lovely trail through subalpine forest, and a traverse through an area badly burned by a fire, but with fine views and marvelous wildflowers. For a measure of solitude, hike in the early morning, before the crowds arrive at the trailhead.

Drive to the Wild Basin Trailhead, as described in Hike 31, and hike 1.8 miles to Calypso Cascades, as described in Hike 32. At the cascades, take the trail to the right, heading west. The trail crosses Cony Creek on two bridges, then leaves the creek to traverse an east-facing slope and enters the area burned by the 1978 fire. Started by lightning at Ouzel Lake, approximately 3 miles away, the fire was the largest in the history of the park, burning 1050 acres. Ten years later, this fire would seem small in comparison to the Yellowstone fire, which burned more than 1000 times as much acreage.

Naturally occurring fires play an important and generally beneficial role in the park. Small, relatively frequent fires create new meadows and shrub lands in a patchwork pattern, thereby providing a rich variety of habitats for plants and wildlife. In this way, fires increase the diversity and populations of flora and fauna. Naturalists know that fire suppression is detrimental. Where natural fires are not allowed, great stores of downed timber and other forest fuels build to dangerous levels. Fire suppression in Yellowstone from 1880 to 1970 contributed to the severity of the 1989 fires, which were fed by ninety years' worth of kindling.

Hiking across this charred mountainside, marvel at the power of fire and the changes it brings. Blackened stumps extend for acres. The area is brightened by the superior views of Longs Peak and Mount Meeker to the northeast and by the bright colors of flowers that have taken over what was once dark forest. Note especially the bright pink fireweed that covers the area. This plant is one of the first to appear after fire strips the land.

Fireweed (Photo by iStockphoto)

Fire created a new feeding area for deer and elk on the open hillside. Watch for them among the fireweed. Admire, too, the innumerable butterflies. Hopping from flower to flower, butterflies sample each blossom through taste organs in their feet. An initial taste determines whether they will insert their long, coiled tongues to sip the nectar.

One activity for the children is to use a small piece of charred wood to make charcoal drawings. Bring a sketchpad and let them draw or make rubbings. Please do not carry out the charcoal; removing natural objects from the park is against regulations.

After 0.4 mile, the trail begins to switchback up to the falls, accompanied by the sound of the rushing waterfall. Continue to climb the rocky slope, following the water music. Ouzel Falls, a magnificent chute of water, plunging a good distance to Ouzel Creek, can best be seen by carefully climbing up the slope on the south side of the falls, just before the bridge over Ouzel Creek. The rocks can be slippery, so children should be closely supervised.

Ouzel Falls was named for the highly entertaining water ouzel, or dipper. Look for this chunky brown bird, which resembles a wren, diving in the rushing water in search of small fish and insects. The superbly adapted dipper is able to walk on the bottom of streams, swim underwater, and fly behind waterfalls. The bird builds its nest on rocky ledges, often within the spray of a waterfall, where its eggs are safe from predators.

Before returning to the trailhead, indulge in a short detour for a marvelous view. Continue up the trail after Ouzel Falls, crossing the bridge over Ouzel Creek. About 100 yards past the bridge is a rocky overlook, offering superb views of Wild Basin, Mount Meeker, and Longs Peak.

Opposite: Hikers take in the view on Trail Ridge.

CHAPTER 3

TRAIL RIDGE HIKES

The trails in this section all lead above tree line, offering magnificent views of surrounding mountains and intimate encounters with the strange and beautiful tundra. These hikes are spectacular and rewarding, but extra precautions must be taken when hiking in the high country. Observe the following guidelines to protect both yourself and the fragile tundra.

FOR YOUR PROTECTION

- Begin hiking early so that you can be off the trail by early afternoon when summer thunderstorms begin. The tundra is a dangerous place during a storm because lightning seeks the tallest object in a landscape, which, unfortunately, may be you.
- Bring warm clothes, including hats and gloves. The average summer temperature is only 50 degrees, and the ever-present wind (averaging 25 miles per hour in the summer) makes wind chill a significant factor.
- Apply sunscreen liberally. The risk of sunburn is greater at high altitudes due to increased ultraviolet radiation.
- Acclimate your group to the park's altitude before trying a long Trail Ridge hike. You'll enjoy the hike more if your body has had a chance to adjust to the thin air.
- Be alert to signs of altitude sickness, including nausea, headaches, dizziness, and shortness of breath. If someone in your group feels uncomfortable, return to a lower altitude at once. Pressing onward would be a serious mistake, especially if children are affected.
- Take it easy; hiking in the high country is more demanding and requires a measured pace.

FOR THE PROTECTION OF THE TUNDRA

- Minimize the impact of off-trail hiking by stepping on rocks whenever possible and by avoiding single-file hiking. Never leave the trail in areas where signs indicate that off-trail travel is prohibited. Such areas include Forest Canyon Overlook (Hike 36), Tundra Trail at Rock Cut (Hike 38), and Fall River Pass Tundra Trail (Hike 40). When in doubt about the permissibility of off-trail hiking, ask a park ranger.
- Never pick tundra flowers; a plant the size of a quarter may be centuries old.
- Carry out all refuse, even organic matter. On the tundra, it can take years for an orange peel to decompose. Furthermore, litter blocks the precious light needed by underlying tundra plants. One naturalist noted that a beer can left behind on the tundra destroys fifty to a hundred years' worth of plant growth and lasts for at least a century.

■ Never enter areas closed for revegetation; it may take a hundred years for trampled tundra to repair itself. Be particularly vigilant in your protection of the tundra—pollution and global warming threaten the sensitive plants and wildlife that inhabit this special region. For more information on these threats, see Chapter 1.

34 INDIAN GAME DRIVE SYSTEM TRAIL

Difficulty: easy
Distance: 0.75 mile one way
Usage: low
Starting Elevation: 11,280 feet; elevation gain, 160 feet
Backcountry Campsite: none
Seasons: summer, early fall
Map: USGS 7.5-minute Trail Ridge

Search for ancient Indian ruins, enter trailless wilderness, spot deer and elk, and enjoy nearly limitless vistas on this excellent hike for older children. For a short hike, head straight to what may be an Indian game drive system (6000-year-old stone walls used for hunting by prehistoric people), or spend hours exploring the surrounding tundra. Because there is no trail to the ruins, a compass and USGS topographic map are necessary—and be sure you know how to use them.

A bit of ancient history will enhance this unusual hike. Archaeologists suspect that the first human presence in Rocky Mountain National Park occurred 10,000 to 15,000 years ago. The finding of crafted stone Clovis projectile points on Trail Ridge suggests that prehistoric peoples occasionally may have used Trail Ridge as an east–west route.

Approximately 8000 years ago, humans began to appear more regularly in these mountains. Numerous projectile points found in the park from this period indicate that seasonal hunting attracted Indians to the mountains and valleys. These ancient people may have constructed game drive systems high on Trail Ridge.

An Indian game drive system is a V-shaped series of low rock walls constructed to funnel game such as elk, sheep, bison, and deer to dugouts at the end of the walls, where Indians lay in wait. Such systems were necessary because natural cover was scarce. More than forty Indian game drive systems have been found along the Front Range.

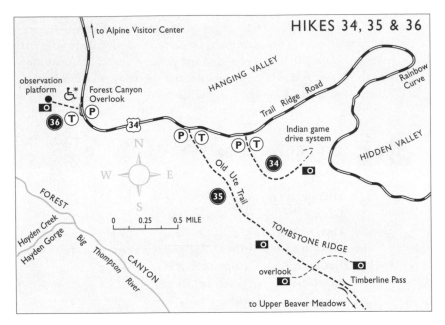

Some archaeologists believe that the rock formations seen on this hike are remnants of an Indian game drive system. The pattern of stones is similar to other game drive systems found in the Rockies. Although some experts question the authenticity of the formation, the hike to the purported relics is still fascinating.

To reach the trailhead, park at a small turnout on Trail Ridge Road, 1.5 miles west of Rainbow Curve. The parking area is the first pullout on the left after Rainbow Curve. For eastbound travelers on Trail Ridge Road, the parking area is the second pullout on the right, 1.4 miles east of Forest Canyon Overlook. To reach Trail Ridge Road from the east, begin at the Beaver Meadows Entrance Station and drive 2.9 miles northwest on US Highway 36 to Deer Ridge Junction. Continue straight ahead on US Highway 34, which at this point becomes Trail Ridge Road. To reach Trail Ridge Road from the west, begin at the Grand Lake Entrance Station and drive north on US Highway 34, which becomes Trail Ridge Road at Milner Pass.

The hike begins at a break in the trees on the thickly covered slope above the turnout. Climb the slope through thick elfinwood on a faint path heading south and over a small rise, emerging from the elfinwood in a level area dotted with islands of *krummholz*. To the right (west) is Tombstone Ridge. Head away from the ridge and around the tree islands in a southeasterly direction.

After hiking through the area of tree islands, arrive at the top of the treeless slope that heads down to Trail Ridge Road. Look carefully on the mountainside

Hiking above tree line offers expansive views.

below. You should see several low rock "walls," badly eroded, in V-shaped configurations, aiming down the mountainside. Climb down for closer examination, but take your time on the steep slope. From the ridge above the slope, enjoy excellent views of the Mummy Range to the north and of Horseshoe Park below.

An early start on this hike brings rich rewards. The *krummholz* woods are a popular habitat for deer and elk in the summer, offering succulent grazing and protection from the wind. Numerous other animals also enjoy the shelter of the *krummholz's* scraggly branches, including snowshoe hares.

Hiking Options:

Just west of Tombstone Ridge is the Upper Old Ute Trail (Hike 35). To reach this trail from the Indian game drive system, hike west through a break in Tombstone Ridge. The Upper Old Ute Trail is clearly visible on the other side of Tombstone Ridge.

35 UPPER OLD UTE TRAIL

Difficulty: moderate
Distance: 2 miles one way
Usage: moderate
Starting Elevation: 11,440 feet; elevation gain, 160 feet
Backcountry Campsite: none
Seasons: summer, early fall
Map: USGS 7.5-minute Trail Ridge

This beautiful tundra trail offers superior views, alpine wildflowers, and Indian history. The easy, mostly level hike leaves you with plenty of energy for exploring

Longs Peak from Old Ute Trail (Photo by Ned Strong)

its many attractions, including off-trail rock scrambling for older youngsters and plenty of wildlife for younger siblings. At dawn or dusk on sunny summer days, deer, elk, and marmots are plentiful. The trail offers the same spectacular scenery as the popular Rock Cut, Fall River Pass, and Forest Canyon Overlook Trails, without the pavement, crowds, and noise.

The Old Ute Trail Trailhead is located on the south side of Trail Ridge Road (US Highway 34), 13 miles from the Beaver Meadows Entrance Station (2 miles west of Rainbow Curve) and 7 miles east of the Alpine Visitor Center (0.8 mile east of Forest Canyon Overlook). Parking is limited at the trailhead; a few more spaces are located a short distance up the road, to the east. The trailhead is marked by a small sign.

Archaeologists believe that prehistoric peoples used the Old Ute Trail for seasonal east–west passage across the Front Range at least 6000 years ago and perhaps as early as 15,000 years ago. Clovis stone projectile points used by Paleo-Indians 10,000 to 15,000 years ago have been found along Trail Ridge. However, it is possible that later Indians might have brought these ancient projectile points to Trail Ridge.

Native Americans regularly used the Old Ute Trail. Although there is no evidence that Indian tribes lived inside what is now Rocky Mountain National Park, the Ute and Arapaho peoples used its meadows for hunting and gathering and traveled across its mountain passes. The Utes resided mainly on the west side of the Rockies, the Arapaho on the east. Both used the rich hunting grounds of the Great Plains and the park's mountain habitats. The common use of hunting grounds led to hostilities and frequent raids across the mountains in the 1800s. One historian recounted the Arapaho belief that the "Man Above created the Rockies as a barrier to separate them and the . . . Utes." Memorable tales of tribal life and battles may be heard at evening campfire programs at the park. Evidence of the Indians' use of this area in the form of arrowheads and stone campfire rings are occasionally still found by fortunate and observant hikers.

The trail begins by climbing a low rise at a very gentle grade. Rock cairns mark the way. To the right is a good view into Forest Canyon; look across the canyon to the high peaks of the Continental Divide.

As the trail rounds a bend, Trail Ridge Road disappears from view. Here, out of sight of the highway, you can imagine what the Utes and Arapaho saw as they crossed over roadless and wild mountains.

To the south, Longs Peak's boxy summit is approximately 10 miles away and almost 3000 feet above you, but on a clear day, it looks well within reach. At this altitude, distances are deceiving. The clarity of the air makes far objects appear closer than they might at lower elevations. This illusion can frustrate hikers for whom a distant peak appears tantalizingly close.

After a quarter mile, the trail heads toward ominous-looking Tombstone Ridge. Look for yellow-bellied marmots sunning themselves on the rocks to the right of the trail. Midmorning and midafternoon are excellent times to watch these chubby relatives of the woodchuck. When startled, they sometimes issue a sharp whistle of alarm (marmots have been called "whistle pigs").

A softer, higher pitched whistle is likely to be the call of the elusive pika, a small, round-eared relative of the rabbit. Called the farmer of the tundra, the little gray pika will most likely be scurrying about gathering flowers and grasses for its winter stockpile. Conservation groups recently filed lawsuits against federal and state agencies, seeking to protect the mountain-dwelling pika against the effects of global warming. Because these small mammals have adapted to cold alpine conditions, pikas are intolerant of high temperatures and can die from overheating when exposed for just a few hours. Once they move to the top of a mountain and find the temperatures still too warm, the pika has no place else to go. By climbing the highest peak in the park, you may be treated to their inimitable squeaks.

Early in the morning, waves of purple peaks define the horizon to the east. Early morning hikers may also catch glimpses of deer and elk grazing on the tundra. Watch for them to the east, after a break in the ridge.

Exploring the ridges is a rewarding and adventurous activity. From atop Tombstone Ridge, enjoy an excellent view of the Mummy Range to the north and winding Trail Ridge Road far below. Do not let children climb unsupervised, however, for the rocks can be slippery and unstable.

Where the trail begins to descend to Windy Gulch, another interesting climb heads off-trail to the right. Head for the rock outcropping just above tree line. This formation looks purposefully constructed, as if Indians had built it to serve as a lookout for game or approaching tribes. The lookout offers splendid views over Forest Canyon to Fern Lake, with Flattop Mountain and Hallett Peak rising dramatically above the lake. Estes Park is visible to the east, Mount Richthofen and the Never Summer Mountains to the west. Again, the rocks can be slippery and unstable.

The lookout marks a good place to turn around. From here, the trail descends to tree line and makes its way to Upper Beaver Meadows, 4.5 miles away, losing almost 3000 feet in elevation from the trailhead.

Hiking Options:
(1) If two cars are available, you can hike a long section of the Old Ute Trail (6.5 downhill miles), from Trail Ridge to Upper Beaver Meadows. (2) The Upper Old Ute Trail can also be easily combined with Hike 34, the Indian Game Drive System Trail.

36 FOREST CANYON OVERLOOK

Difficulty: nature stroll, handicapped access with assistance
Distance: 0.25 mile one way
Usage: high
Starting Elevation: 11,720 feet; elevation loss, 100 feet
Backcountry Campsite: none
Seasons: summer, early fall
Map: USGS 7.5-minute Trail Ridge

Abundant wildflowers, small mammals, fabulous views, and a blast of cold alpine air all await you at Forest Canyon Overlook. A short paved path crosses flowery tundra to an observation platform over vast Forest Canyon. From the overlook, admire the work of glaciers, which carved mountain spires and lake-filled cirques. Across the canyon of the Big Thompson River, 2500 feet below, are the rugged peaks of the Continental Divide. On the rocks below the observation platform, look for marmots and pikas.

To reach Forest Canyon Overlook from the Beaver Meadows Entrance

Take some time to enjoy the view at Forest Canyon Overlook.

Station, drive 2.9 miles west on US Highway 36 to Deer Ridge Junction. Take the left fork and drive US Highway 34—Trail Ridge Road—for 11.1 miles. Forest Canyon Overlook is on the left (west) side of the highway. There is a large parking lot at the overlook.

Although the views from the overlook are truly magnificent, the spot can be desperately overcrowded in the summer. To enjoy the view while listening to the wild wind and the squeak of the pikas, visit Forest Canyon Overlook at dawn or dusk. At that time of day, deer and elk may be grazing on the tundra. Remember to bring binoculars and warm jackets. The first are advisable, but the latter are necessary because of the chilling wind that blows almost constantly at this altitude.

37 SUNDANCE MOUNTAIN

Difficulty: moderate
Distance: 0.5 mile one way
Usage: low
Starting Elevation: 12,000 feet; elevation gain, 466 feet
Backcountry Campsite: none
Seasons: summer, early fall
Map: USGS 7.5-minute Trail Ridge

This is a steep, albeit very short hike that takes you to a rise above Trail Ridge Road. From the rounded peak of Sundance Mountain (actually more like a

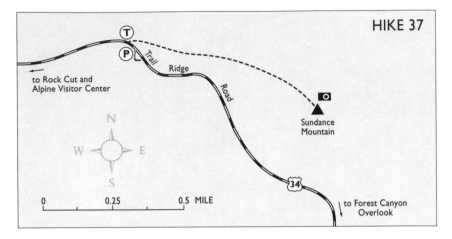

bump), the views are spectacular. This is a fine hike if time is limited or for a child's first climb.

Dress warmly, for it is not unusual for the tundra wind to blow over 30 miles per hour in the summer. Because of the wind-chill factor, a wind of that speed can lower the average 50-degree summer temperature to 28 degrees! Winter winds on Sundance Mountain often reach 70 to 100 miles per hour.

Drive to Deer Ridge Junction, as described in Hike 34. Continue on Trail Ridge Road (US Highway 34) 1.3 miles past Forest Canyon Overlook (if you are approaching from the west, Sundance Mountain is 4.8 miles east of the Alpine Visitor Center). Park at a small turnout on the south side of the highway. Sundance Mountain is visible to the east, across the highway. There is no trailhead sign.

There is no trail up Sundance Mountain; simply choose a route across the treeless tundra. It is impossible to get lost because Trail Ridge Road and the parking area are visible at all times. After you top a false summit, the peak of Sundance Mountain is also always in view. Rather than heading straight up, choose a moderate route that traverses the mountain. Whenever possible, walk on the rocks rather than on the alpine plants.

The brevity of the hike provides time to enjoy the spectacular views. Far to the west rise the Never Summer Mountains, with Mount Richthofen (12,940 feet) rising dramatically above the other peaks of that range. Closer in, look southwest to Forest Canyon and the many peaks rising above it, among them Mount Ida (12,880) and the rounded Terra Tomah Mountain (12,718). To the southeast is the squared summit of Longs Peak (14,255) and its lumpy eastern neighbor, Twin Sisters Peaks (11,428). To the north is an excellent view of the Mummy Range.

This hike also provides an excellent opportunity to observe how glaciers created the dramatic topography of the park. The ice ages began approximately one million years ago. During this era, year-round temperatures that averaged well below freezing kept heavy snowfalls from melting in the summer. Mammoth snowdrifts compacted into ice, forming huge frozen masses in protected areas near mountaintops. As more snow fell, the ice masses, or glaciers, grew into huge tongues of ice 1000 to 1500 feet thick.

Gravity pulled these glaciers down mountains and valleys. Embedded in the glaciers were tons of rock that gouged valley bottoms and steepened valley walls. Successive glaciers scoured the gentle slopes of the mountains, carving the rugged, precipitous peaks that now rise above Forest

Terra Tomah Mountain from the Sundance Mountain Trail

Canyon. You can envision the path and size of these glaciers by imagining that the dense green forest of fir and spruce that covers the canyon to tree line is instead a mass of snow, ice, and rock traveling down the valley. Since the end of the last ice age, approximately 15,000 years ago, conifers have taken over where the glaciers once reigned.

Mount Ida and neighboring Terra Tomah Mountain are a study in glacial contrast. Rounded Terra Tomah Mountain escaped the glacial carving that created the pyramidal shape of Mount Ida. To see this contrast even more dramatically, compare the gentle, unglaciated western slope of Sundance Mountain with the peak's steep, glaciated northern flank. Look over the northern edge of the summit to see how steeply the mountain drops off.

Keep children under close supervision. The modern forces of wind, snow, and ice continue to do the work that the glaciers began. Rock continues to fall from the north side of the mountain to create an ever steeper and more precipitous drop.

The changes in alpine topography are slow and subtle compared to the annual riot of tundra flowers. The short growing season of the alpine zone, less than half that of a more temperate region, nevertheless creates a garden of great variety and rare and delicate beauty. Imagine mountains as spectators; each short season of alpine flowers is like a fireworks display—nearly as bright and just as quickly extinguished.

38 TUNDRA TRAIL AT ROCK CUT

Difficulty: nature stroll, handicapped access with assistance
Distance: 0.5 mile one way
Usage: high
Starting Elevation: 12,050 feet; elevation gain, 260 feet
Backcountry Campsite: none
Seasons: summer, early fall
Map: USGS 7.5-minute Trail Ridge

This trail ascends a flowered tundra slope to reach a fascinating rock formation with superior views. Along the path are informative signs interpreting the natural features seen along the way. At the top is a peak finder that identifies the mountains that entirely surround you. The paved trail is wonderful for those in wheelchairs and for the parents of small children.

Rock Cut is located on Trail Ridge Road, 2.1 miles west of Forest Canyon Overlook and 4 miles east of the Alpine Visitor Center. The trailhead has a large parking area and comfort stations.

This trail is one of the park's most popular walks. In midsummer, the path is crowded, and the parking lot is lined with tour buses. Take this trail in the early

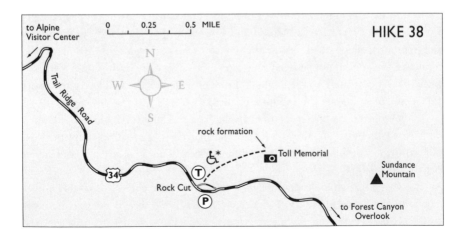

Hikers at Rock Cut on the Tundra Trail

morning, when the winds are calmest and the crowds have not yet arrived. After the hike, stop at the nearby Alpine Visitor Center for a cup of hot chocolate. Dusk is another excellent time for this hike; people are few and the sunsets are spectacular. At dawn or dusk, there is a good chance of seeing deer or elk on the ride up Trail Ridge Road.

The path climbs gently for 0.5 mile to the Toll Memorial, which is located on a rocky bump of Sundance Mountain. The memorial honors Roger Toll, superintendent of the park from 1921 to 1929.

Despite the apparent similarity of the terrain, the trail actually passes several different tundra habitats, each of which supports uniquely adapted plants. The habitats include rocky fellfields, home to cushion plants such as pink moss campion; alpine turfs, which support American bistort and rydbergia (alpine flower); snowbed communities, where snow buttercup and clover-leaved rose can bloom after the late snow melts; and gopher gardens, where yellow alpine avens and blue sky pilot thrive in soil churned and fertilized by pocket gophers.

All these tundra plants are small, generally only a few inches tall. Contrary to what children might guess, these tiny plants are not young. Rather, they are fully formed, mature plants that may be decades old. A fist-sized cushion of moss campion, for example, is probably twenty-five years old or more! Moss campion does not even produce its first blossoms until it is ten years old.

Try a simple experiment with your children. Show them how alpine flowers hug the ground and barely raise their heads above the surface. Then let your children pretend they are tundra flowers. Ask them to crouch down or, even better, lie down on the trail. They will feel a noticeable difference in the temperature close to the ground, for wind speed increases with its distance above the surface. Increased wind velocity, of course, brings greater wind chill and colder temperatures. Alpine plants seek to escape the wind because it robs them of heat and precious moisture, and it tears at them with blowing dirt, ice, and snow.

Next, find a comparatively fast-growing rydbergia, or alpine sunflower, a yellow composite that is the largest, showiest, and one of the most common of all the park's alpine wildflowers. Now ask your children to stand and turn away from the strong, cold wind. They will notice that they are more comfortable with their backs to the wind. So too with the rydbergia, which almost always faces east, away from the prevailing westerly wind. Try using this flower as a natural compass.

If children realize that a plant no bigger than one of their fingers has taken its entire lifetime just to store up enough energy to produce blossoms no bigger than a fingernail, and that the plant must survive ten months of winter each year with winds over 100 miles per hour, the children may look upon such a plant with new respect. You may even see them jump from rock to rock to avoid crushing the alpine flowers on subsequent trips to the tundra.

The trail's first paved turnoff to the right leads to the peak finder at Toll Memorial. The views from the memorial are magnificent. The peak finder identifies mountains as far as 65 miles away. Here too are giant mushroom rocks, geological curiosities that are said to include some of the oldest rocks in the park. The dark heads of the "mushrooms" are over a billion years old.

Farther up the main path, a second rock outcropping to the right provides some climbing for older youngsters. The need to supervise is obvious. The view from the top of these rocks is again spectacular.

Back at the parking lot, carefully cross Trail Ridge Road to look at the rocky slope on the other side of the highway. On sunny days look among the rocks for yellow-bellied marmots and pikas. Look overhead and on the fence railings for the nattily attired black-billed magpie, in formal black and white, and the fluffy robin-sized gray jay.

This trail is a good introduction to more adventurous tundra hikes. If you enjoyed this walk in the "land above the trees," choose another hike from this section for a more intimate encounter.

39 MARMOT POINT

Difficulty: easy
Distance: 0.5 mile one way
Usage: moderate
Starting Elevation: 11,589 feet; elevation gain, 320 feet
Backcountry Campsite: none
Seasons: summer, early fall
Map: USGS 7.5-minute Trail Ridge

This short hike to the top of Marmot Point is a pleasant way to experience the alpine tundra and to stretch your legs after the long ride up Old Fall River Road. This walk, however, sticks close to the road and therefore lacks some of the beauty and serenity of other tundra hikes. Nevertheless, Marmot Point offers magnificent views and a chance to see wildflowers and wildlife.

Drive Old Fall River Road, as described in Hike 24, 1.4 miles past the Chapin Creek Trailhead to a turnout on the right side of the road at Marker 24, just 0.5 mile east of the Alpine Visitor Center (AVC). The turnout is just before a fenced area containing the AVC's water treatment pond. Marmot Point is the cone-shaped peak east of the road. Or drive Trail Ridge Road to the AVC and hike down Old Fall River Road 0.5 mile (elevation loss, 200 feet).

The hike begins by heading up an old roadbed to an unused parking area. A footpath begins from the uphill side of the lot but soon disappears, leaving you to choose your own route to the top of Marmot Point.

In midsummer numerous alpine wildflowers cover the slope. The best way to see the tiny, brightly colored blooms is to crouch down to their level. Many

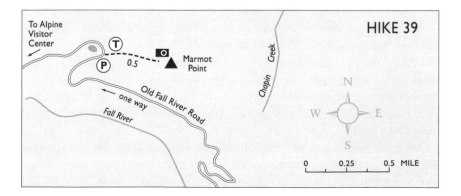

If you're lucky you'll spot a yellow-bellied marmot at Marmot Point.

are no larger than a dime. Their variety and intensity of color, however, more than compensate for their diminutive size. It is a miracle that any flowers can survive on this slope given the fleeting and tenuous eight-week growing season of July. It has been said that there are two seasons on the tundra: winter and the Fourth of July.

The clarity of the air and brightness of the light make the colors of the flowers appear more intense and make the surrounding mountains stand out sharply in detail. There is 25 percent more light at this altitude than at sea level, so distant objects appear deceptively near. The cool tundra air also seems fresher than the air at lower elevations. It is filled with smells of newly melted and newly fallen snow. It seems precious too as you gasp for more of it, while climbing up this relatively gentle slope. The air contains less oxygen than at sea level, so your heart and lungs must work harder.

This is a good hike to look for alpine wildlife. Scan the slopes for white-tailed ptarmigan, a grouse that lives above tree line. Indeed, the male is the only bird that lives on the tundra year-round (females winter below tree line). You need sharp eyes to spot a ptarmigan, for they are almost perfectly camouflaged in their summer plumage of brown and white. The birds are adept at locating each other, however, for ptarmigans are monogamous, reuniting with the same mates each spring.

Look too for the elusive pika. This small, round-eared relative of the rabbit may be seen gathering plants to store for the winter. During the short tundra summer, pikas must gather enough greenery to last for nine or ten cold and barren months. The pika is one of the few mammals who remain active on the tundra in the winter, albeit mostly beneath the protective cover of rock piles. With round bodies, prominent ears, no visible tail, and weighing just five ounces, pikas are irresistibly cute. Loss of habitat due to global warming may soon place these adorable creatures on the Endangered Species list. The park has already lost two lower altitude populations of pikas.

Watch also for the namesake of this hill, the yellow-bellied marmot. This endearing western woodchuck is most often seen on sunny days, warming itself on the rocks. Unlike the pika, marmots prepare for winter by eating themselves to shiny-furred chubbiness. They live off their accumulated fat while they hibernate in rocky dens until spring.

The ropelike mounds of soil on the slopes of Marmot Point are the work of the seldom-seen pocket gopher. As an earthmover, the pocket gopher is almost unequaled. In a single night the gopher can tunnel more than 100 feet! Imagine a network of tunnels roughly one foot beneath the surface of the ground, dug through rocky, half-frozen soil with teeth and claws in complete darkness. Not even earthworms brave the soil at this altitude.

Using binoculars, scan the slopes below the Alpine Visitor Center for grazing elk. You may be surprised to see quite a few elk among the trees.

Marmot Point offers views east and north to the gentle western slopes of the Mummy Range. There are also good views into the valleys of Chapin Creek and Fall River.

40 FALL RIVER PASS TUNDRA TRAIL

Difficulty: easy
Distance: 0.25 mile one way
Usage: high
Starting Elevation: 11,796 feet; elevation gain, 209 feet
Backcountry Campsite: none
Seasons: summer, early fall
Map: USGS 7.5-minute Fall River Pass

A short but steep trail from the Alpine Visitor Center (AVC) climbs to a fine vantage point from which to view the spectacular Trail Ridge scenery. This well-used path at the busy visitor center is usually crowded and windy, but the short walk is worth the effort. Combine this walk with a visit to the AVC exhibits or one of the many activities available at the center.

Everyone will love the view at Fall River Pass—but dress warmly!

The Alpine Visitor Center is located on Trail Ridge Road 17.1 miles from Deer Ridge Junction and 21 miles from the Grand Lake Entrance Station.

The trail begins just west of the Fall River Store, climbing a set of stairs set into the slope. Keep on the path; the tundra is already badly trampled in this area. Because of the slow growth of tundra plants, it will take several hundred years for this damaged area to recover.

In summer, minute tundra wildflowers grace the slope. Take a moment to look for them among the rocks. These small plants hug the ground to escape the chilling, desiccating winds.

The top of the rise brings an awe-inspiring 360-degree view. To the west is the Never Summer Mountains with its permanent snowfields; to the north are Wyoming's Medicine Bow Mountains, 44 miles away; immediately to the east is the Mummy Range; and to the south, Forest Canyon lies more than 2000 feet below. On the west side of Forest Canyon rise the dramatic peaks of the Continental Divide.

Watch also for deer or elk in the Chapin Creek Valley to the east. The grasses and shrubs of the valley make it prime habitat. Binoculars are helpful. Look also for brown-capped rosy finches. The small bird spends summers on the tundra and winters at lower elevations.

After reaching the high point in the trail, descend slightly to an observation platform to the west for more fine views. A sign indicates the role of the glaciers in sculpting this scenery. Sixty square miles of tundra stretch out before you. Take a moment to enjoy the superlative sights. Rocky Mountain National Park contains the largest expanse of protected tundra south of Alaska.

As you appreciate the expansive view from this platform, observe the exceptional quality of the air. According to the Park Service, visibility during the summer is usually at least 85 miles, while on some days visibility may be more than 150 miles. Occasionally, however, visibility is impaired by manmade pollution. Most of the pollution that reduces air quality in the park comes from industrial regions in the Southwest, as far away as Southern California, Arizona, and New Mexico. A monitoring site for atmospheric visibility is located a few miles east of here, at the Gore Range Overlook. At this site, the effects of pollution are monitored to determine the extent of regional emissions.

41 FALL RIVER PASS TO FOREST CANYON PASS

Difficulty: easy
Distance: 1.9 miles one way
Usage: low
Starting Elevation: 11,796 feet; elevation loss, 476 feet
Backcountry Campsite: none
Seasons: summer, early fall
Map: USGS 7.5-minute Fall River Pass

This short walk offers fabulous views and a nearly effortless entry into the alpine environment. Because the elevation gain is slight, it is easily managed by children. Deer and elk may be seen near Forest Canyon Pass.

Drive to the Alpine Visitor Center, as described in Hike 40. The trail begins across the street from the center and follows the former bed of the Old Fall River Road, which was built in the early 1900s and was replaced by Trail Ridge Road in 1934. Fortunately for hikers, the section of the old road from Fall River Pass to Milner Pass has been allowed to return to tundra.

Sounds of birds and the ever-present rushing wind make busy Trail Ridge Road seem far away even at the start of this hike. The wind is a critical factor in determining the look and feel of the tundra.

Its work is evident in the diminutive height of all tundra plants, which hug the ground for warmth and to escape the desiccating and chilling wind. Barren patches of rock, where the wind has stripped the surface bare of soil, are common. In winter the wind can howl across the peaks at over 200 miles per hour. Even in summer it is not unusual to encounter winds of 40 miles per hour. Yet the wind is also life-giving, scattering the seeds and pollen of the alpine plants.

In summer a wide variety of wildflowers grace this trail, including alpine evens, western yellow paintbrush, moss campion, alpine clover, and rydbergia, or alpine sunflower.

The wind is your ever-present hiking companion on the alpine tundra.

Also look for the white-tailed ptarmigan, a common tundra inhabitant that is extremely difficult to spot. The perfect camouflage of this small grouse makes it nearly invisible among the rocks and grasses. If you see a ptarmigan, look for chicks following the adult.

The trail offers tremendous views. To the west is a spectacular view of the Never Summer Mountains. Perpetual snowbanks on their eastern slopes inspired the Arapaho to name the range *Ne-chibe-chii,* translated as "Never-No-Summer."

A short distance down the trail, pass the first of a series of five small ponds. In the mud by the water, look for the tracks of deer and elk. Elk tracks are easy to distinguish by their longer, wider, and more rounded appearance. An elk track measures approximately 4½ by 3 inches, while those of a deer are only 3 by 2¾ inches and are more heart-shaped.

Look into the ponds for the tiny, almost transparent fairy shrimp darting about in the water, its ten legs propelling it here and there erratically. By parthenogenesis (reproduction without the opposite sex) as well as fertilization, the prehistoric-looking fairy shrimp produces winter eggs with a shell thick enough to endure the freezing of its pond.

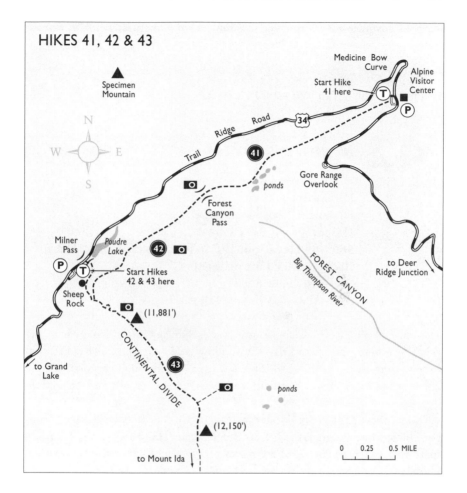

HIKES 41, 42 & 43

Medicine Bow Curve

Specimen Mountain

Start Hike 41 here

Alpine Visitor Center

Ridge Road 34

Trail

41

ponds

Gore Range Overlook

Forest Canyon Pass

Milner Pass

Poudre Lake

42

Start Hikes 42 & 43 here

Sheep Rock

to Grand Lake

CONTINENTAL DIVIDE

(11,881')

43

(12,150')

to Mount Ida

FOREST CANYON

Big Thompson River

to Deer Ridge Junction

ponds

0   0.25   0.5 MILE

After passing the ponds, reach Forest Canyon Pass, where chances are good of seeing elk and deer in the patches of small, gnarled trees known as *krummholz*. During the day, the animals retreat to the *krummholz* for cover. Deer and elk usually feed at dawn or dusk.

Forest Canyon Pass features a superb view into spruce-covered, glacially carved Forest Canyon. Originally, the valley was a deep, narrow, V-shaped canyon eroded about 28 million years ago by the ancestor of the Big Thompson River. During the subsequent ice ages, immense walls of ice, 1000 to 1500 feet thick, flowed slowly from the mountains down this valley. The huge slug of ice carved the canyon into its present U-shaped configuration, broadening the floor of the valley and steepening its sides. This U shape is characteristic of glacially formed valleys and can be seen elsewhere in the park, notably in

Spruce Canyon and the Kawuneeche Valley. From Forest Canyon Pass, retrace your steps to the trailhead.

Hiking Options:
Combine this hike with Hike 42 for a one-way trip of 4.2 miles.

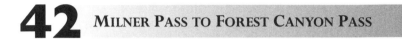

42 MILNER PASS TO FOREST CANYON PASS

Difficulty: moderate
Distance: 2.3 miles one way
Usage: low
Starting Elevation: 10,750 feet; elevation gain, 530 feet
Backcountry Campsite: none
Seasons: summer, fall
Map: USGS 7.5-minute Fall River Pass

This very scenic hike leads above tree line to Forest Canyon Pass, where the views of Forest Canyon and the surrounding peaks are spectacular. The trail travels from subalpine forest to the tundra, passing through two dramatically different life zones. It is an excellent trail for sighting deer, elk, and the wildlife of the subalpine forest.

Milner Pass Trailhead is located at the south end of Poudre Lake. From the Alpine Visitor Center, drive Trail Ridge Road (US Highway 34) 4.3 miles southwest to the trailhead, where parking is available. From the Grand Lake Entrance Station, drive US Highway 34 for 16.7 miles to the trailhead.

The hike begins on the smooth, well-trodden path around the south end of Poudre Lake. The rise in elevation is gradual at first. The trail then steepens and climbs toward the interesting rock formation of Sheep Rock, a half mile from the trailhead. The rock has been so named because of the presence of bighorn sheep in the area, primarily in the summer. Their breeding ground is on the west side of Specimen Mountain, just northeast of the Milner Pass Trailhead. Specimen Mountain, which rises to 12,489 feet, is clearly visible from most sections of the trail.

Please do not approach or harass bighorn sheep. They are extremely susceptible to stress, and the fear of an approaching hiker can actually cause them physical harm. If you are lucky enough to encounter a bighorn on the trail, remain still and silent. The bighorn is a curious animal and, if not frightened, may even approach you!

After Sheep Rock, a rock cairn on the right marks a trail that climbs steeply to the south. This trail leads to the Continental Divide and is described in Hike 43. Stay to the left.

Thus far the trail has passed through a forest of subalpine fir and Engelmann spruce. The two conifers are easily distinguished by feeling their needles. A subalpine fir has flat needles that are rounded at the end and soft to the touch. The needles of the spruce, on the other hand, are more or less square in cross-section and sharp at the tip. To remember the spruce, associate the "s" of spruce with sharp and square. In Rocky Mountain National Park, subalpine forest occurs between altitudes of 9000 and 11,500 feet.

By trapping great quantities of snow, the subalpine forest creates a moist environment. Consequently a wide variety of moisture-loving flowers are found here in the summer, including yellow monkeyflowers and marsh marigolds, white mountain figwort, and tall blue chiming bells. Broom huckleberry, a variety of wild blueberry, provides extensive ground cover in the subalpine forest, carpeting the forest floor in late summer with sweet berries. Also look for subalpine Jacob's ladder, whose flowers are dainty blue and whose leaves have a skunklike aroma when crushed.

During this portion of the hike, be alert for wildlife. While enjoying a snack on one of the downed trees by the trail, watch for golden-mantled ground squirrels and chipmunks, both of which are common here. Far less often seen are weasels and snowshoe hares. You may hear but not see scolding chickarees, or red squirrels, who will most likely be hidden from view high in a tree. Another, more visible scold is Clark's nutcracker, a handsome, gray relative of jays and crows, with black and white wings and a sharp, awl-shaped beak. Its loud dissonant squawking is a familiar sound in the subalpine forest. Other common, more melodious birds of the forest include the fluffy gray jay and the gray-headed junco.

Approximately 1 mile from the trailhead, the trail widens to an old roadbed, where the hiking is easy. The track is all that remains of the western half of the Old Fall River Road, which was built in the early 1900s. The road was in use until 1932, when it was replaced by Trail Ridge Road. The steep eastern section of Old Fall River Road is still maintained and makes an interesting drive.

Climbing toward Forest Canyon Pass, notice how the trees become progressively shorter with elevation. At this altitude the growing seasons are so short that a tree that stands no taller than a four-foot-tall child may be more than four hundred years old. The gnarled, shrubby clumps of firs and spruces that grow near the pass are known as *krummholz,* a German word meaning "crooked wood." The *krummholz* zone is the area right below tree line where trees struggle to survive under tremendously adverse conditions. Strong wind, low temperatures, and blowing snow bombard the trees, stunting their growth and distorting their shape. The trees survive because they tolerate low temperatures and are able to grow close to the ground, where they trap moisture and partially escape the desiccating and destructive winds. Trees on the windward side of a *krummholz* clump provide protection for those in the center and on the leeward side. As the windward trees in the clump die off, the protected trees in their lee extend the clump by layering (i.e., limbs that touch the ground sprout new roots).

The *krummholz* is a favorite habitat for mule deer and elk. In the summer, herds of elk retreat to this area to escape the heat of the lower elevations. The plants growing in and around the *krummholz* provide choice food. The tree islands also provide cover from the winds and cold of the tundra, as well as from the tourists traveling on Trail Ridge Road. Hike this area in the early morning or at dusk for a chance to see the animals feeding.

Continue a short distance above the *krummholz* to Forest Canyon Pass, a magnificent place to explore. The view from the pass is incredible. Mountains and green valleys are visible in all directions, but the peaks of the Continental Divide and the Never Summer Mountains dominate the scene.

The superlative view is not the sole reward of this hike. The tundra is a land of surprises. From a distance it looks gray and barren, but upon closer examination, it is rich with color, diversity, and drama. In the summer, tiny flowers carpet the tundra with multicolored miniature blossoms. With the exception of cold temperatures, growing conditions on the tundra are comparable to those on a desert. In both habitats, plants have to endure insufficient and erratic moisture, intense sun, strong winds, and high evaporation rates. The growing season above tree line is considerably colder and briefer than at lower, more temperate elevations. It lasts only six to eight weeks, during which time the average high temperature is only 50 degrees. For five months of the year, the temperature does not climb above 32 degrees.

Hiking Options:

(1) An interesting short extension to this hike is to walk a half mile farther on the trail to a series of ponds just off the trail. The ponds are visible from Forest Canyon Pass. In the mud surrounding the ponds, elk and deer tracks can be clearly seen. In addition, the ponds contain the prehistoric-looking, almost-too-tiny-to-see fairy shrimp. (2) The trail from Milner Pass continues all the way to the Alpine Visitor Center. The center is 1.9 miles from Forest Canyon Pass (Hike 41). The whole trail is best done (downhill) from the visitor center to Milner Pass. The round-trip distance to the center from the Milner Pass Trailhead is 8.4 miles, with an elevation gain of 1038 feet.

43 MILNER PASS ALONG THE CONTINENTAL DIVIDE

Difficulty: strenuous
Distance: 2.1 miles one way
Usage: low
Starting Elevation: 10,750 feet; elevation gain, 1400 feet
Backcountry Campsite: none
Seasons: summer, early fall
Map: USGS 7.5-minute Fall River Pass

This spectacular high-country hike offers exceptional views on a short but very steep trail. For children (and their parents), there are marmots, pikas, deer, and elk. This hike is a good introduction to the "land above the trees" for older youngsters who don't mind a little bit of tough hiking.

Drive to Milner Pass Trailhead, as described in Hike 42. The hike begins on the Ute Trail. After 0.8 mile, look for a rock cairn on the right that marks the spur trail leading along the Continental Divide. From this point, the trail heads

Mount Ida from the Milner Pass Trail

south. This trail is considerably steeper and narrower than the one just left. Fortunately, tree line is not far away. After approximately a half mile of switchbacks, you reach tree line, on the west side of an unnamed 11,881-foot peak. South of this peak, the hiking is divine as the trail easily traverses a series of unnamed ridges and bumps.

The views along this traverse are worth the effort. The Never Summer Mountains are to the west, Specimen Mountain (12,489 feet) rises to the north, and the trail leads south to Mount Ida (12,880 feet). With such clear landmarks, and with the trail nearly always in view, it is possible to safely hike cross-country and explore. An excellent off-trail destination is the ridge just south of Point 11,881, on the Continental Divide. Walk carefully across the tundra to the top of this ridge. To minimize impact, remember to walk side by side rather than single file, tread lightly, and step on rocks wherever possible. From the ridge, you can see hundreds of feet downslope to a group of unnamed ponds set among *krummholz*. The ponds are often visited by elk in summer. A pair of binoculars will help you find the elk.

Back on the trail, hiking continues to be easy until you reach a second unnamed peak (12,150 feet), approximately 2.1 miles from the trailhead. After this point, the going gets tough as the trail becomes faint or nonexistent and traverses the slope amid loose rock. To add to the difficulty, the grade of the slope steepens considerably. This portion of the hike is not advisable for children and is best attempted by those bent on reaching the tough, but worthwhile goal of Mount Ida (12,880 feet), 2 miles away.

On the way back to the trailhead, look for yellow-bellied marmots sunning themselves on the rocks. According to one park ranger, marmots are born "retired." They spend their days lazily eating, sleeping, and resting in the sun, content simply to watch the world go by.

Also inhabiting the rocky areas of the high country are the pikas. In contrast to the marmots, these small, round-eared relatives of the rabbit are shy and industrious. Unlike marmots, pikas do not hibernate and therefore need a large supply of food for the long winter. Throughout the summer, pikas scurry across the rocks, gathering plants and grasses for their winter food supply. They spread out the greenery on the rocks to dry. When the hay is ready, the pikas then store it in piles beneath the rocks.

Also look for evidence of pocket gophers in the form of serpentine gopher garlands. These long, narrow ropelike mounds are the vestiges of tunnels that gophers dig under the snow in the winter. The disturbed and fertilized soil is thought to provide a good seedbed for tundra flowers.

Opposite: Mount Craig (Mount Baldy) from the East Inlet Trail

CHAPTER 4

WEST SIDE HIKES

The hikes in this section are located west of the Continental Divide. All are within easy driving distance of Grand Lake. The west side of the park is delightfully quieter than the east, and the trails are likely to be far less crowded. The west side is also generally cooler, wetter, and more lushly vegetated. Although west-side vistas are generally less dramatic than those of the east, its trails are well worth visiting. In spring and fall, wildlife abounds in the Kawuneeche Valley. If you are traveling from the east side to the west side, check for local variations in weather. It may be cool and rainy on the west side when the eastern slope is basking in warm sunshine.

The severe epidemic of the mountain pine beetle, fueled by global warming, has devastated the vast lodgepole pine forests of the park's west side. Consequently, visitors must exercise great caution when hiking or camping near stands of dead trees. These areas must be avoided during high winds. Before hiking in areas of dead trees, please consult the precautions described in this book's Introduction. The causes of this epidemic are described in Chapter 1.

44 POUDRE RIVER TRAIL

Difficulty: easy
Distance: 1 to 2.5 miles one way
Usage: low
Starting Elevation: 10,750 feet; elevation gain, 160 feet
Backcountry Campsites: none
Seasons: summer, fall
Map: USGS 7.5-minute Fall River Pass

This hike beside the Cache la Poudre River is a pleasant, meandering journey with no specific goal. It is simply an enjoyable, almost level walk that leads briefly through subalpine forest to the wet, rich deer and elk habitat along the Poudre River. At dawn or dusk the chances of seeing deer and elk are excellent. Try this hike as an early morning excursion, after which you can get a hot chocolate at the Alpine Visitor Center and refuel for another hike. At any hour, the Poudre River Trail is a relaxing, uncrowded hike ideal for spontaneous exploring.

The trailhead is located on the west side of Trail Ridge Road, 4 miles southwest of the Alpine Visitor Center and 17 miles north of the Grand Lake

Entrance Station. From the Beaver Meadows Entrance Station, the trailhead is 24 miles west on Trail Ridge Road. Park at a turnout on the west side of the road, 0.1 mile north of the parking lot for the Crater (Hike 45).

The Cache la Poudre River was named by French fur trappers, who hid a quantity of gunpowder beside the river in the fall of 1836. Returning in the spring for the powder, the trappers found their cache, and thereafter referred to the river as the hiding place for the powder—*cache la poudre.*

The hike starts on a narrow trail through a subalpine forest of Engelmann spruce and subalpine fir. You can easily learn to tell the difference between these two conifers by feeling their needles. If the needles feel sharp, they belong to the spruce; if the needles feel soft, they belong to the fir. In late summer, look on the forest floor for the sweet berries of the broom huckleberry. Look also for wildflowers, including yellow monkeyflowers, white mountain figwort (parrot's beak), and tall blue chiming bells. The names of these flowers graphically (and imaginatively) describe their appearance. See if your children can find these flowers based on their creative names.

After approximately 0.25 mile, the trail leaves the forest to follow the marshy drainage of the Cache la Poudre River. Here the trail is pleasant but occasionally wet as it meanders next to the river and crosses numerous small streams. Notice how the plants and flowers change as the trail approaches and leaves the banks of the river. US Highway 34 is unfortunately just across the narrow valley, and although the road is obscured by trees, car noises may be audible. Early in the morning, however, traffic and noise are negligible.

Look for signs of deer and elk as you walk along the willow-lined trail. Their prints are visible in the moist soil. Elk tracks are easy to distinguish from deer tracks, for elk tracks are larger, wider, and more rounded, measuring approximately 4½ by 3 inches. A deer track is smaller and more heart-shaped, usually only 3 by 2¾ inches. Deer and elk generally graze or browse at dawn and dusk, retreating to the safety of the forest during the day and at night.

The American elk, or wapiti, is an impressive animal. Bulls reach 5 feet at the shoulder and weigh 750 pounds. A mature bull's antlers can span 5 feet and weigh 25 pounds. In summer, elk are reddish-brown on their sides, with a large yellow-white rump patch, and dark brown neck. In fall, their coat turns a darker gray-brown. If you are lucky enough to sight a herd of elk close up, you will not forget it.

Large herds of elk once ranged across the entire United States, from the Atlantic to the Pacific, Canada to Mexico. After the European invasion of the continent, however, the elk population declined dramatically. By 1800 the eastern elk herds were completely gone as a result of market hunting and loss of

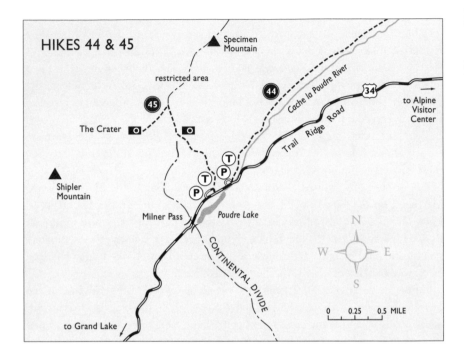

habitat. By 1900, elk survived in the Rockies only in isolated locations. In fact, the current healthy population of elk in Rocky Mountain National Park descends from animals imported from Yellowstone National Park in the 1930s.

Mule deer are considerably smaller than elk. Males stand 3.5 feet at the shoulder and weigh 250 pounds. The deer are reddish-tan in summer and grayish-brown in winter, with a small white rump patch and black-tipped white tail. Their large, mulelike ears are extremely sensitive and can move independently, endowing the deer with a superior sense of hearing. You are likely to see many mule deer throughout the park if you are up early or out at dusk. During the summer, does are frequently seen with their twin spotted fawns, provoking squeals of delight from children who are familiar with Bambi.

Walk as far as you wish along the river. In wet seasons a muddy trail might precipitate an early retreat. Before returning to the trailhead, you may want to ask your children to think like a deer or an elk and tell you why they would choose to live in this valley. Perhaps they will mention the easily accessible water; the wealth of food in the form of grasses, flowers, shrubs, and small trees; the cover provided by the forest in times of danger; the shade of the trees in summer; or the undergrowth where camouflaged fawns can hide.

45 THE CRATER

Difficulty: moderate
Distance: 1 mile one way
Usage: moderate
Starting Elevation: 10,750 feet; elevation gain, 730 feet
Backcountry Campsite: none
Seasons: summer, fall
Map: USGS 7.5-minute Fall River Pass

The trail to the Crater is one of the finest short hikes in the park. It offers verdant subalpine forest, spectacular alpine scenery, and a chance to see one of the most magnificent and elusive of the park's large mammals, the bighorn sheep. The trail travels near their lambing and feeding grounds on the tundra of Specimen Mountain.

Bighorn sheep are particularly sensitive to human disturbance. They generally inhabit remote sections of the park, far from man and other predators, often on precipitous slopes high above tree line. Harassing or even unintentionally startling these sensitive creatures can seriously harm them. For example, fear of approaching humans can generate such stress in the sheep that they suffer cardiac arrest. Repeated stress makes the sheep less resistant to diseases that plague the herds and consequently will reduce their numbers. The bighorn population in the park is fragile, but their numbers have increased in recent years to about six hundred.

To protect the sheep during vital lambing periods, the Park Service prohibits all hiking on Specimen Mountain until midsummer (approximately July 1). After that date, limited access is provided by this trail, but the actual lambing area is always closed to hikers. Because of the fragility of the population, it is *critical* that you observe these restrictions.

The trailhead is located on the west side of Trail Ridge Road, 4.1 miles southwest from the Alpine Visitor Center and 16.9 miles north of the Grand Lake Entrance Station. From the Beaver Meadows Entrance Station, the trailhead is 24.1 miles west on Trail Ridge Road. Parking is available at the trailhead. If the small lot is full, there is additional parking 0.1 mile north on Trail Ridge Road (US Highway 34).

From the trailhead, the trail begins in meadow but quickly enters a mature forest of subalpine fir and Engelmann spruce, switchbacking steeply as it heads for tree line and the open tundra, approximately two-thirds of a mile away.

In the forest notice the variety of wildflowers that love the shade, moisture, and coolness of the subalpine forest. Among the more abundant wildflowers is white mountain figwort or "parrot's beak," whose blossom looks like the tiny hooked beak of a miniature white parrot. Look also for the blue mountain harebell, whose blossom hangs down from the stem like a tiny bell. Because of the flower's shape, the plant is also called a witch's thimble. The harebell is a delectable treat for the elk, deer, pikas, marmots, and sheep.

Another, more familiar edible crop is the delicate-leaved wild blueberry, which covers the forest floor. It produces a blue bloom in early summer and sweet berries in August. Be sure to leave an ample supply for the park's few black bears, which particularly favor them.

One of the most easily identified flowers is the Indian paintbrush, which resembles a small green brush dipped in red or yellow paint.

Proceeding through the forest, watch for squirrel middens consisting of large piles of cone scales and discarded cores, which have been gathered and eaten by red squirrels (chickarees). Beneath such piles of refuse are likely to be large caches of pinecones.

The first views through breaks in the trees are of impressive Specimen Mountain (12,489 feet) to the north. After climbing a little higher, enjoy a more expansive view to the north and east. Trail Ridge Road, the Alpine Visitor Center, and the west side of the Mummy Range are all in sight. Also notice the verdant Cache la Poudre Valley, where a wealth of shrubs, grasses, and sedges creates a rich summer buffet for deer and elk (see Hike 44).

As you approach a rocky area near tree line, look for the Colorado blue columbine, one of the most beautiful of the park's flowers. The blossoms of the columbine, whose name is derived from the Latin *columba,* meaning "dove," were thought to look like circles of doves dancing around the stems. The Colorado blue columbine's inner layer of white petals do resemble the backs of doves, set off by the outer sepals of blue, which mimic the clear Colorado sky. Native Americans used a tea made from columbine leaves to cure fevers and headaches.

On the trail, look for tracks of deer and elk. At tree line, notice the long ropelike mounds of dirt left by pocket gophers. These energetic excavators can tunnel more than 100 feet in one night. The animal was named for its cheek pockets, which open to the outside instead of into its mouth. The pocket gopher gathers seeds in his cheeks and then empties his cheek pockets by turning them inside out, just as we would empty a pants pocket. Special muscles snap the pockets back into place.

Above tree line, the view west to the Never Summer Mountains is excellent and continues to improve as you climb higher. Follow the narrow path as

Hikers near the rim of the Crater

it heads toward a saddle between Specimen Mountain and the Crater. At the saddle, a sign indicates the restricted lambing area. Find a comfortable perch here to watch for bighorn, or ascend to the top of the Crater on the faint trail to the left. Views from the top of the Crater are magnificent.

From either the Crater or the saddle, enjoy a good view to the northwest of Mount Richthofen (12,940 feet), the highest peak in the Never Summer Range. Below you to the west is the Kawuneeche Valley. The small mountain directly southwest of the Crater is Shipler Mountain.

If you see one sheep, you will probably see many. Rarely do bighorn sheep travel alone, for they are gregarious animals with a highly evolved social system. Look for sheep on the west side of the Crater and on the rocky western slopes of Specimen Mountain. Binoculars would be useful. In summer and fall the bighorns have dark brown coats and a large white rump patch and black tail. Rams can grow to 3.5 feet at the shoulder and may weigh up to 400 pounds; females are considerably smaller. Both males and females have horns that grow continuously throughout their lives. A healthy and mature ram's horn will reach a full and magnificent curl on each side of its head. A three-quarter curl indicates that a ram is approximately ten years old. In contrast, a ewe's horns are short and spiky, like those of a young ram.

During the fall mating season, rams compete for ewes by butting heads. The sound of the rock-solid horns slamming together can be heard a mile away. Despite the force of these cracks, dueling rams seldom hurt each other, and usually the smaller or weaker ram simply withdraws out of exhaustion.

Bighorn sheep are diurnal, so daytime hours are the best time to look for them. You are fortunate if you are able to observe these magnificent creatures.

Though millions of bighorn sheep once roamed the Rockies, only small herds survive today, owing to extensive market hunting in the late 1800s, loss of habitat, and infection by diseases of domestic livestock.

46 LULU CITY

Difficulty: moderate
Distance: 3.6 miles one way
Usage: moderate
Starting Elevation: 9010 feet; elevation gain, 350 feet
Backcountry Campsite: none
Seasons: summer, fall
Map: USGS 7.5-minute Fall River Pass

This very pleasant, almost level walk along the Colorado River leads to the site of a mining boomtown of the late 1800s. Although not much remains of Lulu City, the trail is rich with the ghosts of miners. Discover abandoned cabins, ruins, and mines, and for more inspiration, take along the well-written account of Lulu City, which is available at park visitor centers.

The Colorado River Trailhead is on the west side of US Highway 34, 10.5 miles north of the Grand Lake Entrance Station and 10.5 miles southwest of the Alpine Visitor Center. There is a parking lot at the trailhead.

This hike is a good choice if you are uncertain of the stamina of your group, for the following intermediate goals make good turnarounds: (1) the first abandoned mine (1.2 miles), (2) the cabin ruins and second mine (1.3 miles), (3) the Shipler Mine (2 miles), (4) the Shipler Cabin site (2.4 miles), or (5) the beginning of the old stage road (2.7 miles).

From the trailhead, the trail heads north and immediately climbs a short steep hill, but beyond the hill the trail is nearly level. For much of the way, the path is wide and smooth, allowing two people to stroll abreast. Many varieties of wildflowers line the trail, and the trees are alive with the sounds of birds and chattering red squirrels.

At 0.6 mile from the trailhead, the trail to Lulu City (La Poudre Pass Trail) splits from the Red Mountain Trail, which heads left. Take the right fork, which continues north along the east side of the Colorado River, almost always keeping within sight of the water and sometimes meandering right up to it. There are many good picnic spots along the river, and the bank makes a fascinating playground for youngsters.

The headwaters of the Colorado River lie 7 miles up the trail to the north at La Poudre Pass. This gentle singing stream is the start of the great river that carved the Grand Canyon and on which the entire Southwest relies. From this point in the Rockies, the river flows more than 1400 miles to the Gulf of California.

After approximately 1.2 miles, a spur trail climbs steeply uphill to the right to an abandoned mine. This is one of the numerous mine shafts dug into Shipler Mountain, probably between 1870 and 1900. Do not enter the mine.

After returning to the trail, come to another set of paths, one leading to the right, another to the left. The path to the right leads to a second abandoned mine, this one boarded up and scarred with graffiti. The path to the left leads to cabin ruins, where there is evidence of a stone fireplace. Notice that the foundations of the cabins are remarkably small. Most of the houses built by prospectors were built hastily, often only seven logs high and roofed with poles and dirt. Most miners did not winter at their mining sites, but retreated to warmer, more populous areas until spring.

Shipler Mine is approximately 2 miles from the trailhead. The site is marked by a large tailings pile on the right. This rocky slope is an excellent place to see yellow-bellied marmots. These western woodchucks inhabit rocky areas and enjoy napping on the sun-warmed rocks. In late summer, wild raspberries ripen near the trail at the base of the tailings.

Enjoy the peaceful meadows on the former site of Lulu City.

Shipler Mine is an interesting mine to visit. To reach its entrance, carefully climb the slope to the north of the tailings. Do not attempt to climb up the tailings, for the pile is unstable. Do not enter this mine without a park ranger. The Park Service runs guided hikes to the mine during the summer. For more information, check with the park visitor centers.

Continue down the trail 0.4 mile to the ruins of Joe Shipler's cabin, at the edge of a beautiful subalpine meadow. Joe Shipler, a miner, lived here with his family from 1876 until 1914. Comfort stations are located just behind the cabins.

Beyond the cabins, notice unhealed wagon-wheel ruts beside the trail, evidence of the stagecoach road that once brought mail, provisions, and hundreds of prospectors to Lulu City. Also notice the new tree growth on either side of the trail, indicating the swath of road that was cut almost a hundred years ago.

At 3.4 miles, come to a trail junction. The right fork leads north to Little Yellowstone Canyon. Take the left fork to Lulu City, a short 0.2-mile downhill. On this last leg of the trail, walk through a fine stand of aspens, which are particularly beautiful in the fall.

At the site of Lulu City the trail opens up to a lovely flowered meadow—a wonderful picnic spot with safe, easy access to the river. Children will enjoy the chipmunks, golden-mantled ground squirrels, and gray jays. The meadow is bordered on the west by the picturesque peaks of the Never Summer Mountains. Toilet facilities are located after a small bridge.

Explore the undergrowth to find cabin foundations, tailings piles, and rusted pieces of machinery. Very little remains here of what was once a bustling boom town. It is hard to imagine that 100 square blocks were laid out, named, and marketed by ambitious city planners.

The dreams of those coming to Lulu City were as grand as the scenery. Dubbed "The Coming Metropolis of Grand County," the town thrived between 1880 and 1883, peaking at a population of 500. During this time, stagecoaches arrived five times weekly from Grand Lake and Fort Collins. A hotel with linen, silver, and fine china served well-to-do travelers. The town supported liquor, hardware, clothing, and grocery stores; two sawmills; and a two-cabin red-light district. But the mines at Lulu City produced only low-grade ore, which was unprofitable to mine in the absence of a nearby smelter. Consequently, Lulu City was largely abandoned by 1883.

Unfortunately, one of the most enduring signs of Lulu City's mining is the deposition of iron manganese precipitate (an orange deposit) along the banks of the Colorado River. Throughout Colorado, similar drainage from long-abandoned mines now endangers precious water sources. The state is currently seeking solutions to this dangerous legacy of its mining heritage.

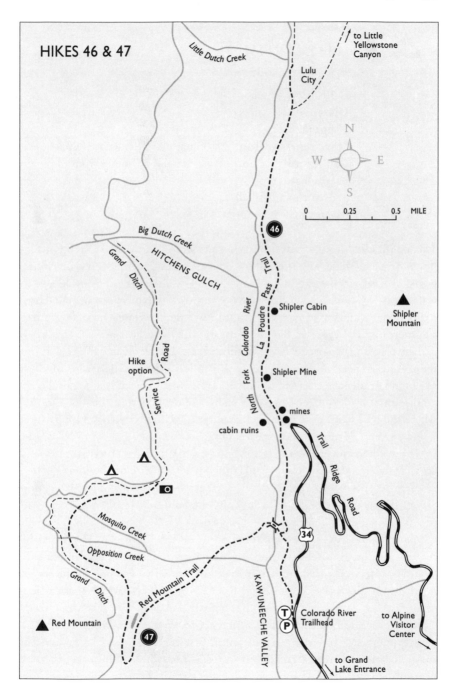

HIKES 46 & 47

Little Dutch Creek

to Little
Yellowstone
Canyon

Lulu
City

N
W — E
S

0   0.25   0.5   MILE

46

Big Dutch Creek

Grand Ditch

HITCHENS GULCH

Colordao River

North Fork

La Poudre Pass Trail

Shipler Cabin

Shipler
Mountain

Service Road

Hike
option

Shipler Mine

mines

cabin ruins

Mosquito Creek

Opposition Creek

Grand Ditch

Red Mountain Trail

Red Mountain

47

Trail Ridge Road

34

KAWUNEECHE VALLEY

Colorado River
Trailhead

to Alpine
Visitor
Center

to Grand
Lake Entrance

T
P

47 Grand Ditch

Difficulty: strenuous
Distance: 3.4 miles one way
Usage: low
Starting Elevation: 9010 feet; elevation gain, 1200 feet
Backcountry Campsites: 3.2 and 3.5 miles from the
   trailhead
Season: summer, fall
Map: USGS 7.5-minute Fall River Pass

This uphill climb to the water diversion project of the Grand Ditch is a sur-prisingly scenic hike. The trail offers verdant forest, scenic views, marmots, pikas, several small cascading streams, and a somewhat sobering lesson in water conservation. The service road next to the ditch provides an abundance of good views and a very easy walk high above the Kawuneeche Valley. In late summer, the trail is one of the best for sampling wild berries.

Drive to the Colorado River Trailhead, as described in Hike 46. From the trailhead, head north for an easy 0.6 mile to the junction with the Red Mountain Trail. Take the Red Mountain Trail west crossing the Colorado on a substantial bridge. After a pretty meadow, enter a mature subalpine forest, where the trail steepens. Climb for 0.2 mile to the first crossing of Opposition Creek, a very clear, fast-flowing stream.

The trail ascends moderately for another half mile, then crosses a rocky area, with views to the east of magnificent green mountain ridges. Aspen trees grow among the rocks, framing the views and making this section especially pretty in the fall. Throughout the summer, bright pink fireweed provides a stunning contrast to the gray rocks.

Aspens and fireweed are common to areas that have been disturbed by fire, rockslides, avalanches, or logging. Aspens regenerate themselves quickly from root networks that survive in the soil; when an opening in the forest is created, as by a fire, the roots generate new suckers, which form a new colony of aspens. Fireweed colonizes disturbed areas by means of seeds equipped with long silky threads, which act like parachutes in the wind. The paratrooping seeds invade after a natural disaster and quickly germinate in the bare soil. Fireweed's rapid growth helps hold the soil in place, thereby preventing erosion.

The golden-mantled ground squirrel looks a lot like a chipmunk but it is larger and its stripes don't reach its face.

Native Americans enjoyed the taste of fireweed and, reportedly, Russians long ago used it to make beer. More locally significant, fireweed is a favorite food of the grizzly bear in the northern Rockies and of the elk in this park.

This rocky slope is a good place to rest, sample wild raspberries, and watch for marmots and pikas. Below is a fine view into the Kawuneeche Valley, through which the young Colorado River twists and turns.

Leave this rocky area to travel south, and then switchback north through a rich subalpine forest consisting of Engelmann spruce, subalpine fir, and aspen. The forest floor is colorful with purple and white wildflowers. Wild blueberries sport delicate blue flowers in midsummer and tiny purple berries at season's end. This fine forest walk offers diversity, dappled sunlight, songs of birds, and lush scents.

After another rocky and open area, the trail passes a small pond, home to a large variety of creeping, crawling delights for interested youngsters. Watch for water boatmen, whirligig beetles, and midges.

Beyond the pond, the path reenters the forest and rises again. After crossing Opposition and Mosquito Creeks, continue uphill another 0.6 mile to the Grand Ditch. The views are fabulous. Walk along the service road in either direction. Just about 0.2 mile north, find a backcountry campsite west of the trail. To the south, aptly named Red Mountain rises dramatically. Mount Cumulus looms to the west, Howard and Lead Mountains to the north. The long Kawuneeche Valley is visible below. The nearly level road provides miles of effortless hiking. Those hiking southwest will find a campsite at the ditch, 3.5 miles from the trailhead. Although a sunrise would be magnificent from this spot, the uphill hike to the campsite with loaded packs would be very strenuous.

The Grand Ditch was an early attempt to divert large quantities of water to the arid lands east of the Continental Divide. The vast eastern prairies had rich soil but too little rainfall to sustain agriculture. Inventive farmers coveted the heavy snowfall on the western slopes of the mountains, whose meltwater flows west, not east. Their solution in 1890 was to build a diversion ditch to capture the melting snow and empty it into an east-flowing river. The ditch was begun at La Poudre Pass to catch water that ordinarily would have drained into the Colorado River. At its completion in 1936, the 20-foot wide, 6-foot deep ditch reached 14.3 miles.

The Grand Ditch had many effects. The scar on this mountain range is visible a great distance away, and severe erosion is evident on the slopes. The ditch also cut the flow of the North Fork of the Colorado River in half, adversely affecting the once thriving fish population.

It is now clear that irreversible loss of habitat, destruction of wilderness, erosion, and the loss of fish and wildlife may result from construction of dams, reservoirs, and water diversion projects. Given these risks, conservation is the only acceptable long-term solution. In Denver, single-family homes consume 65 percent of the water in the metropolitan area, and half of that amount is used to water lawns. The price for green grass, measured in lost wilderness, tamed rivers, and destroyed habitat, is too high.

Hiking Options:
A good destination along the service road is Hitchens Gulch, 1.7 miles north. Wildflowers bloom along the Gulch, through which Big Dutch Creek runs east to meet the Colorado River.

48 HOLZWARTH HISTORIC SITE

Difficulty: nature stroll, handicapped access with assistance (buildings are not accessible)
Distance: 0.75 mile one way
Usage: moderate
Starting Elevation: 9100 feet; elevation gain, none
Backcountry Campsite: none
Seasons: spring, summer, fall
Map: USGS 7.5-minute Grand Lake

In the scenic Kawuneeche Valley, at the foot of the Never Summer Range, the rustic cabins of the Holzwarth Historic Site remain just as they did a century ago when they comprised the Never Summer Ranch. A trip to this turn-of-the-century guest ranch makes a fascinating and scenic walk.

The Holzwarth Historic Site is located on US Highway 34, 7.8 miles north of the Grand Lake Entrance Station and 13.2 miles west of the Alpine Visitor Center. There is a parking lot and picnic area at the trailhead.

From the parking area, a dirt road crosses the Colorado River and travels a level 0.5 mile to the Holzwarth Historic Site. Easily managed by wheelchairs and strollers, this road provides a pleasant walk through the wide Kawuneeche Valley, through which the Colorado River flows for almost 7 miles. At the cluster of cabins that make up the original ranch, bring out your guide, "Never Summer Ranch" (available at park visitor centers), and take yourself on a self-guided tour of the site. Open for your inspection are kitchens, bunkhouses, a taxidermy shop, old sleds, wagons, and more. The site reveals the rugged simplicity of guest ranching in the 1920s, when the West was still young. During the summer, park rangers lead entertaining interpretive walks to the site. Check at a park visitor center for schedules.

Aspen bark grazed by elk

Visitors owe the preservation of this portion of the Kawuneeche Valley to the generosity of John Holzwarth, the former owner of the Never Summer Ranch. Before the ranch became part of the park, Holzwarth received numerous lucrative offers from speculators who wanted to build resorts on his property. Fortunately, Mr. Holzwarth declined these offers and earmarked the land for conservation. At age seventy-one, he stated, "I can live with and die knowing that this valley will be for all and not a select few."

49 KAWUNEECHE VALLEY AT BOWEN/ BAKER MOUNTAINS

Difficulty: nature stroll, handicapped access with assistance
Distance: 0.5 mile one way
Usage: low
Starting Elevation: 8864 feet; elevation gain, none
Backcountry Campsite: none
Seasons: spring, summer, fall
Map: USGS 7.5-minute Grand Lake

This trip follows an unpaved road 0.5 mile through the wide and scenic Kawuneeche Valley. The level road, closed to vehicular traffic, gives every hiker, even those in wheelchairs, the opportunity to travel through the wide river valley, away from paved surfaces. Although the scenery is not spectacular, the valley views are very fine, and the trail is usually uncrowded. At dawn or dusk, look for deer or elk.

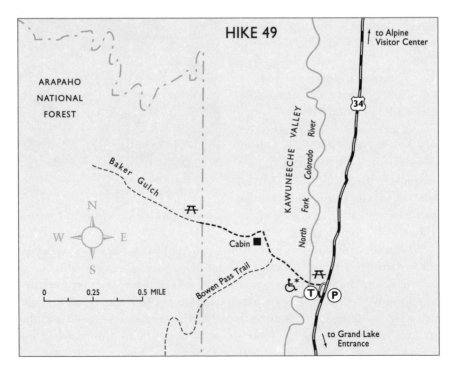

The Bowen/Baker Trailhead is located on the west side of US Highway 34, 6.4 miles north of the Grand Lake Entrance Station and 14.6 miles southwest of the Alpine Visitor Center. There is a parking lot and picnic area at the trailhead.

The old road starts out at the end of the picnic area and heads directly west across the valley. Enjoy a fine view of the Never Summer Mountains and the 7-mile-long Kawuneeche Valley, through which the North Fork of the Colorado leisurely courses. The pyramid-shaped peak to the west is Baker Mountain (12,397 feet). At the west end of the valley, the road divides. Take the fork on the right, leading to the Baker Gulch Trail.

After circling around a cabin, the road continues into a forest of lodgepole pine and aspen. A hike in the autumn amidst the aspen's golden fall foliage is recommended. Since this trailhead is not heavily used, the walk is quiet and lovely. The sounds of birds and squirrels can be clearly heard. After a half mile, the road ends (at the start of the Baker Gulch Trail and Arapaho National Forest). Secluded picnic tables are at the end of this road.

50 COYOTE VALLEY NATURE TRAIL

Difficulty: self-guided nature stroll, handicapped accessible according to federal accessibility standards
Distance: 1-mile loop
Usage: low
Starting Elevation: 8766 feet; elevation gain, none
Backcountry Campsite: none
Seasons: spring, summer, fall
Map: USGS 7.5-minute Grand Lake

This charming 1-mile loop trail offers superbly easy access to a wonderfully scenic and educational trail. Set on the edge of the Kawuneeche Valley, the level path parallels the Colorado River, enabling those with wheelchairs and strollers to enjoy a beautiful part of the park. Come early in the morning or at dusk to view a wide variety of wildlife. At any time, enjoy a picnic on tables at the meadow's edge.

The Coyote Valley Trail is located 5.4 miles north of the Grand Lake Entrance Station and 2.3 miles south of the Timber Creek Campground.

The trail begins in an old fir-spruce forest. Just opposite the trailhead sign, find an Engelmann spruce more than two hundred years old. A few yards down the trail to the right, an even larger spruce is estimated to be over three hundred.

As you walk this new trail through this ancient valley, consider the changes these trees have witnessed.

Cross the Colorado River over a stone bridge, and then turn right for the nature trail. Straight ahead a picnic area loops beneath the pines. Stroll slowly; this trail was built for comfort and contemplation. Waysides provide benches and interpretive signs every 200 to 400 feet.

The Coyote Valley Trail is named for the broad valley through which it travels. Just before this park was created, elders of the Arapaho tribe were asked to recount the ancient names given to the land. They called this valley *Kawuneeche,* meaning "valley of the coyotes." Today, coyotes can still be spotted in the meadow hunting small rodents and grasshoppers, and their calls are frequently heard at night. Look for their scat on the trail. Its shape is doglike, but its telltale sign is the presence of undigested fur.

This valley was once a rich gathering and hunting ground for the Arapaho. Many of the plants they picked for food and medicine remain. White and purple penstamen, wild parsley, yarrow, yellow sulfur flower, and pink pussy toes are just a few. The willow that lines the riverbanks supplied supple weaving materials as well as analgesic from its bark. Lodgepole pine (a grove is just ahead) provided narrow and lightweight poles for tepees.

Colorado cutthroat trout once thrived in the Colorado River, whose headwaters lie just 14 miles north at La Poudre Pass. Unfortunately, a water diversion project, the Grand Ditch, diverted about half of the river's volume, severely affecting fish habitat by reducing water flow and increasing the river's temperature. Observe the ditch by looking northwest to the eastern slope of the Never

Looking for elk on the Coyote Valley Nature Trail

Summer Range, where a horizontal line scars the slope (easily spotted because of the erosion it generated). The Kawuneeche Valley is still a gorgeous place to fish, but anglers will find it challenging.

Time has not been so hard on the mammalian population here. The old fir-spruce forest east of the river remains home to porcupine, weasel, pine marten, and chickaree. In the heat of day, elk also seek refuge in the forest. Along the river, recently introduced moose may be found. Most dramatically in the spring, early summer, and fall, large elk herds graze the meadow. The valley is a prime viewing spot for the elk's mating rut in the fall. Visit between September 1 and mid-October, at about forty-five minutes before dusk, to hear and see this unforgettable spectacle. There are few sights as stirring as watching elk run through the golden meadow against the superb backdrop of the snow-capped Never Summer Mountains.

Proceed down the path, passing a pond on the right, where children can search for minnows or tadpoles. Confirmed inhabitants of the pond include fairy shrimp and midges. Continue following the path as it loops through a grove of lodgepole pines at 0.5 mile from the trailhead. At the north end of the trail, pause at a viewpoint to appreciate the majestic peak of Baker Mountain (12,397 feet) rising behind beautiful Green Knoll. Some hikers may want to continue beyond the established trail to explore the area north along the river. Using the river as your guide, it is impossible to lose your way.

Those who wish to remain on the trail can take their time ambling back to the trailhead.

51 | GREEN MOUNTAIN LOOP

Difficulty: strenuous
Distance: 7-mile loop
Usage: low
Starting Elevation: 8794 feet; elevation gain, 858 feet
Backcountry Campsites: 2.4, 2.8, 2.9, and 5.1 miles
  from the trailhead
Seasons: summer, fall
Map: USGS 7.5-minute Grand Lake

This long, uncrowded walk through a shady coniferous forest features an aspen grove, numerous creeks, a flowered meadow, and the scant remains of a nineteenth-century ranch. Although some visitors may find the miles through

The distinctive "doghair" forest on Onahu Creek Trail

dense pines monotonous, this hike has a feeling of isolation that is not found on the park's more visited trails. Backpackers can find shady and secluded camp-sites along Onahu Creek, about 2.5 miles from the trailhead, and at Big Meadows, about 5.1 miles from the Onahu Creek Trailhead but only 1.9 miles from the Green Mountain Trailhead.

Drop hikers off at the Onahu Creek Trailhead, located on the east side of US Highway 34, 3.2 miles north of the Grand Lake Entrance Station and 17.8 miles southwest of the Alpine Visitor Center. Park at the Green Mountain Trailhead, located 0.6 mile south of the Onahu Creek Trailhead on US Highway 34, and then rejoin your group by walking north along the highway or on a path parallel to the highway. Find this path by continuing due north shortly after the sign for the Green Mountain Trailhead.

The trail begins among aspen trees that have been liberally grazed by elk, which eat the bark when other food is scarce. Bulls eat the bark in the fall and winter, while cows seem to do so in the winter and spring. The bark may have some coagulative properties that aid the cows in their birthing season.

Soon after leaving the aspens, enter a dense and extensive "doghair" stand of lodgepole pines. Although these trees are spindly pole timber, they are probably 70 to 150 years old. Lodgepole pine forests often have a large number of toppled trees because their root systems are shallow, making them vulner-able to what foresters call "windthrow," the uprooting of trees by wind. Fallen trees remain on the ground for a long time because the rate of decomposition

202

is slow at this altitude, where soils are too cold for many of the organisms that aid in decomposition.

Along this portion of the trail, children can play an alphabet game by finding letters in the configurations made by the fallen trees. A second trail game is mental "pick up sticks," in which children look at a maze of uprooted trees and try to figure out which tree could be removed without tumbling the pile.

As you progress up the trail, young firs and spruce appear. These trees represent the next stage in the forest succession. As they grow, they will shade out, and thus eventually kill, the sun-loving lodgepole pines. Notice also the rocky mountain junipers, whose berries smell like gin when crushed. Growing on the forest floor is broom huckleberry, providing a green shag carpet and sweet berries.

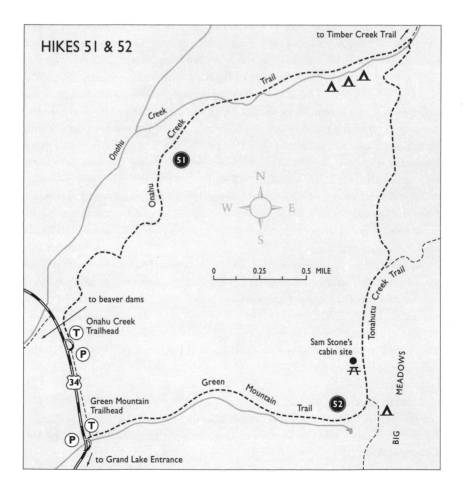

Listen for the sound of red squirrels, or chickadees, which chatter angrily in the trees overhead. Finding one is difficult, however, because the squirrels are skilled ventriloquists. Look for their nests, made of twigs and leaves and placed high in fir trees. Listen also for the mountain chickadee, which calls out its name over and over.

At 2.2 miles from the trailhead, the trail levels out and follows Onahu Creek. Walking along the bubbling creek is a pleasant change. Big rocks by the creek and a series of bridges make nice picnic spots. In this area there are three campsites, located 2.4 to 2.9 miles from the Onahu Creek Trailhead.

After crossing the last bridge over Onahu Creek at 2.9 miles, arrive at the junction with the Timber Creek Trail. Bear right (south) on this trail; signs at the junction clearly mark the way. This portion of the trail traverses a north-facing slope through a mature forest of Engelmann spruce and subalpine fir. As the trail climbs higher, the lodgepoles return. After 1.2 miles, arrive at the junction with the Tonahutu Creek Trail, which enters from the east. Proceed south (right) on the Tonahutu Creek Trail to Big Meadows.

The 0.7-mile walk along the edge of Big Meadows is very pleasant. The wide meadow is filled with wildflowers and long grasses. Wild strawberries grow by the trail and bear fruit in late summer. Deer and elk tracks can be seen. Toward the south end of the meadow are the scant remains of the ranch of Sam Stone, including his cabin and barn. In the early 1900s, Sam Stone attempted to grow hay in this meadow. Despite his lack of success at farming, he must have been cheered by the beautiful view out his door.

Near the south end of the meadow is the Big Meadows campsite, 5.1 miles from the Onahu Creek Trailhead. This campsite is an excellent and easy back-packing destination when approached from the Green Mountain Trailhead, only 1.9 miles away (see Hike 52).

At the end of the meadow, the Green Mountain Trail comes in from the west to join the Tonahutu Creek Trail. Bear right (southwest) at this junction, 1.6 miles from the Green Mountain Trailhead. Once again, the trail is well marked.

This is the last leg of the loop. The trail passes a second, smaller meadow frequented by deer and follows a small musical brook all the way back to the Green Mountain Trailhead.

Hiking Options:

Across the road from the Onahu Creek Trailhead, and 0.1 mile north, is a fisherman's trail leading to a series of large beaver dams and lodges along the Colorado River.

52 BIG MEADOWS

Difficulty: easy
Distance: 1.8 miles one way
Usage: low
Starting Elevation: 8794 feet; elevation gain, 606 feet
Backcountry Campsite: 1.9 miles from the trailhead
Seasons: summer, fall
Map: USGS 7.5-minute Grand Lake

This is a short hike through subalpine forest to a pretty, flowered meadow by the ruins of an early settler's ranch. The trail was originally the wagon road to the ranch, and to this day the path remains wide and smooth. At dawn or dusk there is a good chance of seeing deer. The meadow is also a superb place to view the rut of the elk in the late fall. Backpackers will find an excellent campsite at the meadow, just 1.9 miles from the trailhead.

Drive to the Green Mountain Trailhead, as described in Hike 51. There is a parking lot at the trailhead. A musical brook accompanies the trail to the

Sam Stone's cabin at Big Meadows

meadow. Look for the tasty ground cover of wild blueberries and the less abundant, but equally delicious, wild strawberries. Feel free to sample, but remember
that it is against park regulations to carry out more than a small quantity of edibles
for your own consumption. It is best just to taste, and leave the rest for the next
hikers or the park's wildlife.

The trail climbs moderately to Big Meadows, passing two small wet meadows
along the way. Look for deer in these openings, especially very early or late in the
day. Listen for the pleasant chirping of mountain chickadees and the angry scolding of the chickarees, or red squirrels.

Big Meadows, 1.8 uphill miles from the trailhead, is a large, open meadow
that provides welcome change from the shady trail. Many wildflowers grow
amid the grass. Look for shrubby cinquefoil, a five-petaled yellow flower. Native
Americans and early settlers discovered many valuable uses for this member of the
rose family. The roots dry beautifully and are reputed to taste like sweet potatoes.
Other parts of this plant were used to treat stomach ailments, fevers, toothaches,
and infections. Look also for pink elephantheads, which mimic tiny elephant
heads with upturned trunks and floppy ears. A herd of heads is arranged verti-
cally on each stalk.

The trail leads to the remains of two log structures, the cabin and barn of Sam
Stone, who attempted to harvest hay here in the early 1900s. You walked up his
pleasant wagon road to arrive at this meadow. After toiling for years at his largely
unsuccessful hay operation, he left this site to prospect, unsuccessfully, for gold.

This is a great spot for a picnic. Golden-mantled ground squirrels and
chipmunks come for lunch, but resist feeding them. It's easy to tell the difference between the ground squirrel and a chipmunk. The golden-mantled ground
squirrel is much larger and has stripes only on its sides. The chipmunk has
stripes on its back and on its face. In addition, the chipmunk is quicker and
more nervous, rarely sitting still for more than a moment.

Watch also for the fluffy-headed gray jay, a common resident of the subalpine forest. The gray jay is slightly larger than a robin and is primarily gray,
with white markings on its forehead and neck, and black on the back of its
head. You may also spot a weasel on its almost constant hunt for prey. To fuel
its long, tubular body, the weasel must eat an amount equal to two-thirds of its
body weight per day. Hunger and instinct drive this intrepid predator to attack
animals up to thirty times its size. Look also for deer and elk tracks on the trail;
the animals themselves are not likely to appear here in midday.

At the south end of the meadow, 1.9 miles from the Green Mountain
Trailhead, is a campsite that would make an excellent destination for a family
backpacking trip. A night at this site would simulate Sam Stone's experience of

almost a century ago. Stories about prospectors, Indians, or early settlers would greatly enrich the experience for children (see "Recommended Reading").

After exploring Big Meadows, retrace your steps, this time all downhill, back to the Green Mountain Trailhead.

Hiking Options:

This trail is one section of the Green Mountain Loop Trail, described in Hike 51.

53 NORTH INLET MEADOWS

Difficulty: nature stroll, handicapped access with assistance
Distance: 1.2 miles one way
Usage: moderate
Starting Elevation: 8540 feet; elevation gain, none
Backcountry Campsite: 1.2 miles from the trailhead
Seasons: spring, summer, fall
Map: USGS 7.5-minute Grand Lake

This hike heads down an unpaved road to a meadow popular with campers and picnickers. Summerland Park, only 1.2 miles from the trailhead, is a short and easy destination for backpacking families.

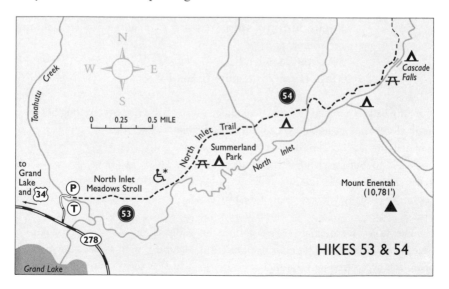

HIKES 53 & 54

Drive to the Tonahutu/North Inlet Trailhead. From US Highway 34 in Grand Lake, turn east onto Colorado State Highway 278. After 0.3 mile, come to a fork. Keep left, and drive 0.8 mile to a dirt road. Turn left again and follow this road past a parking lot, up a hill, and over Tonahutu Creek. The parking lot for the Tonahutu/North Inlet Trailhead is just after the bridge.

The hike begins at the east end of the parking lot and follows the dirt road, which is closed to traffic. The gently rolling road is easy to walk, although it may be wet and muddy in places. The road, which borders private ranchland, passes flowered meadows with grazing horses and cows, set against a background of rocky peaks. It feels like a stroll down a fine country road.

After 1.2 gentle miles, reach sunny Summerland Park, which is usually populated with tents and picnickers. Summerland Park is a very easy backpacking destination and is a good place for a summer lunch. There is plenty of open space for children to explore. An accessible stream flows along the southern edge of the park.

54 CASCADE FALLS

Difficulty: strenuous
Distance: 3.5 miles one way
Usage: moderate
Starting Elevation: 8540 feet; elevation gain, 300 feet
Backcountry Campsites: 1.2, 2, 3, and 3.5 miles from the trailhead
Seasons: summer, fall
Map: USGS 7.5-minute Grand Lake

Cascade Falls is a wide, raucous, magnificent waterfall. The trail is a long but easy walk along a sunny, unpaved road and then through moist, shady subalpine forest. The falls are an excellent destination for a picnic.

Walk to Summerland Park, as described in Hike 53. Beyond the sunny, often crowded, park, the mostly level trail enters a forest of lodgepole pine and aspen. Eventually, the lodgepole forest gives way to subalpine fir and Engelmann spruce.

The valley increasingly narrows, and the walls of the mountains rise more steeply on each side. The cliffs are beautiful, dripping with moss, glowing wet from this area's frequent summer rainstorms. A variety of moisture-loving wildflowers thrives beside the trail.

At 3.5 miles from the trailhead, arrive at Cascade Falls, where the sound of crashing water drowns out any conversation. There is good exploring and rock scrambling both above and below the falls. Vantage points above and below offer unique perspectives of the wide torrent. Children need to be closely supervised when approaching the falls, for wet, mossy rocks are slippery. The large flat rocks above the falls provide superior places to picnic.

55 ADAMS FALLS

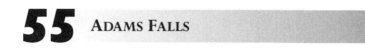

Difficulty: easy
Distance: 0.3 mile one way
Usage: high
Starting Elevation: 8391 feet; elevation gain, 79 feet
Backcountry Campsite: none
Seasons: summer, fall
Map: USGS 7.5-minute Shadow Mountain

A very short walk leads to one of the most magnificent waterfalls in the park. Get an early start to avoid the crowds. Early-morning hikers may also be rewarded with a sparkling rainbow made by the rising sun shining through the falls.

The East Inlet Trailhead is located near the West Portal of the Alva B. Adams Tunnel. From US Highway 34 in Grand Lake, turn east on Colorado State Highway 278. After a third of a mile, the highway divides; take the road to the left, which leads away from the village, and drive 2.1 miles to a large parking lot. The trailhead is at the east end of the lot.

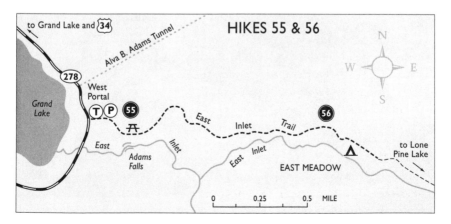

Watch children closely when you take in the view over Adams Falls.

The wide path to the falls is lined with lodgepole pines and aspens. The trail heads uphill moderately, so for the smallest hikers the short distance to the falls is a blessing. This hike is a good one for children because most motivated youngsters over age four can walk the entire distance. Reaching the falls without the aid of an adult should bring great pride to a young hiker.

Adams Falls is impressive and imposing. Torrents of water tumble down a wide gully, then rush into a narrow canyon with tall rock walls. The power of the water is felt in the rising spray and the thundering sound of the water sweeping over the rocks. Explore the area around the falls, but supervise children carefully. The wet rocks are slick and can be dangerous.

Hiking Options:

A good addition to this short hike is to continue east beyond the falls to a series of scenic meadows, 1.4 miles away (see Hike 56).

56 EAST INLET MEADOWS TRAIL

> **Difficulty:** easy
> **Distance:** 1.7 miles one way
> **Usage:** low
> **Starting Elevation:** 8391 feet; elevation gain, 159 feet
> **Backcountry Campsite:** 1.5 miles from the trailhead
> **Seasons:** summer, fall
> **Map:** USGS 7.5-minute Shadow Mountain

This pleasant, nearly level walk leads to magnificent Adams Falls and beyond to a series of meadows rimmed by mountains. The scenery has a gentle beauty that is enhanced by the solitude of the uncrowded trail. There is plenty of opportunity to explore the meandering East Inlet as it winds through the meadows and to look for beavers and muskrats along its banks. A superb backcountry campsite is an easy 1.5-mile hike from the trailhead.

Drive to the East Inlet Trailhead and hike to Adams Falls, as described in Hike 55. During the short, steep climb to the falls, you gain more than half of the total altitude gained on this hike. After enjoying the truly impressive waterfall, continue east on the trail, following the East Inlet. This river is one of two water courses that flow down from the Continental Divide into Grand Lake. The other river, to the north, is called North Inlet.

The river above the falls is lively and noisy. The path follows the river through a shady forest of lodgepole pines and aspens. Large rocks line the trail, some in interesting formations. To the left of the trail, look for an aspen tree tenaciously growing from the scant soil on top of a boulder. Aspens can grow in areas that are too rocky, wet, or infertile for other trees.

Aspens are easily identified by their small, trembling leaves and whitish-gray bark. They are one of the few deciduous trees found in the Rocky Mountains, but they are widespread and abundant in the range. In the fall, aspens turn brilliant yellow or orange, providing a dramatic contrast to the deep greens of the more abundant conifers. Aspens are usually found in disturbed areas, including places that have recently burned, been logged, or have been subjected to avalanches or rockslides.

The smallest puff of wind causes aspen leaves to tremble. The quaking aspen's scientific name, *Populus tremuloides*, reflects this trembling motion. The quaking is caused by the way the leaf is attached to its long slender stem. An early missionary to the north country recorded that superstitious woodsmen believed that Jesus was crucified on a cross made out of aspen and that the tree has been trembling ever since.

Approximately 1.3 miles from the trailhead, arrive at the first of two meadows. The view is lovely across the meadow. At the east end stands Mount Craig, or Mount Baldy, as it is commonly called in Grand Lake. This impressive 12,007-foot mountain is well named, for it has, in fact, a treeless rock dome for a summit. A variety of wildflowers grows by the river, which is easily reached by spur trails.

You can spend time at this small meadow or continue to East Meadow, a larger meadow, 0.5 mile farther down the trail. Right before reaching East Meadow a sign announces the East Meadow Campsite. This site, 1.5 miles from the trailhead, is an easy backpacking destination for a young family. The meadow is an exquisite, uncrowded place to camp.

As at the first meadow, Mount Baldy presides over East Meadow. The East Inlet snakes through the meadow in horseshoe curves. Spur trails lead to the water. There are signs of beaver activity along the river, so look carefully for lodges and dams. During the day, you are unlikely to see a beaver because they are usually active after dusk. Watch for them if you are camping at East Meadow or hiking very late in the day. Muskrats also frequent this habitat and may reside in abandoned beaver lodges. At dusk watch for deer.

If you're not spending the night, take a leisurely walk to the east side of the meadow. At its east end the trail starts to gain altitude as it makes its way to Lone Pine Lake, 5.5 miles east. This is a good place to turn around. In late summer, your walk back is enhanced by snacks from wild raspberry bushes along the trail.

RECOMMENDED READING

The books and periodicals listed below promote an understanding, appreciation, and respect for the environment. Through reading, children can build upon their park experiences and prepare for their next outdoor adventure.

The Rocky Mountain Nature Association is a great source of books about the Rocky Mountains. The Association runs book concessions at park visitor centers and the Moraine Park Visitor Center. Proceeds from sales benefit park educational programs. For a free mail-order catalog, write the Rocky Mountain Nature Association, Rocky Mountain National Park, Estes Park, CO 80517, or call (970) 586-1258 or visit www.nps.gov/romo/supportyourpark /rmna.htm.The following organizations also offer excellent nature books on a wide variety of topics:

- National Wildlife Federation, www.nwf.org.
- National Geographic Society, www.nationalgeographic.com.
- The Sierra Club, www.sierraclub.org.

BOOKS FOR CHILDREN
Field Guides

Alden, Peter. *Mammals: A Simplified Field Guide to the Common Mammals of North America*. Boston: Houghton Mifflin Co., 1987.

Arnosky, Jim. *Secrets of a Wildlife Watcher: A Beginner Field Guide*. New York: Beech Tree Books, 1991.

_____. *Wild Tracks! A Guide to Nature's Footprints*. New York: Sterling, 2008.

Jones, Charlotte Foltz. *Colorado Wildflowers: A Beginner's Field Guide*. Helena, MT: Falcon Press, 1994.

Peterson, Roger Tory. *Birds: Simplified Field Guide*. Boston: Houghton Mifflin Co., 1986.

Seacrest, Betty R. *Rocky Mountain Birds: Easy Identification*. Boulder, CO: Avery Press, 1993.

Stall, Chris. *Animal Tracks of the Rocky Mountains*. Seattle: The Mountaineers Books, 1989.

Watts, Tom. *Rocky Mountain Treefinder*. Rochester, NY: Nature Study Guild, 1972.

Games and Activities

Kreider, Elizabeth. *High Country Games: An Environmental Activity Book*. Estes Park, CO: Rocky Mountain Nature Association, 1984.

Larson, Helen Henkel. *Rocky Mountain National Park Coloring Book*. Eureka, CA: Earthwalk Press, 1993.

Peterson, Roger Tory, and Peter Alden. *A Field Guide to Mammals Coloring Book*. Boston: Houghton Mifflin Co., 1987.

Peterson, Roger Tory, and Frances Tenenbaum. *A Field Guide to Wildflowers Coloring Book*. Boston: Houghton Mifflin Co., 1982.

General Nonfiction

Amsel, Sherri. *365 Ways to Live Green for Kids: Saving the Environment at Home, School, or at Play—Every Day!*. Avon, MA: Adams Media, 2009.

Bird, Isabella. *A Lady's Life in the Rocky Mountains*. Nabu Press, 2010.

Cooper, Ann. *Above the Treeline*. Denver: Denver Museum of Natural History Press, 1996.

_____. *In the Forest*. Denver: Denver Museum of Natural History Press, 1996.

Cornell, Joseph Dharat. *Journey to the Heart of Nature*. Nevada City, CA: Dawn Publications, 1994.

Dolson, Sylvia. *Bear-ology: Fascinating Bear Facts, Tales and Trivia*. Masonville, CO: PixyJack Press, 2009.

Evans, Lisa Gollin. *An Elephant Never Forgets Its Snorkel*. New York: Crown Books for Young Readers, Inc., 1992.

Freedman, Russell. *Buffalo Hunt*. New York: Holiday House, 1988.

Gordon, David, Laurie, and Cambria. *Down-to-Earth Guide to Global Warming*. New York: Orchard Books, 2007.

Haluska, Vicky. *The Arapaho Indians*. New York: Chelsea House Publishers, 1993.

Hirshi, Ron. *Headgear*. New York: Dodd, Mead and Company, 1986.

Javna, Sophie. *The New 50 Simple Things Kids Can Do to Save the Earth*. Kansas City: Andrews McMeel Publishing, 2009.

Paluso, Beth. *The Charcoal Forest: How Fire Helps Animals and Plants*. Missoula, MT: Mountain Press Publishing Company, 2007.

Parker, Steve. *Pond and River*. New York: Alfred A. Knopf, 1988.

Pettit, Jan. *Utes: The Mountain People*. Boulder, CO: Johnson Books, 1990.

Robson, Gary. *Who Pooped in the Park: Rocky Mountain National Park*. Helena, MT: Farcountry Press, 2005.

Robertson, Kayo. *Signs Along the River: Learning to Read the Natural Landscape*. Boulder, CO: Roberts Rinehart, Inc., 1986.

Smith, Lucy. *Improve Your Survival Skills*. Tulsa, OK: Usborne EDC Publishing, Inc., 1996.

Picture Books

Aronsky, Jim. *Come Out, Muskrat.* New York: Lothrop, Lee and Shepard, 1989.
_____. *Deer at the Brook.* New York: Lothrop, Lee and Shepard, 1986.
Donahue, Mike. *The Grandpa Tree.* Boulder, CO: Roberts Rinehart, Inc., 1988.
Fourment, Tiffany. *My Water Comes from the Rocky Mountains.* Lafayette, CO: Moonlight Publishing, 2009.
George, Jean Craighead. *One Day in the Alpine Tundra.* New York: Thomas Y. Crowell, 1984.
_____. *One Day in the Woods.* New York: Thomas Y. Crowell, 1988.
Gilmore, Jack. *Year at Elk Meadow.* Boulder, CO: Roberts Rinehart, Inc., 1986.
Landstrom, Lee Ann. *Nature's Yucky: Gross Stuff that Helps Nature Work.* Missoula, MT: Mountain Press Publishing Company, 2003.
Mazur, Rachel. *If You Were a Bear.* Three Rivers, CA: Sequoia Natural History Association, 2008.
Plumb, Sally. *A Pika's Tail.* Jackson, WY: Grand Teton Natural History Association, 1994.
Steptoe, John. *The Story of Jumping Mouse.* New York: Mulberry Books, 1984.

Fiction

Connolly, James E., ed. *Why the Possum's Tail Is Bare and Other North American Nature Tales.* Owings Mills, MD: Stemmer House, 1985.
George, Jean Craighead. *Julie of the Wolves.* New York: Harper & Row, 1972.
_____. *My Side of the Mountain.* New York: E. P. Dutton, 1975.
Mowat, Farley. *Never Cry Wolf.* Boston: Little, Brown and Company, 1963.
Rawlings, Marjorie Kinnan. *The Yearling.* New York: Collier Macmillan Publishers, 1938.
Savage, Deborah. *A Rumour of Otters.* Boston: Houghton Mifflin Co., 1986.
Seuss, Dr. *The Lorax.* New York: Random House, 1971.

Periodicals

National Geographic Kids. National Geographic Society, P.O. Box 98199, Washington, D.C. 20090. Ages 8–14.
Ranger Rick. National Wildlife Federation, 11100 Wildlife Center Dr., Reston, VA 20190. Ages 6–12.
Your Big Backyard. National Wildlife Federation, 11100 Wildlife Center Dr., Reston, VA 20190. Ages 3–5.
Zoobooks. Wildlife Education Ltd., P.O. Box 28870, San Diego, CA 92128. Ages 1–12.

BOOKS FOR PARENTS
Sharing Nature with Children

Brown, Tom, Jr., with Judy Brown. *Tom Brown's Field Guide to Nature and Survival for Children.* New York: Berkley Publishing Group, 1989.

Caduto, Michael J., and Joseph Bruchac. *Keepers of the Earth: Native American Stories and Environmental Activities for Children.* Golden, CO: Fulcrum, Inc., 1997.

_____. *Keepers of the Night: Native American Stories and Noctural Activities for Children.* Golden, CO: Fulcrum, Inc., 1994.

_____. *Keepers of the Animals: Native American Stories and Wildlife Activities for Children.* Golden, CO: Fulcrum, Inc., 1997.

Carson, Rachel. *The Sense of Wonder.* New York: Harper & Row, 1984.

Cornell, Joseph Bharat. *Sharing Nature with Children.* Nevada City, CA: Dawn Publications, 1979.

Masterson, Linda. *Living with Bears: A Practical Guide to Bear Country.* Masonville, CO: PixyJack Press, 2006.

Pfaffmann, Garrick, and Hillary Forsyth. *Family Field Guide to Rocky Mountain Plants.* Basalt, CO: BearBop Press, 2007.

Ross, Micheal Elsohn. *The Happy Camper Handbook.* Yosemite National Park, CA: Yosemite National Park, 1995.

First-Aid Books

Carline, Jan D., Martha J. Lentz, and Steven C. Macdonald. *Mountaineering First Aid: A Guide to Accident Response and First Aid Care, Fifth Edition.* Seattle: The Mountaineers Books, 2004.

Natural History

Armstrong, David M. *Rocky Mountain Mammals: A Handbook of Mammals of Rocky Mountain National Park and Vicinity.* Boulder: University Press of Colorado, 2008.

Buccholtz, C. W. *Rocky Mountain Park: A History.* Boulder: Colorado Associated University Press, 1983.

Cutts, Gretchen S. *Potions, Portions, Poisons: Indian and Settler Plant Uses.* Estes Park, CO: Rocky Mountain Nature Association, 1985.

Dannen, Kent and Donna Dannen. *Best Easy Day Hikes: Rocky Mountain National Park,* Guilford, CT: Falcon, 2002.

_____. *Rocky Mountain Wildflowers.* Estes Park, CO: Tundra Publications, 2005.

_____. Rezendes, Paul. *Tracking and the Art of Seeing: How to Read Animal Tracks and Sign.* New York: HarperCollins, 1999.

Fisher, Chris, Don Pattie, and Tamara Hartson. *Mammals of the Rocky Mountains.* Renton, WA: Lone Pine Publishing, 2000.

Peterson, Roger Tory. *Peterson Field Guide to Birds of Western North America.* Boston: Houghton Mifflin Harcourt, 2010.

Whitney, Stephen. *Western Forests.* New York: Alfred A. Knopf, 1985.

Willard, Beatrice, and Michael T. Smithson. *Alpine Wildflowers of the Rocky Mountains.* Estes Park, CO: Rocky Mountain Nature Association, n.d.

Zwinger, Ann. *Beyond the Aspen Grove.* New York: Random House, 2002.

Zwinger, Ann, and Beatrice Willard. *Land Above the Trees.* New York: Harper & Row, 1989.

INDEX

ABOUT THE AUTHOR

Lisa Gollin Evans received her B.A. from Cornell University, then obtained a J.D. from Boalt Hall School of Law. Since 2006, Ms. Evans has worked as senior administrative counsel for Earthjustice, a nonprofit environmental law firm.

Evans believes the best way to create tomorrow's environmentalists is to expose children to the wonders, beauty, and excitement of nature. Her books include *Lake Tahoe: A Family Guide, An Outdoor Family Guide to Acadia National Park, An Outdoor Family Guide to Yellowstone and Grand Teton National Parks,* and *Sea Kayaking Coastal Massachusetts.* She has also written a nonfiction book for children, *An Elephant Never Forgets Its Snorkel,* which was named an "outstanding science book for children" in 1992 by the National Association of Teachers and the Children's Book Council. Evans lives with her husband and three daughters in Marblehead, Massachusetts.

THE MOUNTAINEERS, founded in 1906, is a nonprofit outdoor activity and conservation organization whose mission is "to explore, study, preserve, and enjoy the natural beauty of the outdoors . . . ." Based in Seattle, Washington, it is now one of the largest such organizations in the United States, with seven branches throughout Washington State.

The Mountaineers sponsors both classes and year-round outdoor activities in the Pacific Northwest, which include hiking, mountain climbing, ski-touring, snowshoeing, bicycling, camping, canoeing and kayaking, nature study, sailing, and adventure travel. The Mountaineers' conservation division supports environmental causes through educational activities, sponsoring legislation, and presenting informational programs.

All activities are led by skilled, experienced volunteers, who are dedicated to promoting safe and responsible enjoyment and preservation of the outdoors.

If you would like to participate in these organized outdoor activities or programs, consider a membership in The Mountaineers. For information and an application, write or call The Mountaineers Program Center, 7700 Sand Point Way NE, Seattle, WA 98115-3996; phone 206-521-6001; visit www .mountaineers.org; or email clubmail@mountaineers.org.

The Mountaineers Books, an active, nonprofit publishing program of The Mountaineers, produces guidebooks, instructional texts, historical works, natural history guides, and works on environmental conservation. All books produced by The Mountaineers Books fulfill the mission of The Mountaineers. Visit www.mountaineersbooks.org to find details about all our titles and the latest author events, as well as videos, web clips, links, and more!

 The Mountaineers Books
1001 SW Klickitat Way, Suite 201
Seattle, WA 98134
800-553-4453
mbooks@mountaineersbooks.org